# THE POET AS JOURNALIST

## AS JOURNALIST

*Life at The New Republic*

# THE POET AS JOURNALIST

## Life at The New Republic

*Reed Whittemore*

*The New Republic Book Company, Inc.*

*Washington, D.C.*

Published in the United States of America
in 1976
by The New Republic Book Company, Inc.
1220 Nineteenth St., N.W.
Washington, D.C. 20036

Most of the pieces in this book appeared first in *The New Republic*, but "Checks and Balances: The Poet in the Bank" appeared first in *Cultural Affairs*, "The Soviets' Problem—Or Is It Ours?" appeared in *The Nation*, "The Writer as Runaway" appeared first in *The Review of Existential Psychology*, and *"The Poet as Effete Snob,"* having been delivered at Carleton College as part of the regular Ward Lucas lecture series, appeared first in *The Michigan Quarterly Review*.

**Library of Congress Cataloging in Publication Data**


Whittemore, Reed, 1919-
  The poet as journalist.

  I. The New Republic.    II. Title.
AC8.W475    081    76-14897
ISBN 0-915220-16-4


Printed in the United States of America

To Nancy and Gilbert Harrison

# Contents

# THE KULCH

# The Poet as Journalist
# (Life at The New Republic)

1.

There was a time, the storybooks relate, when English teachers knew what they were doing. It was the time when a student's knuckles were rapped when he said "ain't" and when everybody read *Julius Caesar* and *The Vicar of Wakefield* and equivalent turkeys, read them and knew that they were good because teacher said so. It was the time when a whole satchelful of literary and verbal values was decreed and taught and the making of Americans was a sensible and straight-forward enterprise. It was in short a golden time, a time for the children of either new immigrants or old settlers to grow toward a common cultural felicity, taking off their hats in the house and not using "like" as a conjunction.

But then, the storybooks also relate, came the revolutions, beginning with the literary revolution against the old conventions like the sonnet, passing through the language revolution against English domination of American usage, and ending with a grand social-cultural smash in the sixties, during which it was discovered that *everything* that had *ever* been taught in the schools by the oldtimers had been a lot of bunko to preserve the status quo.

Whether or not the stories in the storybooks were true, clearly enough had happened in the country's classrooms by the time of the seventies to make any English teacher insecure in his teachings. If he were an old teacher with tenure and crusty ways, he might profess to be unswayed, might adhere tenaciously to the old standards and vote religiously against any possible English department reform; but even he would know in his inner heart that the old dispensation was no more, and would therefore drink an extra martini before supper. And if he were a young teacher, he would have less to hold on to; he would have only a bookish notion of what the old standards had been, and he would see daily that his students had even less than that, that the school administration had even less than that, and that from the McLuhanites to the Linguists to the Social Scientists to the Black

Studies people to his own Creative Writers there was an impression floating in the air that the old standards were not only moribund but also, where still effective, vicious. Under such circumstances he could only find himself encouraged to be a follower rather than a leader, that is, a teacher giving his students not what the ages had prescribed but what the students themselves in their wisdom thought they wanted. And what was *that*?

Once the boys wanted to be firemen and that was a joke, and the girls wanted to go on stage and that was a joke too. All their elders knew that they would get over their romantic professions and settle into common sense and the family trade (and children), that is, learn to be the selves they had inherited. But Jack Kerouac came along to change all that, saying that the most romantic profession of all was no profession at all (or possibly writing, which was the same as no profession at all), and saying too that one *could*, if one were strong, hang on to no profession at all, did not have to succumb to the System.

Kerouac described the new nirvana well in 1958 in his book *The Dharma Bums*. He said that once when he was hitchhiking easterly through Arizona he was picked up by a moral and hardworking truckdriver and that he quickly taught the truckdriver both how to cook a steak over a desert fire and how to live. He said that the truckdriver had "a nice home in Ohio with wife, daughter, Christmas tree, two cars, garage, lawn, lawnmower, but he couldn't enjoy any of it because he wasn't really free"—not free at least until Kerouac got hold of him. Kerouac set out to teach him to be free and then teach the rest of America to be free—that is, teach everybody how to dispose of the nice home and the Christmas tree—and he did such a good job (reinforced as he was by dozens of other writers and noisy System protestors) that pretty soon there emerged, as the universe now knows, a complete alternative "life style" with levis, long hair, pot, and the rest.

That style not only played hell with the nice homes and Christmas trees but did other things of which Kerouac could also approve, such as converting hordes of middle-class young persons into wild zen poets; but in the end it did not meet the main Kerouac specification of providing freedom. No, the alternative life style worked out just the way Kerouac didn't want it to on that score; it became a system in its own right with its own forms, prescriptions, assumptions, conventions right down to how tight the jeans should be and what the wild zen poems should be wild about. For there was one quality of the

American soul that Kerouac and the others overlooked when they set out on the road to the new freedom; it was a universal quality too, but the Americans seemed to have more of it than anybody; it was an indisposition to *be* free.

"Don't conform" was the cry, but conformity remained the need. The new Americans did not want to be free any more than the old Americans had wanted to be free; they merely wanted to be enslaved by new, different masters, not the oldtime WASPs and the oldtime grammar and prosody. There were plenty of new masters waiting to oblige. They quickly moved in.

So the English teachers sat on the sidelines and watched the new masters move in, watched and didn't do anything because their teaching trade had not taught them much about power plays and because, as one of the new masters himself put it, the scene was ripe for a takeover. The new master in question was Tom Wolfe, he of the "new journalism." What he said was directed at novels only, but he might well have been talking about the rest. He said that he and his journalist friends discovered in the sixties that they "had the whole crazed obscene uproarious Mammon-faced drug-soaked mau-mau lust-oozing 60s in America all to themselves."

He was partly wrong of course. There were others beside the new journalists seeking to possess the territory (Wolfe made the statement, appropriately, in a chapter about the new journalism entitled "Seizing the Power"), others of the likes of Kerouac, for example, who had little flair for journalism but plenty for the expression of the *private* sensibility of the lust-oozing sixties, and still others with straightforward political designs upon sixties power, not to mention the aforementioned power-hungry Linguists, Social Scientists and Black Studies people, all of whom had their own plans for replacing the status quo. But Wolfe was certainly on sound ground in observing that the journalists—that is, the ones with the feel for the lust-oozing sixties—suddenly found themselves possessed of powers they had not known they had, powers extending into literature.

In the old days the journalists, as Wolfe put it, had had a low opinion of their own trade, and when they entertained elevated thoughts, they imagined themselves going off into the woods for a siege of *serious* writing, which was never journalism but always literature, usually novels. The sixties scene changed all that for them. They discovered that they didn't have to go off into the woods at all to use their creative resources but could stay right at the journalist trade and do their serious expressing there. Why? Because the novelists, the real old woodsy ones, had defected from reality, departed from the manners and events of the contemporary scene, had decided it was not for true artists to go out and *look* at the world but to stay home with their thoughts and navels. By that decision, Wolfe felt, they had lost the world completely; therefore the journalists were not only able to take the world over from them but were able to "wipe out the novel as literature's main event." Touché. But what he didn't say about the wipeout—aside from the fact that it was not, and he knew it was not, total—was that it gave to the journalists authority over the molding of minds that they were unaccustomed to exercising, gave them in other words an opportunity (which they rushed in to accept) to lead the way into the new slavery that was destined to replace the old slavery.

The new slavery had been creeping up on us for some time anyway, so was not all Tom Wolfe's doing. TV had been heavily responsible, making the immediacies of contemporaneity even more immediate and putting us more at the mercy of national, as opposed to local or regional, imperatives than ever before. But if TV had pointed the way by bringing the here and now of the world right into the parlor, the new journalists added something that TV could not add, since TV was lowbrow and aimed at ten-year-olds. The new journalists added Significance and Art. And of course Wisdom.

More than anything else the takeover by journalists of art and the profundities weakened the English teacher's authority since for generations what he had had (or thought that he had had) that the journalists and other new entrepreneurs did not have was Truth and Beauty, plus the myth that Truth and Beauty were eternal, or near enough to the eternal to put those who lived by daily ephemera at a disadvantage. But now someone had intervened to decree that Truth and Beauty inhered to the daily ephemera and not the eternal. In the early part of the century not even journalists had heard of *that* decree. As H.W. Boynton, one of the literary journalists of the turn of the century, put it, a journalist then was "contemptible only when by some falsetto method he attempted to lead the public into fancying that it was getting literature of him." There were, it is true, a few literary characters of the period who professed to admire the journalistic mode—H.G. Wells was the most celebrated of these and went around bragging that he was not a novelist but a journalist, which meant that he was not like Henry James—but their bragging did not keep them from writing novels, that is novels in the old sense whose characters' resemblance to anyone in real life was alleged to be coincidental. The result was that they did not live up to their announced journalistic intentions but continued to enforce the traditional distinctions between journalism and literature. And as for the rest, the everyday working journalists, they were as sure as the literary people that the gap between literature and journalism was clear and unambiguous, leaving Truth and Beauty to literature while journalism picked up something less than that, something journalists needed not to be ashamed of but needed not to put on airs about either. Those were the good days for English teachers.

### 2.

I have been an English teacher for nearly thirty years now, have watched the decline of my profession with some sorrow, and watched the inflexibility of the professionals of the profession in the face of the decline with more sorrow; but this book is not so much about English teacher troubles as about the new troubles that journalism seems to be leading us to. I put my foot into journalism for four interesting years (1969-1973) when Gilbert Harrison hired me to be literary editor of *The New Republic.* Most of the reviews and essays in this volume are from that magazine and that period (though a couple are from earlier *TNR*s when I was a frequent contributor, and a few others are from unrelated publications), and while Harrison was always anxious to leave me to be as literary as I chose in the magazine's back pages, the journalistic spirit did creep into both my writing and my editing, partly because I was working against weekly deadlines and partly because the mere act of working for an essentially journalistic enterprise gave me a journalist's yearnings, yearnings to be, as a recent ad for Quadrangle Books put it, "on top of everything." The promoters of Quadrangle Books think that one stays on top of everything by being up-to-date, and for a book company owned by *The New York Times* that is a natural thought. But for someone like myself bred up in the older faith that one achieves topness merely by ascending to the top of a thinker's tower and sitting there thinking—that, and reading what earlier tower thinkers thought—for such a person the *TNR* experience was a novelty. It made me simultaneously aware of how cloistered I had been in the palmy days of my writing for quarterlies and how cloistered I was in another and new sense when riding along with the press and TV (for I became a TV critic too). The articles here reflect the latter cloistering most. They are a record of a mind that lived close, for four years, to the doctrine that knowledge and wisdom come to those who are up-to-date and stay there constantly, never letting a fad or fashion or major event slip by unnoticed into the night. I came to fear that doctrine, and to grow nostalgic for the old days of Beauty and Truth, but I came to believe it partly too. Certainly I lived it.

Not that *TNR* offices had a hectic newspaper air with James Cagney reporters buzzing in and out swearing and smoking. John Osborne appeared *very* quietly from the White House at irregular intervals to write his *"Nixon Watch,"* but when he appeared he was invisible, closeted in a tiny office (though swearing and smoking); and every Wednesday—or sometimes as late as Thursday morning— Harrison himself would emerge shyly from his struggles with his weekly lead to ask for last-minute facts and figures; but mostly the magazine amazed everyone, and particularly the managing editor David Sanford who was as invisible as the rest of us, by its capacity to appear on schedule when nobody could be seen doing a thing. Life was grey and quiet at *TNR*. Harrison was himself an impetuous, quick-moving man, but he managed to create an atmosphere opposite to that around him. He could red-pencil a manuscript faster than any editor I have known—and usually do a good job too—but he was also determined to be respectful of leisure and timelessness. He let his contributing editors alone when they were working on big projects; he didn't insist on production quotas from the staff and certainly didn't push me to be as timely in the reviewing of books as I pushed myself. He was determined to be respectful of the magazine's long literary tradition, was himself an authority on early modernist literature, especially the writings of Gertrude Stein, and had no illusions about the progressive incapacity of *TNR*, and of weekly publications in general, to compete with TV and the big papers in being journalistical-ly on top of everything. Under his mostly benign rule (though those he red-penciled sometimes did not find it benign) the magazine seemed to have a momentum of its own that had built up as a result of its regular appearance for sixty years; it was in all superficial aspects calm, out of the weather. I could therefore sit in the pleasant shabby literary office on the ground floor and and look out at the poor hurrying hordes on the sidewalk as if I were simply not a part of all that.

But then the mail would come in (see my essay, "Climbing the Wall"), and the printer would call to say that a page of a manuscript had been lost, and a reviewer from New York would call to be angry at what I proposed to do with his review (for I had learned to red-pencil too), and, chiefly, my typewriter would tell me that I needed to produce a magazine page's worth of written wisdom on it by sunset. Journalists, all true journalists, are accustomed to the typewriter's call, but I was not. Though I had been a writer all my life, and had been able to school myself to write fast and loose when the spirit was upon me, I was not accustomed to writing fast and loose for somebody else's spirit. Was the new discipline not good for me? Probably. And aside from having to meet close deadlines I had to learn to stay on top of articles right through the printing process—that is, be a sort of one-man band for the magazine's back pages—and so I benefited, became more competent, more capable of coping with the world than I had been when I was merely a grubby teacher writing petulant complaints in student margins (I was, though, still doing that too). Yet while I was learning—under pleasant conditions—what journalism had to teach me, I was also learning what I did not want to learn, and now wish journalists in general could partly unlearn: to keep my feelers out for the current and hot. And I was learning how to achieve instant mastery of the current and hot, the basic journalistic doctrine that has effectively replaced the old literary doctrine of permanence.

Ezra Pound, an oldtime hater of journalists, put the hex on them once by saying that they had absolutely no minds of their own but functioned only to tell the public what the public wanted to hear. (The poet's obligation on the other hand, EP hurried to point out, was to tell the bloody public what it did *not* want to hear.) Well, to live with journalism even as comfortably as I lived with it at *TNR* was to discover that EP was right. It was to discover that as a journalist one pretty much had to write about what the public seemed to think one *should* write about, and one had to take the positions that the public seemed to expect—that, or suffer from having no public.

But it was also to discover what EP apparently didn't, that journalists, though slaves to the public taste, were also and at the same time the public's leaders, the public's tyrants of taste. Their motion was circular. They harkened to the big stories and competed madly with each other in bringing the public the delights of national scandals and tragedies, but they also moved in on the stories and came to govern their destinies. And of course told the public what to think of the stories. Perhaps EP failed to see this side of journalists, their enormous authoritarianism, because he was such an authoritarian himself, but more likely the journalists he grew up with simply did not show as much authority as the new modern breed. (For a discussion of the difference, see my essay on Teapot Dome reporting.) The new modern breed's faith was in journalism's capacity for instant mastery of *anything*. If the *Washington Post* felt that it was running out of material to fill its giant stomach, it would pack off a star reporter to report on, say, the city of New York by a week from Sunday; and the reporter would take on the assignment and begin his feature story with the rich and sappy junk that had formerly been only the province of (bad) literature:

> *New York—Man was not meant to emulate the mole. Yet every day four million New Yorkers enter a subterranean world of noise and foul air, dim lights and dirt, vandalism and crime. They burrow into their manmade tunnels, surrounded by the sight of decay and the slogans of the ubiquitous graffiti artists who scrawl their symbols on all visible subway surfaces. They are jostled, harried, pushed and pulled as they hurtle down sections of track laid nearly three-quarters of a century ago, past stations that were once gleaming ornaments of the city and are now begrimed relics of a better era. They travel in this nether world because they must; their livelihoods depend on it.*

That paragraph was a beginning that Harrison would have red-penciled within five seconds, though he was in general an admirer of its author, Haynes Johnson; but Harrison was old-school and thought reporters should be reporters, not singing birds. The singing birds had descended on the *Post* and on the *New York Times*, sure of their capacity instantly to sing any song and also to persuade their public to sing along with them.

Then there were the new-style investigative reporters, triumphing on the Watergate scene. The Watergate reporting was remarkable, some of it, and its catastrophic effect on the Nixon administration was a steady tonic for all non-Nixonites; but its very success bred a lot more of the new journalistic self-confidence in instant mastery than the more arrogant and aggressive members of the profession needed, the Jack Andersons and Seymour Hershes. The destruction of Senator Eagleton by the press was an early instance (see my piece on this, p. 106) and an innocent one, relatively. Later the investigative reporters, some of them, would become instant judges of character as well as of events and institutions, would not hesitate to indulge (and to announce their indulgence) in plain fictions and would assume that the average American citizen had a sort of native-born obligation to tell an investigative reporter what an investigative reporter wanted to know. (If the citizen didn't, he was automatically one of the bad guys, though the chances were good that what he told would be distorted and maliciously used.) EP would have found such conduct merely characteristic of reporters, but since I was surrounded by reporters with scruples (though even the most scrupulous, I discovered, had a very loose view of how direct a direct quote had to be), I could still be shocked by bad journalistic practice but able to live comfortably with journalism's new powers otherwise.

Moreover, while I was working at *TNR* I was also still frequenting poet circles where several sensitive souls never read newspapers at all but measured their days instead by precious images that they personally pulled out of the air and pinned to paper. As I commuted between these worlds, I worried sometimes about my own identity and the preservation thereof—and I think the tension that was in me then shows in these essays. On the one hand I was trying to set literary folk straight for their failures to write about the society around them, and on the other I was trying to set journalists, and media people, straight, for knowing too much too soon, and for believing in nothing but flux.

Poetry was what I knew best, and so poetry was what I farmed out least for review—yet poetry was also, I felt, the sickest of the sick genres of literature; poetry was what made me want (sometimes) to be a journalist. I could not impose more than one poetry review every month or so upon *TNR*'s slim back section, but when I did review poetry I could readily work off adrenalin and feel better—though what I said had absolutely no effect on poetry's sickness and merely made enemies for me among some of the more influential sick poets. Oddly I found that the place where I did seem to exert a measure of influence was where I was most ignorant, that is, in television. For more than two years I wrote a not very regular TV column that I had begun casually while in a hospital with nothing to do but be sad and watch the tube. Harrison was strong on the column from the beginning, and it was he who thought up my pseudonym, Sedulus. The pseudonym was settled upon innocently, not as a device for grand concealment but simply to make it possible for more than one person to write the column (several writers other than myself tried their hand at it at the beginning) and also for me to write the column and yet review books too. (It was conventional not to have a writer's name appear twice in any one issue.) The purpose of the column was obscure, but I think now that I thought of it as a pragmatic way for me to decide what a TV column should be about *anyhow*. I did eventually decide; I decided that it had to be about what any long-term column about journalism or the other current and hot media had to be about. It had to be about the new slavery. The trouble was that Harrison didn't agree with me there.

The column was a cinch at the beginning, before I had my big subject. At the hospital I would scribble comments about particular programs on the backs of envelopes, and then dictate into a machine brief program reviews. When I left the hospital, I was able to move out into the politics of TV, writing columns that took the pulse of the FCC occasionally or tried to analyze what Nixon's media man Whitehead was up to (I never really did find out). These were easy too, being a matter of fairly straight reporting on current decisions and statements. The columns also had the merit—at least the program reviews had the merit—of being about matters that everybody right down to the thumbsucking set was familiar with—a pleasant change for an aging poetry reviewer.

But the ease of doing them, and the familiarity of the material, turned out to be dubious assets for the long pull, at least for me. The simple occasions for the columns encouraged simple responses to them. Writing for an intellectual liberal weekly, I found that the occasions encouraged in me the simple, pat, patronizing responses to TV that liberal intellectuals mostly adopted. In other words the occasions were naturals for the sort of journalistic predictability that EP had complained about and that most journalists accept, consciously or unconsciously, as a condition of their professional being. The trouble with me was that I didn't think of myself as a professional, had been trained to avoid stock responses, and had learned that lesson so well that if I had a predictable tic it was of avoiding, or trying to avoid, the predictable.

Another nonprofessional was Helen Featherstone who wrote one of Sedulus's best columns, a long early considerate study of *Sesame Street. Sesame Street* was then, and is now, the darling of public broadcasting; it was the right-thinking liberal's answer to commercial children's shows, the ones with the violent cartoons and the advertisements for sweets and cardboardy cereals and overpriced unsafe toys. But Mrs. Featherstone gently took a different line toward *Sesame Street*, in other words failing the intellectuals by questioning their pet show. She found the show honest and well-intentioned, but she said that some of the good intentions had gone astray. The complaint of hers that caused, as I recall, the most stir among *TNR* readers was that the show's social good intentions had produced prettified social relations on the screen, that is, a falsifying of life's cruel social facts. The many angry letters that we received as a result, especially from TV cleaner-up groups who wanted to know what side we were on *anyway*, were early evidence for me, as I worked myself into the column, that the column was where the action was, but the action wanted to be slave action, canned action, everybody nodding and clapping, or booing and hissing, at the same time. I admired the Featherstone column and wanted to be complained about too.

So I tried to be as unaccommodating as she to right-thinking. I praised the Lucy shows for example and other forms of moron TV comedy (though not steadily; I couldn't stand *Hogan's Heroes*), and I gave approximately two cheers for Arthur Fiedler's pop concerts, though they became more and more pop and the audience at them could be watched and heard singing such catastrophes as "Take Me Out to the Ballgame." (See page 95.) To keep my batting average up I matched my illiberal praise with illiberal complaints—complaints, for example, about the pretentiousness of some of the "serious" and belligerently cultural shows. Slowly it became apparent to me, and maybe to my readers too, that my basic target was not any of the individual shows, good or bad, but the general slavery, that is, TV and media conditioning. As I wrote the columns I found that I kept wanting to find out why and how TV produced or encouraged the responses that it did. But Harrison didn't want me to.

Harrison was ready to back me on particular shows, even when he thought I was being a fool about them, but my new vast subject came to annoy him immensely. When he was annoyed, he behaved like a true journalist with me—he would red-pencil my generalizations and scuttle whole pages of my lovely radical truths about our slave culture—and I then behaved like a misunderstood antijournalistic radical from another country, looking as if I had just been censored (as sometimes I had) and as if I were wondering (as sometimes I was) how long, oh Lord, it would be before the decaying bourgeois world would stop addressing itself to trivia and start asking good basic questions. It would be, I discovered, long indeed if Harrison had his way, but I persisted anyway and generous Harrison gave me more rope than he wanted to.

I began by questioning the narrow focus of liberal criticism of TV, the focus on cigarette advertising or false claims for headache remedies, saying that we were neglecting more sinister though less obvious TV norms (see "Wormy Norms", p. 90), neglecting a variety of pressures the medium was constantly applying to the poor addled brains of the public as well as to the medium's own performers. It wasn't long before I was questioning the media in the large—and Harrison didn't like things in the large. My favorite topic came to be the conditioning of journalists, which therefore came to be one of Harrison's least favorite topics. Knee-jerk liberals had been a steady target for conservatives, but what, I wanted to know, about knee-jerk reporters, liberal or conservative? Was a press free that felt obliged to concentrate half its forces in the wastes of the city of Washington? that was driven by its own internal competitions to focus upon one or two big stories at a time? that was lemminglike in its rush to those stories? and that was uniformly so myopic in its handling of the stories that it couldn't bring itself to any sort of awareness of the extent to which it was not just reporting the stories but creating them? No, my reply kept emerging, the press was not free, or only free to be bounced from one crisis to another at high speed.

So it was of that kind of conditioning that I had Sedulus write when he should have been reviewing *Hee-Haw,* and the piece on Senator Eagleton's destruction was perhaps the high point. Even Harrison did not, as I recall, complain about that one, and for my pains with it I found myself on a Sunday morning TV talk show. Everybody was interested—my position was provocative—but the trouble was that nobody agreed. That unhappily became Sedulus's regular trouble. He had plenty of readers, but he was always on the wrong side.

For the wrong side in the days of Watergate was to be against the journalists; and to be against the journalists was to be identified with the Nixon-Agnew camp. (After one of Sedulus's columns John Osborne even brought the news from the White House that somebody terribly high in Agnew's office had thought well of the column—the kiss of death).

### 3.

Aside from the Sedulus columns and the literary reviews I also undertook to be knowledgeable about the state of the culture and took on reviews of books in the social sciences, in history, in education. After all, one of the early pieces I had written for *TNR* had been about the stock market (p. 222), and if as a salaried scribbler I could write about the stock market, could I not write about anything? Just like the new journalists? No, I slowly discovered that I could not write about anything; I didn't have enough arrogance for it, though from the point of view of my academic colleagues at the university I must have looked like just another one of the enemy. I remember listening in wonder, even after I had been at *TNR* for three years, to an assistant to a prominent columnist for the *New York Times* as she asked me over the phone if I could fill her in on the current state of poetry so that she could fill her boss in on it and, in a couple of days, he could toss off a column on it. The columnist had attained such grace that he didn't need to talk to the likes of me himself to do his column, and he didn't himself have to look at any of the poetry either. I was still not learned enough in the ways of journalism for that, having to read the books I reviewed and having to admit occasionally to vestigial ignorance. As part of my general reaction against the know-it-alls I tended, therefore, to choose know-it-all books for review so that I might do battle with them. It was a case of taking arms against the sea in all cases, but the "kulch" section of this volume accordingly reflects some of the concerns of the Sedulus section.

In all the sections I was discovering—and perhaps this was my only discovery; I was no Columbus—that the power of the dispensers of words was not where it had been. For anyone like myself who had come out of the old place and tried to contend in the new place the shift was sure to be greater than his cogs could readily adjust to—and so my wheels spun raggedly. If as a professor I had become intolerant of my colleagues for being Luddites, I found that among the journalists I was myself a Luddite and rather proud of it. So I was not sorry to leave off editing the back of *TNR* after four years, though it had been good to me and though it was itself an oldtimer suffering from the new tyrannies. I had had enough of keeping up, so went off to write a book about a poet (William Carlos Williams, who also hated journalism), and to vegetate, and to wonder what the world was coming to.

# POETRY

*There are eleven reviews in this section (printed in the chronological order of their appearance in* **The New Republic***), plus two short obits for Eliot and Pound (also written for* **TNR***), plus two longer essays on poetry. Maybe it is an indulgence to include Cole Porter and the Beatles among the poets here, but without them the section, and poetry, would be duller.*

# Kenneth Koch

### THE PLEASURES OF PEACE
*by Kenneth Koch*

Some poets, some very good poets, like to stand on edges.
Wordsworth was always on the edge of bathos, and frequently fell over. Whitman was always about to lose his tonsils, and I can't say for sure that he didn't. What was Shakespeare in danger of?—perhaps of being the writers he stole his plays from.

Kenneth Koch is always on the edge of nonsense or frivolity, or of a bottomless pit of images, fancies, soft squirmy words. Take his well known early poem "Fresh Air"—it is a marvelous "fit" (as in Lewis Carroll) on the sad state of divine poesy. In it the edge he teeters on is between mock and deadly serious, or perhaps between rational statement and yawp. The poem is a dramatic display of supermanner, with Koch trying to see how extravagantly he can gesture without dislocating his elbow. His new book, *Pleasures of Peace,* is an even more extravagant version of the same game, with gesture or manner displacing statement or content as thoroughly as Koch can manage. "Fresh Air" was reduceable to some freshman's miserable precis: "Mr. Koch disapproves of the sterility of academic poetry and criticism;" but much of the new work is further out, beyond reduction. Does anybody want to exegete "O Labrador, you are the sexual Pennsylvania of our times?"

Better not try. These are anti-interpretation days. The oracle Susan Sontag has advised us to cultivate an erotics rather than a hermeneutics of art, and surely Koch's latest poems, like Ashbery's and many lesser gamesmen's, suggest that he agrees. His poems may be compared musically with a long jam session (oh ancient phrase) on "Ain't She Sweet" or, more tonily, compared with Beethoven's "Diabelli Variations" where the original waltz is merely the departure point for the concert. Koch is a master of such music. He is marvelously various and inventive. He can play the names of the forty-eight states (he hasn't got to fifty yet) as if they were the complete works of Beethoven, and do the same with sounds, faces, islands, with the phrase "sleeping with women," with erotic proper names, in short anything he finds worthy of gaming with.

Sometimes he adds a harebrained plot, as in the poem "Scales" where he follows a singer's laborious ascent of do-re-mi three times, and the descent once, and then has her reach too low, hemorrhage on fa and die.

Clever. Funny. But that is the curse of the game too. When the poems fall over the edge they are last-days-of-the-empire stuff; the reader wants to put Koch to work in a salt mine.

There are good and ponderous reasons for such excesses of manner. Seriously to set about saying things in poetry gets harder and harder (and never was easy) simply because everything has already been said and said badly in bad prose, and keeps being said more and worse. We're awash in statement. "What oft was said but ne'er so well expressed . . ." is a joke of poetic policy when practically every "what" a poet can think of has been said so oft that it has achieved the vigor of "Ain't She Sweet" before he gets to it. At least that seems to be Koch's position on truths in poetry: they are dead ducks in this age of truth overkill, unless you treat them *as* dead, in which case the deader the better.

The title poem, my favorite, takes that deadest of ducks, peace, and improvises around it. Koch presents himself as writing a poem for peace in competition with one Giorgio Finogle who is also doing one. Giorgio throws himself out of a window for peace, which slows up his poem. Koch keeps on, meanwhile making love for peace and parodying solemn statements of lovers.

He finishes his poem and then gives us samples of the reviews of it: "Great, man! "Dead, man!" "I will expect you at six!" Meanwhile, back at the world, monkeys and boats and "all the really important mountains" are for peace, and we emerge sweaty, after 16 pages, with our freshman paraphrase: Nothing is more futile than being for peace.

Over the edge? I don't know but I think so. I had hoped that something more than the usual manner would be displayed in the poem, for the poem is in part a complaint against the manner, a complaint against the wild and futile gesticulations of pacifists. I was looking for Koch to come clean, speak straight from the shoulder about peace, about anything. He didn't, and rightly or wrongly I was disappointed. The poem is so good I would have liked it to be serious too.

Where is the future of the mode? For the unsubtle imitators of

Koch—and there seem to be a lot of them—the future is over the edge
into dada, mockery of mockery, absolute non-statement. But for Koch
the future is unclear because he obviously has the capacity, if not the
inclination, to be thoroughly rationalist in his verse, and to play a
number of other roles than those he chooses.

Since I like Koch but don't like the nonsense world that much of
his poetry edges toward, my inclination is to pray for him to come back
from the edge. I'm dubious of the results of the prayer, though. Koch
might reply by writing a poem about it:

> *They are praying for me in Andalusia—or is it the bathroom?*
> *They are praying and I hear them, the worms,*
> *They are perfecting me into a service station.*

1969

# A.E. Housman

### THE CONFINES OF CRITICISM
### by A.E. Housman

Eight and fifty years ago A.E. Housman delivered at Cambridge a lecture conceived in bitterness at what was happening to scholarship. He singled out an Oxford man, Algernon Charles Swinburne, for special blame. Swinburne had taken as a masterpiece one line by Shelley that Housman wanted to demonstrate was unfinished (Housman couldn't demonstrate Shelley's dissatisfaction with it for sure; hence the publishing delay of eight and fifty). The line—"Fresh spring, and summer, and winter hoar"—wasn't important but the Swinburne procedure with it was. Swinburne had abandoned observation and tradition for epithet; he had gone overboard. He had said that "the melodious effect of the line's exquisite inequality . . . was a thing to thrill the veins and draw tears to the eyes of all men." If he had played scholar, Housman felt, rather than violinist he might have noted the good reasons for Shelley's dissatisfaction with his own line, might have noted that the line was short a foot and a season—and having noted that he might have let his readers judge for themselves its exquisiteness.

The year (1911) of Housman's lecture was also the year of the publication of the eleventh edition of the Encyclopedia Britannica, a great year, maybe the last great year of a dying cause. In 1912 came *Poetry* of Chicago followed closely by Ezra Pound, T.S. Eliot, the War and all those other persons and events we now associate with the invention of modernity. Housman was above all else not modern; he was a crusty old Latinist who concluded his lecture with a spirited diatribe against keeping up with the Joneses, what he called "servility shown toward the living." The servility was often found "in company with a lack of veneration for the dead." Housman counseled thinking "more of the dead than the living" (can any one imagine such counsel now?) and added:

> *The dead have at any rate endured a test to which the living have not yet been subjected. If a man, fifty or a hundred years*

*after his death, is still remembered and accounted a great*
*man, there is a presumption in his favor which no living man*
*can claim; and experience has taught me that it is no mere*
*presumption. It is the dead and not the living who have most*
*advanced our learning and science; and though their*
*knowledge may have been superseded, there is no supersession*
*of reason and intelligence . . . If our conception of scholarship*
*and our methods of procedure are at variance with theirs, it*
*is not indeed a certainty or a necessity that we are wrong, but a*
*good working hypothesis.*

Remarkable words. The Cambridge Press editors must have felt very daring in resurrecting them. Yet Pound, though he hated Housman and was in his prime the noisiest advocate in Europe of making it new, would not have denied the past its due as so many poets and critics do now, and he would have been delighted with Housman's attack on Swinburne. Until recently most modern students of literature would also have gone along with Housman's major premises, though perhaps thinking of Housman himself as an old fuddy duddy. The past *was*, literarily, depended on, until recently, by all camps, and the extravagances of Swinburne's showbiz criticism were deplored.

When I was in college the Swinburne sort of thing could be found, however. It was for example well represented by Professor Billy Phelps at Yale, and both the old scholars and the New Critics could agree to deplore Billy. Billy was a great popularizer, a legislator of lowbrow tastes, an addict like Swinburne of purple appreciations. Looking back I realize now that nearly the whole of my literary education, in works ancient or modern, was designed to combat what Billy encouraged.

Particularly he encouraged the vice that I.A. Richards, another Cambridge man, inveighed against: the stock response. Housman and the old scholars believed that independence from faddish current opinion could be achieved by respecting ancient texts and ancient authority. The New Critics tended to favor the authority of the texts alone. The difference was sometimes construed as that between the inductive and deductive mode, and it was a difference that seemed, in 1940, to threaten the destruction of English Departments course by course and brick by brick; yet throughout that civil war Billy and his kind remained for both sides a greater threat than destruction. When he retired at Yale in 1940 most members of the literature faculty were overjoyed; they felt that education could now resume.

Now another thirty years have passed, of which ten have been the

Terrible Sixties. The sixties discredited evenhandedly the old scholars and the New Critics, leaving English departments on the ropes and increasingly dependent for their clientele upon offerings of that non-course called Creative Writing (imagine what Housman's lecture on Creative Writing would have been like). The sixties also reintroduced the postures of Swinburne and Billy Phelps with a vengeance, in the form of what Susan Sontag, who is not to be blamed for the *whole* thing, called an erotics of criticism. If the Howling Seventies give us more of the same, literary people of my generation will die even sourer than Housman.

A modest reversal is pleasanter to contemplate: a thermidorean reaction. Some semblance of the past's authority would be restored, and the mind's role in creation and criticism would again be acknowledged. Suddenly students would discover quaint old characters like Housman, and would loftily tell their parents about them. Eventually *New York* might publish a spread about Housman, together with wild bearded poets busily counting their feet.

Perhaps the Cambridge Press had the same crazy dream before they issued this book. In any event, here, in a mere fifty pages, is a past so remote as to be attractive, and an academic position so stodgy it's radical. Read Housman; he's the most.

1969

# The Beatles

### THE BEATLES ILLUSTRATED LYRICS
*edited by Alan Aldridge*

I was kingpin of my age group," said John. "The sort of gang I led went in for things like shoplifting and pulling girls' knickers down."

"We had masters who just hit you with rulers, or told us a lot of shit about their holiday in Wales or what they did in the Army," said Paul. "Never once did anyone make it clear to me what I was being educated for."

George had some school complaints too: "Some schizophrenic jerk just out of training school would just read out notes to you which you were expected to take down . . . Useless, the lot of them . . . They were trying to turn everybody into rows of little toffees."

Unlike the others poor Ringo didn't have a chance to rebel as a child, and he didn't have "the education to do anything clever" because he was sick all the time. He stole a few items from Woolworth's—"just silly plastic things"—but he was a late bloomer and the last Beatle to join up. He felt out of things for a while but made the scene at last— and received time in the authorized biography of the Beatles by Hunter Davies (1968).

The quotations above are from that biography, maybe the first authorized biography ever deliberately devised to make its subject(s) look bad. The sixties suddenly made possible large monetary rewards for praising and promoting dropouts and dropoutism. The Beatles found out early where big money was—it was in good anti-bourgeois vice—and with remarkable prescience they then hung close to the appropriately dissentious fads, right through LSD and the mysterious East, until they reached their present rich old age of 28 (average). For as John put it in the *new* book, "You see we're influenced by whatever's going."

John might have added, had he not been modest (he *did* say once that they were bigger than Jesus, but that was in Nashville), that they were not only influenced but influences. One of my children was just four when the first Ed Sullivan Beatle program occurred, and the "yeah yeah yeah" in a stirring love song released him instantly from whatever small influence we had upon him. His head began to bob, he stamped his feet, he went off to find a drum, make a toy guitar—and grow hair. He has never recovered.

The new book, containing most of the lyrics the Beatles have themselves written, is another instance of their clever tactics. The lyrics are not bad but they would have looked naked and skinny if they had been left by themselves. Certainly not revolutionary. The problem of the book was to find something to accompany a lyric on a page, something equivalent to Beatle noise; and the problem was handsomely solved with pictures, hundreds of wild, sexy, psychedelic, *noisy* pictures.

Half the new artists of the now world were harnessed to the job, and the result is extremely now. The editor Alan Aldridge is himself a clever young now dropout with appropriately long hair, and he describes his occupation with a phrase that covers the book itself: he is in the business of "graphic entertainment." In graphic entertainment as in music the Beatles continue to let whatever's going influence them. The book, priced low for so much genuine nekkid art, will sell like hotcakes and breed dozens of publishing imitations, some perhaps even using Dante or Shakespeare's sonnets as a lyrical base (Think! the Dark Lady!—I shdnt have mentioned it.)

What is impressive about the lyric entertainment in the book is how simple and sentimental and corny most of it is without the accompanying dissonance. Those who take deep soundings into the meanings of Beatle words should pay attention instead to the meaning of musical bronx cheers—for they are where the big Beatle profundity lies. A few lyrics have innuendoes about drugs and sex, and a few are openly porn, notably "Why don't we do it in the road?" but mostly they are straightforward love lyrics out of the twenties. Tin Pan Alley had its innuendoes too but people just laughed at them. Now in our age of revolution we are asked, by editor Aldridge among others, to revel in solemn ambiguities and hidden meanings; but the revel of the lyrics simply does not reside there. It resides instead in a bright and mildly tricky verbal surface enforced by, of all things, rhyme and meter:

> *Michelle ma belle*
> *Those are words that go together well.*

And:

> *It feels so right now, hold me tight,*

*Tell me I'm the only one,*
*And then I might*
*Never be the lonely one.*

Those are deep like Irving Berlin. Ah, but editor Aldridge would have
me look in the *deep* songs such as those in the Sgt Pepper album where
there are deepnesses about going on trips and even a bit of Liverpool
phallic. Yes, and there is surrealism too, as in lines like "keeping her
face in a jar by the door." But despite Aldridge's protestations the lyrics
remain simple even as the Beatles themselves keep saying they are
simple. Their very first song, composed by John and Paul together,
remains the model for at least a third of the lyrics. It begins undeeply
with a clever little syntactical twist, its only distinguishing feature
aside from the fourth line's "who-ho":

*Love, love me do,*
*You know I love you.*
*I'll always be true*
*So please love me do, who ho love me do.*

Another third of the poems is like the first third except that Romantic
Love is ridiculed or denied. The following sour lyric, for example,
would seem to be a sort of parody of romantic songs in which the girl is
going away and the boy is heartbroken:

*Do what you want to do,*
*And go where you're going to,*
*Think for yourself,*
*'Cos I won't be there with you.*

In such songs the Beatles are little boys throwing snowballs at
stovepipe hats. Yet they also constantly pay their respects to the hats
by keeping the "I love yous" and the simple rhymes and rhythms as a
base.

The third third of their collection is of course the deep third,
containing numbers with exotic imagery from the land of the lotus
eaters, plus a few ironic dialogues in which they play the roles of
unpleasant bourgeois types ("Revolution," "Try to See it My Way,"
"She's Leaving Home"). These songs are more than just tricky, and
perhaps I cheat here by underemphasizing them and emphasizing the
other two-thirds of the Beatles' repertoire—the Beatles can afford to
be cheated. Anyway it was the deeprooted conventionality of the first
two thirds of the selection that most impressed me. I was oddly taken

back in my mind to the old Orson Welles movie *Citizen Kane*, in which the mystery of the old man's last death-bed word, "Rosebud," as well as the mystery of what had made him tick all his life, is laboriously sustained to the very dramatic end when the flames of Kane's great house as it burns finally consume a small sled in the attic. On the sled is the word "Rosebud."

Tin Pan Alley is the Beatles' rosebud, and a convincing rosebud it is for four young capitalists selling 225 million records and saving the British pound. But what *should* be the rosebud for four of the world's leading dissenters? Neither honest art nor thoroughgoing dissent has ever accommodated itself well to money and middle class opportunism. The Beatles have ringed their art with layer upon layer of dissonance, but in the still heart of most of the lyrics the deep truth is revealed. Hell of a way to run a revolution.

1969

# The New York Poets

GREAT BALLS OF FIRE
*by Ron Padgett*

OLT
*by Kenneth Gangemi*

T o one of those who are now called the New York Poets I once said grandly that it was impossible for a poet not to make any sense at all in a poem. Since then the New York Poets have proved me wrong hundreds of times. Ron Padgett is a leader among these poets, though he is young; and according to the blurb with his book he is about to turn out an anthology of the New York Poets. He is therefore a master of nonsense, and also apparently a teacher of it. Great balls of fire.

But who are the New York Poets? Their name for themselves must be a joke, perhaps derived from that other joke, the San Francisco Poets. The New York Poets are an entity—clique?—with poetic notions largely inherited from Frank O'Hara, Kenneth Koch and John Ashbery.

E.E. Cummings would have called the entity a nonentity, because he didn't believe that genuine, gilt-edged poets went around in groups. Poetry, he said, was strictly an individual proposition. Yet he probably would have liked a good many of the individuals in the (non)entity. Padgett seems, for example, endlessly inventive and goodhumored; he would have been a "yes" force for Cummings. Each poem is a fresh start for Padgett, a new game; and he collects marvelous gewgaws like the following:

> *Steve is suffering from a severe old.*
> *LaSalle and his hand explored*
>   *Louisiana.*
> *The cadet saluted the Ten Commandments.*
> *The Wicks sent the box of wax to*
>   *the monks by express.*
> *The foreigner examined the ruined*
>   *Latin.*

He can also make sense too when he wants to, which is not often. In one poem he tells us that the terrible brain of Mussolini should not be brought to our country, but should be placed in the Smithsonian Institution in Washington. In another poem he observes that the first line of a poem he wrote wasn't really a very good line, and wasn't his line but his wife's, who didn't mean it. And then there is this:

> Let's take a string quartet
> Playing one of Beethoven's compositions
> We may explain it as the scratching
> Of a horse's hair against a cat's gut;
> Or we may explain it as the mind
> Of a genius soaring up to an infinite
> Horse's hair scratching against an infinite cat's gut.

Profound, I say, and sound. Unfortunately very little of this book moves in the direction of statements that an old sense-monger like me can construe *as* sense. Instead the game is to avoid sense, to live a twenty-four hour day receiving random signals from all over and exploring every random fancy that enters the head. This apparent motivelessness can have real charm—the poem is there because it's there because it's there. It can be a fine antidote to high rhetoric, bigthink and puritan uplift generally, what D.H. Lawrence described scornfully as the American urge to crack the whip and "get things inside a barbed wire corral."

It can also, though, be boringly self-indulgent. It is a poetry of the supermarket, with the poet throwing anything and everything into his basket, rolling it forth, and saying, as if we had an obligation to care, "look what *I* found!"

I don't know if Kenneth Gangemi thinks of himself as a New York Poet, and anyway this particular volume is prose; but what he is doing in clear syntactical prose is very much of a piece with what they call poetry, and I don't want to argue genres. How we can live with the New York Poets (in poetry or prose) as a force, a collective, an aesthetic hippopotamus rolling through our time, I don't know. Their now most worn device is that of the listing. They all can list sweet nothings for pages and pages. In *Olt* Gangemi has written three sketches of the life of an idle mind committed to listings. That mind collects oddities from newspapers and billboards and heaven, and spews them forth endlessly as its body goes about its mundane business:

*Robert Olt picked up the newspaper and began to read. Japan was building mineral-extracting ships that propelled themselves through the sea by ejecting the water they had processed. A gas explosion had blown off sixteen manhole covers. The Pope had warned against "the virus of rationalism." A breed of chickens had been developed that laid nothing but double-yoked eggs. The Marine Corps had hired a team of psychiatrists . . .*

The prose is straightforward; the listings sometimes have the wit and excitement the New York Poets seem to be looking for; and if Gangemi's little book had appeared in isolation, it would deserve praise. But in the context of what are now years of this stuff, plus the threat of a long novel from Gangemi possibly in the same vein, I think I should hold my enthusiasm in check.

1969

# Charles Olson

LETTERS FOR ORIGIN
*by Charles Olson*

Charles Olson died four months ago. He was a difficult and eccentric writer and teacher, whose followers and admirers, though not numerous, are firm in their loyalty to his talent and way of art. An outsider comes to him best through a celebrated but now aging Grove Press anthology, *The New American Poetry* (1945-60), edited by Donald Allen, where both his verse and verse theory (though he professed to hate aesthetics) are well represented. The book at hand, a collection of letters, is an extremely private document, and the editor, Albert Glover, seems to have been determined to keep it so (by carefully omitting from the book the "scholarly clarifications" that he concocted as doctoral dissertation for the State University of New York at Buffalo). It does, however, display the intensity of the man, and something of his life and character, as well as illuminating some of his notions of "projective verse." It should be put with his first book, *Call Me Ishmael*, as background material for the poems. *Call Me Ishmael*, published in 1947, is an odd but telling reconstruction of *Moby Dick's* origins in Melville's mind and experience. Olson concentrates on the Pacific as SPACE and TIME (Olson loved capitals), and on Shakespeare's dark plays as a source of the character Ahab. The new *Letters For Origin* show us not Ahab or Melville but Olson himself contending with primal elements on dry land, and using for a whaleboat a little magazine called *Origin,* edited by Cid Corman. With the naivete of the best and worst of those who have entrepreneured in little magazines, he apparently did think of himself as vaguely in Ahab's position as he shipped off his manuscripts to Corman. The magazine, published for four or five years in the mid-fifties, is no longer even available at the Library of Congress (which recommended to me that I go to the New York Public Library or Kyoto, Japan for it), so it may not seem a very seaworthy craft. But to Olson it was. His poems had appeared only spottily elsewhere, until Corman came along. Corman offered him and Robert Creeley great quantities of space—comparable, I suppose, to the Pacific—and Olson set forth with the vigor of all great American entrepreneurs to achieve a conquest.

Corman was an affable collaborator mostly, and Olson displayed great affection for him except when he talked back. Olson praised him particularly for wanting to organize the first issue of *Origin* so that it could be read "from cover to cover as a single effect"—shades of Edgar Allen Poe. Olson wanted a magazine, like a poem, to be a "FIELD OF FORCE"; he disapproved the way most magazines were broken up into sections of poetry, fiction, and criticism, and he filled Corman's ear with diatribes against conventional categories. Insistently he spoke of getting down, or back, to primary things; in the middle of their correspondence, as if to prove his point, he took off for Mexico to study Mayan culture. With the elemental on land or sea he professed to be at home; there he sought, with Ahab, honesties.

And as in Ahab there seemed to be in Olson a sort of elemental confusion of motives. Was the act of writing a poem (or publishing a magazine, or hunting a white whale) undertaken in the name of inner illumination or outward conquest? Was striking behind the mask war or art? Was it revenge against a cruel world or the pursuit of truth? If an inner search, why so much concern for constructing, like a blooming rhetorician, "effects"? A doctrine of effects in Poe's hands had a fine decadent air about it—but in Olson's the doctrine contradicted the search for the honesties and primal necessities he kept harping on. It seems he wished to be artful and artless at once.

His poems as well as letters display the difficulty. His two most ambitious anthologized poems, "The Kingfishers" and "Maximus of Gloucester," are both elaborately sophisticated constructs, but to the end of simplicity and wholeness. They preach the wholeness of elemental organic life but they are themselves patchwork composites after the manner of a Pound *Canto*.

Olson's hero, aside from Melville, *was* Pound; Olson matched Pound's yearnings for the Chinese and the Greek with his own for the Mayan, and he assumed with Pound that one could move freely out of the cultural trap one was born to—a common American delusion—into something more basic, truer. Also with Pound he divided his energies confusingly between escaping the culture and trying to set it straight, and therefore like Pound he found his devotion to art constantly being interrupted by his need to be a pedagogue.

It must have been the pedagogue as much as the artist in him that made him worry about "effects," but a pedagogue with only the haziest notions of how the "effects" might be received by an audience. Like Pound, when he set forth on an artistic conquest, he entertained extremely grandiose notions of what he was about. Ahab did too, but at least he was grandiose within the frame of whaling, an odd but worldly occupation. Olson seems to have had no such frame; he was out in the Pacific alone with his poems and his theory.

Olson's confusion about the size of his poetic ventures is both Poundian and American. In recent years particularly we have been treated to an enormous amount of romantic fudge about the uses of poetry. From the private life of the poet with his poem to the big bad world outside seems a big jump to the worldly. It did not to Olson, and it does not to most of the young in art. They imagine both truth and conquest to attend solemnly upon their acts of art, yet they are extremely misty about what truth it is they are seeking and what conquests they can reasonably expect.

A very different kind of poet, Wallace Stevens, constantly meditated on the powers of poetry, and kept coming to modest conclusions. He once said, for example, that poetry was a way of getting the day in order—he meant by that, as I read him, the poet's or his reader's *private* day. In contrast Olson seems to have thought of art as a way of plumbing the day, or making it over—and making it over for everybody. Thus, alongside Olson, Stevens is apt to look like a dilettante, not serious, not really committed—and at one point in his letters Olson says as much about him. Yet it was Stevens who could on the one hand describe beautifully the range of an artist's conquests (I think of "The Idea of Order at Key West"), and on the other acknowledge the presence of the "fatal dominant X," destroyer of poets.

The Stevens kind of perception I miss until very late in Pound; that great man was benevolently but sometimes absurdly Quixotic. I miss it also in Olson, but his last works I do not know. I suspect that its absence ultimately brought them both great disappointments; their fatal white whale was perhaps their own expectations.

1970

# From "Howl" to OM

## INDIAN JOURNALS
### by Allen Ginsberg

Allen Ginsberg's "Howl" was based on the extraordinary premise that it described the "best minds" of Ginsberg's generation. (To qualify as a best mind one had to be on drugs, on the road and a Ginsberg acquaintance.) Also it had extraordinary sales, probably attributable to its pornography. Yet it was a strong poem, a poem of great energy; it had a way of gobbling up complaints about it. Within a few years of its publication (1956) it had joined a small number of earth-moving angry poems of this century, poems that poets (and people) who come after have been unable to ignore.

Because of "Howl," poets writing in the sixties became ill-at-ease manufacturing their tried-and-true delicate nuances. Fashion decreed that they howl instead. Ginsberg's poem had the effect of a sort of natural disaster. The country deserved it—and poetry deserved it—but it was a disaster nonetheless, one that left us in a state of poetic emergency. Rightly or wrongly, "Howl" knocked hell out of earlier images of what best minds say and do. Not only was it descriptive of a vast social-spiritual death, but it provided a villainous cause, the god Moloch who in the poem is simply the System. Not since the thirties had the System had such an inclusive raking over—in fact, "Howl" singlehandedly did much to restore the thirties vogue of super-colossal system-damnation we are still suffering from, and it did so without providing a Marxist antidote. It was what D. H. Lawrence would perhaps have called a death-energy poem.

Having dropped his bomb, Ginsberg looked around for a next step—and that of course was to rehabilitate us. Any powers effectively restorative of the blasted American landscape would obviously have to come from outside the country; and so, with the remarkable timing that has marked his career Ginsberg went thoroughly Eastern. His *Indian Journals* (March 1962-May 1963) described in prose and verse his heavily hallucinatory (morphine) daily experiences in India where, with Peter Orlovsky, he scouted out nirvana and suchlike for us: "heaven: a place beyond shit and desire."

My impression is that he didn't find it (heaven), nor did he escape "clinging to my human known me, Allen Ginsberg." He also failed—if the Journals are evidence—to get very close to India. He describes encounters with a variety of holy men—and provides us with a few snapshots of them—but the encounters are tourist-like in their brevity and incompleteness. The significant life of the book is (1) the inner life of the poet reflecting on poetry, America, death, love, personality; (2) the private life of the poet in a room with Orlovsky; and (3) the life of the astonished alien observer seeing for the first time India's squalor and grandeur. The squalor he is good on; it offends him far less than American tawdriness; he displays no middle-class goose pimples about dirt and starvation, and he has an understandable obsession for the constant proximity of death in India—the skeletons living and the corpses burning:

> boy chased three cows out of the rectangle garden of fire—they were eating up a corpse litter prematurely—or horsing around in the way—the nearby corpse masked in white shroud lay back in the flames & turned black, knees hanging down, the veil burning away and one ear sticking too far out . . .

On the grandeur, particularly at the Taj Mahal, he is weaker; he is driven to tears and exclamation points like Richard Halliburton himself: "O Spoken with Stone! O Socialist Architecture!" Indeed? But whether meditating, making love or touring the streets and temples, he emerges forever as A.G. from Paterson, N.J.—*not* made over by drugs or by the cultural distancing.

I must confess to what must by now be obvious, a passionate disapproval of all the sudden easy Easternness that descended on the American sensibility in the sixties. To me it was, and still is, a screaming defeat for the whole revisionary machine of youth; and so I naturally look on Ginsberg as a wicked pied piper. My "error" here, however, has not been, I believe, in failing to respect Eastern thought as she is thought in a loin cloth under the Howrah Bridge in Calcutta, but in failing to respect it in young middle-class Americans, to whom a guru is like a new exotic flavor at Howard Johnson's.

For the devotee the fascination of *Indian Journals* will presumably be in seeing where and how the saint who brought OM to Chicago had his basic—i.e., oriental—training. For me, the non-believer, the fascination is mostly less pleasant; it is the fascination of seeing close-up the kind of cheaply acquired religious experience—hop the plane, get the drugs—that has come to take hold of so many so fast in the last few years. For me this second stage in the Ginsberg saga has been even more calamitous than the "Howl" stage. The first had the genuineness of anger and despair about it—it was home grown and home felt—but the second has been clouded by great expectations, expectations that Ginsberg himself sometimes manages to temper with solid observations and with his striking death-obsession, but that his devotees infallibly leave raw: nirvana in the pad, nightly, forever. There is terror for me in their misconceptions of what inner fantasy-life can make of the stony world; and Ginsberg is one of the breeders of that terror. Saintly he may indeed be as a private sinner—I do not question his private credentials—but he has also been a most influential loudmouth, an eccentric evangelist for an apocalyptic faith (and aesthetic) that has in my opinion competed pretty well with Moloch in mind-destroying. In various parts of *Indian Journals* he runs down the apocalyptic most effectively.

> *"Skin is sufficient to be skin, that's all it ever could be, tho screams of pain in the kidney make it sick of itself . . ."*

Yet the fantasy-Ginsberg is what the destroyed ones pick up.

As an addendum I should note that Allen Ginsberg has written an introduction to a newly published volume of verse, *Morning in Spring,* by his father, Louis Ginsberg (Morrow, $1.95), in which A.G. prophesies, ambiguously, the country's return to his father's kind of verse. Beyond OM?! The father is an excellent craftsman in a mode that (I say without malice) Ezra Pound might have described as popular magazine verse fifty years ago, largely because it displays occasional inversions and tum-te-tum, and speaks abstractly without guile about life in general, like Arthur Hugh Clough or, later, Ella Wheeler Wilcox. Allen Ginsberg has never been strong on Pound's precepts either, though a praiser of Pound. His new prophecy is hard to believe, but yes, it *would* be grand to go beyond OM, almost anywhere.

1970

# A Poetic Leader Without Guitar

### THE LIFE OF MAYAKOVSKY
*by Wiktor Woroszylski*

Thirty years or so of progressive annoyance with that dubious entity called modern poetry have persuaded me that modern poetry will never come to much so long as it keeps doing what it has been doing: finding the surrounding culture contemptible. Maybe the culture is contemptible, but that's not my point.

I agree that the nonmodern poets, the sweet things who have found good in the culture, haven't done well, but that's not my point either. They were not good poets. We have had good poets but pitifully little poetry, because the good poets—I am thinking of English and American white poets—have had little to be affirmative about except their own poor battered selves.

To know why the culture and the poets have been apart— and all the good poets have thoroughly documented the reason for separation—is not enough. Knowledge will not help produce the poetry it would be healthful to have. But even less healthful is pretending that England and America have been living through a glorious age of poetry for the last half-century. English Departments and publishers may need to kid themselves into a bit of glory to keep the money flowing, but aside from the economics of the thing I think it is time for a little honesty. The poets my generation grew up reading— Eliot, Yeats, Pound, Stevens and so on—and the poets who started the new poetry of the sixties—Ginsberg, Ferlinghetti, Corso and so on— are alike in their incapacity to live with the culture. Eliot's incapacity and Ginsberg's incapacity are different, and of course their poetry is different; but they are both of the hate-the-culture party, and so are *all* the important moderns, old and new, of no matter what aesthetic persuasion. The role of serious modern western literature has persistently been, except in Communist countries, the role of the dissident. And dissidence, though it may be necessary, does not produce the poetry the world pants for.

The alienation will continue. My guess is it will deepen. But poetry—and literature in general—will not be, can never be, the better for it. We have an enormous poetry machine, an enormous literary machine, endlessly spewing clinkers—and the cause is clear: the machine is endlessly committed to refusing to serve any central social cause, committed to a variety of salvations of the self, a wide assortment of ye olde capitalist anarcho-individualist alternatives to what V.L. Parrington a long time ago called (and I hated him for it) literature of the mainstream.

Nobody thinks of Parrington any more. Or MacLeish. They are the central Kulch side of life that Western intellectuals, remembering many failures, are bred up to dismiss. And of course nobody *ever* has thought seriously of Washington or City Hall or any possible central administrative entity as a way to bring together the Kulch. Nobody, that is, who can be said to be a significant shaping spirit in literature.

As an American, one does not I think understand Mayakovsky's mad gyrations as a Soviet enthusiast and revolution-booster without drawing certain analogies between the Russian and American experience. So let me be personal and describe my private experience with Kulch, especially Washington. Washington shares the look of Moscow and the Party in that it has always been a big part of the mass cultural thing the American literary intellectual can't stand. Starting with Thoreau, or even earlier, 19th century intellectuals were appalled by Washington, but it was Henry Adams who first solidly elaborated upon the intellectuals' complaint. Adams was a snob about Washington, and Washington was nearly as bad then as it is now: it was all rhetoric and no mind, it was power and emptiness, it wasn't human, it was (and is) something to be snobbish about.

My pre-World-War-II college generation took in the Thoreau-Adams views of bureaucracy and Washington. The views were part of our classroom education in the past, and important to us; but we were more nearly affected by what the thirties depression had done to Washington. It had produced the New Deal and the new contempt for Washington manifested by the likes of my FDR-hating physician father, who sat at home with high blood pressure created by the horrors of a save-the-world federal government. My father didn't understand the modern-poetry kick I went on, and he remained a good

Book-of-the-Month-Club person as I developed into a snob about best sellers and had my own brief theoretical love affair with Washington; yet he could be kind and sympathetic about my poetry, my little magazines, my Ezra Pound—no problem there. He remained unappeasable only by Washington; and when and if I ever displayed the slightest affection for FDR he went silent. He did want us to win the war, but otherwise the whole national scene remained an abomination for him. The oddity is that he and my modern-poetry friends, whom he couldn't understand, were in agreement: Washington was the end.

That Washington was the end I had forgotten when I came to it as poetry consultant for the Library of Congress in 1964. I had been holed away in Minnesota for two decades, where the Cowles newspapers and modern literature and sheer prairie had kept me well insulated from Washington; but I needed only a week or two at the Library to sense the enormity of the spiritual clash between the Library's poetry post and the Feds surrounding it. I have never been treated so well, never been made so much of as a poet as I was that year at the Library, but the cause was not I; the cause was the post. Nobody, in Washington or out, has ever quite believed that post. Washington is not supposed to have poets, certainly not an official poet; the whole notion is ridiculous. Yet, courtesy of Gertrude Clarke Whittall, Washington keeps having one official poet. I know of no better post in the world than the Library of Congress post to sense the foreignness of Washington from the literary sensibility, a foreignness that is the foreignness of all bureaucracy, all big government, all large-scale non-individualist thought from whatever it is that the Thoreaus, Eliots, Orwells, Ginsbergs, Mailers, even Beatles stand for. I lived for a year in Washington dazed by the inexplicable pleasantness of the Library post, then returned to Washington a year later to be properly the outsider that Washington demands artists be. That was 1966.

But in 1966 the peace movement was strong and the intellectuals were moving in on Washington from all over, and especially from NY, to set the government straight. Sitting in Washington as a new literary native I saw for the first time with my own eyes the magnitude of the contempt for Washington these visitors had. They thought *nobody* could live in Washington and not be tainted.

How much of American utopian life has in its heart a march on Washington. And how different has been the Russian experience, with its perhaps misplaced but nonetheless real faith in the central thing that is Moscow. At first sight it is thus the remoteness of the Mayakovsky experience from the American experience that is striking. In our country Mayakovsky would have been a New York or Hollywood figure, a success story in the individualist vein like Chaplin (or perhaps somebody more mercantile—Bob Hope?—I can't find an appropriate entrepreneur-*artiste*)—but in his own country Mayakovsky became rapidly an agent of the revolutionary bureaucracy, a soldier in the mainstream that was Moscow. He would have made a grand poetry consultant at the L of C.

He was one of the prime exhibitionists of all time. Wherever he was the center of the world was. That he should have been a champion of socialist realism is a laugh, but he was that too. He was also a futurist—which at the time of World War I was like being a surrealist, something way out and disorderly. And he was insistently central at the same time. Amazing. He began being a poet by being a 15-year-old rebel, jailed for printing revolutionary material. His poetry itself was a sort of afterthought to his personality (in his poet-as-person get-up he is insistently reminiscent of our guitar poets). In 1913—he was by then 18—he persuaded his mother to sew him up a brightly striped tunic, and the tunic demonstrably made him a poet before he opened his mouth (he was an extraordinary physical presence anyway—tall, strong, handsome, fierce, funny), and the tunic therefore became, just as the revolution itself began to take shape, a fuzzy symbol of rebellion, futurism, whatall. Soon he was making with the fame and money by circulating in his tunic, reading poems, and being Mayakovsky. Wherever he was he was at home, and a leader. By the age of 24 he was an old pro as a poet, a film actor and producer (he rewrote a Jack London story into a "scenario about a Russian poet who overcomes all obstacles in his fight against conservative tastes and gains fame and riches") and a fixture as a revolutionary. He was and he was not an establishment figure; he was and was not of the new people's government. At "The Poet's Cafe" in 1918 he introduced the People's Commissar for Education, who thereupon attacked the futurists for their anarcho-individualism but praised Mayakovsky. Maybe, thought the commissar, Mayakovsky could "attract the masses and tinge futurism with an element of popular art," as other futurists could not; yet Mayakovsky was also, in the commissar's mind, obviously a bit of a freak. He was that in the minds of the futurists too.

In the early years of the revolution Mayakovsky was apparently a popular, certainly a ubiquitous performer, who kept his ties with the anarchistic, egocentric futurists, yet also sold himself as a worker and a propagandist for the working class (he did posters as well as instant epic poems); he was full of "I" but he was also tired of the "trifles" of private loving and suffering that he had written about in the near past:

> Comrades,
> give us a new form of art—
> an art
> that will pull the republic out of the
> mud
> ("Order #2 to the Army of the
> Arts.")

In 1918 one Nikolai Punin said of him, in a review: "Mayakovsky, after all his street rhetoric, has now placed himself in a square like a monument and, as the first among futurist poets, has clearly said 'we.' At that moment he ceased to be a romantic and became a classic."

Maybe. But he was a romantic again the next week. Mayakovsky built friends and enemies, and identified with changing movements and causes, with great casualness; but he remained throughout his changes a fixed public symbol, something to talk about rather than someone to know, a dependable undependable whom everyone could use as an instance of something. Even Lenin could profitably refer to him (1922):

> Yesterday I came across a poem by Mayakovsky on a political theme. I do not count myself among the admirers of his poetic talent, though I fully admit my lack of competence in that sphere. But it is a long time since I have felt so satisfied from a political and administrative point of view. In that poem, the poet utterly derides and mocks the Communists because they confer and debate all the time. I do not know whether it is good poetry, but I promise you he is absolutely right from a political point of view. . . .

As the revolution took hold and the inexorable issues of the individual's place in the hungry utopia sharpened, Mayakovsky's own place, I gather, grew less sharp. He was born, as so many commentators observed, to revolution, he was at home with it the moment it was mentioned; so there was never any problem in his becoming some sort of leader in it, with or without guitar. If he had been at the Library of Congress it would have been marvelous; he would have held poetry readings in the parking lot of the Capitol rather than across the street in the Library's staid Coolidge Auditorium. He would have inspired cab drivers; he would have thrown confetti at conservative southern congressmen and at the same time been recognized as part of the government machine. Yet as bureaucracy grew to define itself in Moscow Mayakovsky, despite his enormous will to be an artistic prostitute and to stand for anything whatever so long as it was the people's wish, came to feel more and more lonely. He had always, I gather, been somebody delightfully optimistic about democracy on a vast stage in front of thousands who wouldn't speak to his neighbor, and he had always been able to produce fuzzy public statements in verse by the yard, which did not really get to the quick of his own or anybody else's character—broad brush strokes of cartoonist, publicist, poster artist—and he had therefore depended for success upon nobody inspecting his work too closely. In the twenties, both sides moved in on him. Commissars kept seeing through to his undoubted anarchism, artists kept seeing his incurable opportunism—and so the game was up; he sickened and eventually committed suicide. Yet even trying to straddle the thing, as he did, is a sort of lesson to those of us who came later. The L of C would have been the place for it.

Woroszylski's volume is not really a biography. It's a compendium of remarks, mostly public remarks, about the post. It does not take us behind the scenes, behind the dramatic mask that Mayakovsky wore, and so we are left with precisely the kind of emptiness at the center that perhaps the Soviet experiment has ultimately demanded of its artists. That emptiness might well have been the price we would have paid for nondissidence in our arts over here, had we gone the way of Russia. And yet there is something about Mayakovky's career that is not at all foreign to the American way of art. We have been suckers for a variety of public artists, both sentimental (like McKuen) and futurist (like Warhol), and Mayakovsky had a bit of both these in himself. We have desperately wanted a powerfully built yea-sayer, with or without beard, for a national poet, and in his absence (Frost never quite made it; he was too soft-spoken and finally too negative, at one with all the other dissidents) we have had to settle for nonpoets like Billy Graham. Somehow literature itself has always failed us; the yea-sayers have had to wander off into music and religion.

Not only could we use a Mayakovsky, but we could use the nonliterary literary criticism that surrounded him. Our literary criticism has been impoverished by its snobbishness; we now have as a result the most primitive kind of lit crit growing up among our radicals, who are having to do the socialist thing all over as if there were no precedents, having to do it over because what we have left them they simply don't understand. How do you apply Brooks and Warren to Bob Dylan? Our younger set with its new vision of poetry as a street art—and fiction as something in the drug bag—may find Mayakovsky and his critics more useful than our conventional canons of criticism. They may even be ripe for a bit of indoctrination in the ways of bureaucracy, rather than those of Greenwich Village. I mean criticism in this vein:

> —*The past seven years of socialist construction are poorly reflected in the poem* [a 1927 poem by Mayakovsky called "Good"]
> —*The New Economic Policy . . . demands that we praise the joy of life, the fascination of the arduous march toward communism.*
> —*If you want to know, the work of art of the highest order today is political propaganda.*

This sort of comment would be mixed in with the lovely immensities of the country existing beyond the bureaucracy, beyond even New York; it would be a manifestation of the relevance business, but built into a tradition of criticism rather than all uppity fresh.

New York publishers are giving us a new run on Mayakovsky. Besides the book reviewed here there is a reissue of *The Bedbug and Selected Poems*, edited by Patricia Blake, plus *How are Verses Made?* Nobel prize-winner Solzhenitsyn is also being pushed; *For the Good of the Cause* was reissued last winter by Praeger, and two new biographies as well as a collection of stories and poems will appear this spring and summer. Such publications are late in the coming. We need to understand socialist realism more than we do, and to live with our "new" criticism less than we do—not to be good socialists but to put the poet back with the hicks where he (sometimes) belongs, and to look again at the possibility, however faint, of social and institutional affirmation as a part of the literary scheme of things.

1971

# Poets and Leaders

### THE PRISON DIARY
### OF HO CHI MINH
*translated by Aileen Palmer*

**A**ll good American school children are obliged to write at least one bad two-line something and call it *haiku*. They learn thus to count syllables, to search for punchy revelations in lily pads and perhaps, if they are really learned, to tie these activities in with the ancient Western phenomenon of Imagism. What they do not learn thereby is anything about poetry, Western or Eastern. Or so at least I have concluded after taking in my full teacher's quota of the student Orient.

Ho Chi Minh's *Prison Diary* was written in verses (and in Chinese rather than Vietnamese) thirty years ago while Ho was a prisoner of Chiang Kai-shek. Haiku the verses are not, but related to haiku. They emerge in English as quatrains with mechanically five-stressed lines rendered the more mechanical by persistent half (or perhaps ⅛) rhymes, and they do remind me of student haiku, a connection that is not Ho's fault and perhaps not wholly the translator's fault but depressing anyway. And to think that Bantam is printing 500,000 for a starter.

The reader is better off, but not much, if he tries to forget that Ho's verses are verses and instead reads them prosaically as the record of an extraordinarily cruel experience in a great man's life. Ho was accused of being a spy: he was jailed, fed only one bowl of rice every meal, put in leg irons at night (or sometimes strung up with rope), obliged to sleep without mattress or blankets, driven out to repair roads, robbed, deprived of tobacco, given no opportunity to bathe, and generally kicked and dragged about by petty officialdom for months. His testimony to these events would have been of interest if it had been written in the plainest prose. Unfortunately it was not so written; the poetry keeps showing, and showing with a labored infelicity that makes each quatrain look like the product of a cut rate Chinese-American rhetoric factory:

*The Water Ration*

*Each of us has a ration of half a basin of water*
*For washing or brewing tea, according as each may choose:*
*If you want to wash your face, then you must go without*
*    brewing tea:*
*If you want a drink of tea, then you have to go without washing*
*    your face.*

Or:

*Moonlight*

*For prisoners, there is no alcohol nor flowers,*
*But the night is so lovely, how can we celebrate it?*
*I go to the air-hole and stare up at the moon,*
*And through the air-hole the moon smiles at the poet.*

Or perhaps instead of a labored balancing of lines there will be nothing but the plainest exposition in a quatrain, and it will come out as a four-line shaggy-dog tale that the reader thinks must have had *something* else going for it in the original or Ho wouldn't have bothered.

*From Lungan to Tungchun Jail*

*The land in this region is vast but very poor,*
*So the people are thrifty and industrious,*
*They are suffering this spring from a severe drought, we are*
*    told:*
*Only two or three tenths of the land can be sown for crops.*

Or:

*On The Train To Laeping*

*After scores of days travelling wearily on foot*
*Today we board a train.*
*Although we have to sit on piles of charcoal*
*At least this is much better than having to walk!*

Ho lost a couple of rounds with me as I read this book. Beyond the duteous line-filling and the heavy balancings I sensed a deficiency of imagination, commonplaceness of thought that can never be wholly blamed on translation. Take for example the following quatrain, which seems to be basically one of the best in the book despite its English flabbiness:

### Tsingming Festival

*On the day of the Tsingming Festival falls a monotonous drizzle.*
*The inmates of the prison felt the pangs of acute sadness.*
*'Liberty, where are you?' we ask, and the warder points*
*To the official government residence far away.*

Sharpen that up; take away the weak modifiers "monotonous" and "acute," the schmaltz of "pangs" and "far away," and the awkward tense switch; and it might be good. But it would still be wholly conventional thematically, just one more round of the nothing-to-lose-but-your-chains blues of which so much of the book is composed. My point is not to deride the theme but put these verses in their appropriate political context and observe that Marx has been here. It is party-line stuff, sharpened by actual experience but still rootedly doctrinaire.

Ho became, after these writings, one of the great doctrine commissars of modern times, and presumably these verses are before us now because of his political eminence, not his blithe spirit; so we should not be surprised at the appearance of doctrine. But the point is that the book *is* being published as poetry; the labored quatrains that should have been rendered in prose are all sitting there lumpishly; and the poetic spirit not only of Ho but of the East itself in comparison with the materialist West is being affirmed somehow (in 500,000 copies). Many readers recalling their innocent haiku struggles will doubtless think of Ho as a dreamer, a maker of idylls, and put his verses squarely on the scene at American school exercises or state poetry society shindigs—for the rather conventional prettiness is frequently there in Ho as if he were poet laureate of a midwestern state—and they will miss the political roots of his conventionality, miss the point that Ho was wholly alien to our poetic tradition on most counts.

Ironically, a *Russian* poet or novelist could not move into the big time in American publishing the Ho way at this point in history; he would instead have to produce a book notorious in the homeland for being anti-system and *un*doctrinaire. The Ho case thus appears an odd case in our cultural relationship with communist art and thought, a case in which we gobble up that which is essentially antithetical to our individualist tradition, and digest it perhaps without ever having known what it is.

The Vietnam war is largely the reason for the oddity—for Ho came to assume heroic stature even among his enemies—but the American romance with haiku has surely had something to do with it too. And with Ho now scheduled to jump forward as a student favorite it would seem to be time for oppressed teachers of haiku to dream up ways of distinguishing, for students and themselves, between old-time patrician Eastern literary figures like Li Po, with their many affectionate later Western admirers, and a modern Eastern revolutionary who also happens to mention the moon, mountains and fig trees. An interesting exercise, for example, would be in trying to demonstrate to a resistant Creative Writing class that the following poem by Ezra Pound was closer in spirit to Ho's enemy and imprisoner Chiang Kai-shek than to Ho:

*Epitaph*

*Fu I loved the high cloud and the hill,*
*Alas, he died of alcohol.*

I doubt that Ho would have demonstrated much interest in an aesthete and sybarite who loved high clouds. Also the sudden deliberate bathos of the switch to alcohol, which is the poem's whole *raison d'etre,* is a bit too clever, too frivolous for Ho. Fu I's decadence, and the poet's benign amusement about it, would not have pleased Ho much; he would have adopted a more severe, chastising tone than EP's. Then too EP's poem is much sharper, more abrupt than Ho's verse; it presents its theme rather than talking about it (Pound's incessant poetic commandment), and as a result it is an excellent example of the sort of aestheticism modern Western writers have found so refreshing in Chinese literature, an abrupt, non-rhetorical handling of material that the doctrinaire political poet cannot afford to adopt. A political poet has to be more explicit—even to the point of banal sloganeering— about themes and morals if he is going to win a war, which is why Western poets never have won a war. Ho knew how to win a war and his verses show it.

One can of course argue that our poets with high-cloud tastes could learn something from Ho—learn, that is, to "make poems including iron and steel," but my point here is not that, not for or against iron and steel; it is merely that we should not confuse the high-cloud tradition with the other. What I fear is that 500,000 American high-cloud addicts will dutifully read Ho and *like* it, and then solemnly think to themselves that after all Ho was only writing the sort of thing Robert Frost might have written if *he* had been in prison. The next thought to that is, "What's wrong with us? Why is it that we cannot have poets as political leaders?" The question has no ready answer—and brings up all sorts of other unanswerable questions about our positivist lives—but certainly cannot be settled by the moral injunction, "come off the high cloud, bub." By Western standards the Ho verses must I think be adjudged to be bad verse despite or because of their romance with engagement. For better or worse the crucial separation in our culture between the aesthetic and the political will presumably continue.

1971

# Inventiveness and A White Tie

COLE
*edited by Robert Kimball,*
*introduction by Brendan Gill*

I n the roaring traffic's boom/ In the silence of my lonely room" is feeble verse by any artistic standards one might find floating around a nobby place like Yale University. "Boom" is not apt except as a rhyme and musical noise, and the combination of "boom" and "roaring" is flabby padding. Also the later information that the lover thinks of his sweetie night and day (in traffic or room) is plain platitudinous romanticizing right out of, yes, tin pan alley. Nobody will take "Night and Day" off the shelf as divine poesy, yet a hundred million or so of us are still around unable to forget its silly lines, or Fred Astaire singing them to Claire Booth in the play, Ginger Rogers in the movie).

We remember "White Christmas" too, of course, by an even lesser poet. Both Cole Porter and Irving Berlin learned early that to make a tune "catchy" was part luck and part sweat, with the sweat coming from a tight weaving, syllable by syllable, of words, melody and beat, so that the big thud of the thing would come through under almost any conditions, such as a noisy shower. (There are no such tight fittings of words and music any more. Nobody lisps in numbers.) As for the lyrics' message, that had to be clear clear clear, and simple simple simple (with variations). When "Night and Day" hit the best seller list in 1932 Irving Berlin wrote Cole to say he was "mad" about it, adding, "I think it is your high spot. You probably know it is being played all over, and all the orchestra leaders think it is the best tune of the year." Welcoming Cole into the fold. Was there any difference between whatever it was Cole brought to popular song from Yale (class of 1913), where he loved Robert Browning as William Lyon Phelps had told him to, and what Irving Berlin brought to it from having been, in the words of *Who's Who,* "educated in public schools, NYC, two years only"?

Yes, in many respects there was a terrific class difference. What is surprising is how little that terrific difference came to in terms of other qualities in the songs than manner, tone. Apparently the great American home was (and is) willing to accept highbrow and lowbrow corn with equally indiscriminate enthusiasm. Just keep it corn.

Brendan Gill (Yale, '36) notes in his fine introduction that when Cole came to the Broadway scene first he didn't want to be contaminated by it. Berlin "warned him that if he wanted to get work from theatrical producers he had better acquaint himself with the corner of Broadway and 42nd Street where, if his name was recognized at all in the twenties, he was written off as an expatriate highbrow." But Cole instead rented a "large and costly apartment on Fifth Avenue" that was, "except geographically, . . . even farther from Broadway than Paris and the Lido were." The boy from Peru, Indiana, had not only gone to Yale (where, with the second biggest allowance in his class—there's an exotic bit of data—he made a senior society, was Leader of the Glee Club and a member of the Whiffenpoofs, and of course wrote "Bingo Bingo") but had also married mighty high, and had sailed abroad to join the best expatriate people, and had set up shop as "a sort of gentleman composer, moving at a measured height above the squalid scramble of the market place." The result in the early twenties was that his ambition, which was deep and fervent, was thoroughly frustrated; in 1926 he had in his own words "given up all hope of ever being successful on Broadway" and was living in Venice in the Palazzo Rezzonico, where Robert Browning had died, and creating such a ruckus as an American nouveau that a fashionable Russian complained bitterly: Cole had "started an idiotic night-club on a boat moored outside the Salute . . . They are teaching the Charleston on Lido Beach! It's dreadful!" Yet only a few years later Cole was fully committed to Broadway shows, being obviously self-conscious about the nature of his popularity but hardly disliking it. A now famous letter from Cole to Paul Whiteman in 1937 put Cole's dilemma neatly. He had written a version of "Rosalie" that he liked very much, but Louis B. Mayer found it highbrow. Mayer said, "Forget you are writing for Nelson Eddy and simply give us a good popular song." So Cole angrily did; that is, he rewrote "Rosalie" in the form we now know ("Won't you make my life thrilling/And tell me you're willing/To be mine, Rosalie, mine"), and Mayer was delighted but Cole was not. The song became a hit. When Irving Berlin congratulated him Cole said, "Thanks a lot, but I wrote that song in hate and I still hate it." Berlin replied, "Listen, kid, take my advice, never hate a song that has sold a half million copies."

Whatever the merits of that immortal moral it seems useless to worry about some high seriousness in Cole that was knocked on the head by the world's Louis B. Mayers. What Cole was truly serious about was not being serious. At least there is no evidence in the book that Cole had grander aims than the songs we have. By grander I do not mean artier but meatier. His art, given the demands of musical comedy, big bands and big box office, is not to be scorned, and wherever one touches it it is of a high order of precision and sophistication; but it remains a thematically empty art, an art insistently blind, for example, to trouble around it—Cole's own or America's. It is like a circus band playing furiously while the tent burns. How Hollywood and Broadway have managed to march along in their musical comedies for so long, especially through the thirties, with so little to say is a sociological problem of some moment, but for Cole that emptiness became a happy context for his inventiveness— and also, one may guess, a way of spiritual survival. "You're the Top" is the most extravagant instance available of where his horsepower went, with its sixty gorgeously-rhymed tropes about tophood ("You're a rose/You're Inferno's Dante/You're the nose /On the great Durante," etc.), but all the songs have the same primary formula. It worked and worked.

Early in his career, before the great machinery of show-writing gobbled him up, one can detect a little devil occasionally driving him to comments beyond the musical-rhetorical gamesmanship that became his life. For instance at Yale he once wrote an angry short piece on the banalities of New Haven's then new Taft Hotel and there is also a song—comic but toughly comic—about the literary snobbery of Yale's Elizabethan Club. But in general his aim was to fit sparklers to platitude, not rock the boat. He was a genius at it, yet to see all the lyrics of his famous songs sitting in a row in these pages is to be struck by how mechanically at last his talent fulfilled this destiny.

Brendan Gill has nightmares about the unchangingness of Cole's face, from childhood on through the good years to the years of suffering (he was terribly injured in 1937); and in this he sees a key to Cole's character: the child in him remained in the ascendant throughout, so that he brought to the grave "not the ravaged face of an old man but the ravaged face of a young one." Add to this another kind of unchangingness—a persistence of tone, an insistence on always looking gay, untroubled, urbane even when in mortal trouble—and one gets the impression of a mask that became a man.

It is a beautiful non-book, so good that maybe non-books should now be admitted into the sanctum of book-books; it is a sort of biography kit with which each reader, guided by Gill's introduction and the careful collatings of editor Robert Kimball (who must also be Yale, class of something, for this is a Yale bag) can put together his own Cole Porter with appropriate personal shadings of approval or disapproval, depending on such matters as the reader's age, college, favorite bands and dance steps. And it is also, I think, a striking book to be confronted with in the seventies, when most of the worlds over which Cole presided—and anyone over 40 or 50 will admit that he presided over a lot—seem to have vanished. Cole was a beautiful specimen of a rather special kind of determined hedonism in life and art. Deeply built into his views was the notion that if you went out to dance and sing you went out to dance and sing. You turned off the social relevance, the troubles in office, home and heart, and you did the Charleston. It was a serious view, and it had its adherents all through the jazz age and into the swing age. If Cole, because of his commitment to musical comedy and other frivolities, seems now more brittle and less-to-be-reckoned with than Hemingway, say, or Edna St. Vincent Millay, he is nonetheless a wholly serious phenomenon in the American past, perhaps the more serious ultimately because he *did* write brittle little songs all his life rather than novels and throaty sonnets. His commitment was total to what our new earnestness must inevitably think of as merely evasion. To put Tom Lehrer or Bob Dylan up against Cole is to sense the difference. Have we gotten better?

The ways of emptiness are many. Cole's life may seem now in part a tragedy because a self seems to have gotten lost somehow and somewhere between the joke-rhymes; certainly an outsider is hard-pressed to know, looking at what Cole left behind, what Cole's heart belonged to beside the daddy of his genre. And yet the hundred million of us who have partaken of him late drunk happy unhappy in movie playhouse dance hall must have found *something* there, something primal, something beyond the white tie and tails and fixed Fred-Astaire smile that now seem, in our serious world, snobbery, evasion, all the bad things. Personally I think the something will turn out finally to be the gayety, the genuine joy in the songs. I think they are primal in their energy, in the *urgency* of their singing life, past the money and mechanics. I think they do add life to life way down.

My four-year-old wanted to dance to all Cole's songs the other night and I took that as a good sign. I gather from Brendan Gill's introduction that he too doesn't know quite what to make of the complications of the Cole legend, but he ends flatly with an extravagance that was Cole himself: "the face and the voice and the songs are one and they will never grow old, never die." A wonderful book.

1971

# On the Shelf

### EPISTLE TO A GODSON
*by W. H. Auden*

T his is quiet poetry—sometimes serene, sometimes politely caustic. Auden's is a masterly talent out of what now appears as another era; he is here preoccupied with age, sickness, death—and perhaps most of all with what it is like to feel that one has been put away on a shelf:

> *Our earth in 1969*
> *Is not the planet I call mine.*

I think there is a sense in which Auden put himself on a shelf a good many years ago when his verse came reiteratively to proclaim man's incapacities, his inability to take charge, direct his fate; and indeed he has perhaps become our greatest poet of the shelf. But in the new volume the shelf is even higher in the closet, and on it he sits meditating—with himself, or imaginatively with a few old friends. It is the friends who will have to say whether America was what chiefly made him come to feel shelved, and therefore drove him first to buy a house in Austria and spend his summers there, and then to leave this country entirely for his homeland; but an outsider's impression is that his is not a readily localizable isolation. Though he is certainly not impressed by some of America's worldly triumphs like the moon landings, and though he does take offense at such American glories as bad, or no, manners and permissive education, his isolation would nonetheless seem to be largely the non-prejudicial isolation of an extraordinary mind that ultimately finds its solidest comforts in its own workings.

The characteristic movement of his poems is circular, a slow and leisurely jaunt around some fixed point—an object, an event, an idea. In a volume a few years back he went through his Austrian home room by room, dwelling upon the properties and meanings of each. Before that he wandered through the physical world examining islands, lakes, mountains, winds, limestone. And before *that* he cogitated, always in extremely elegant verse, upon Christ, Freud, *The Tempest* and whatnot, with, in each case, an analogical playfulness that, had it been painting, would have emerged as highly ornamental renderings (bric-a-brac and squiggles) of simple basic forms. In other words his verse centers have usually been large and obvious like a statue in a park, with the poet's game one of sitting down in front of the statue and letting the sight of it develop in the mind a series of themes, projections, fancies. Thus it is a contemplative art, an art for a lonely and unbugged visionary on a park bench. Or shelf. A very early and much anthologized version of the virtues of shelfdom is his sonnet "Who's Who," in which an activist who climbs mountains and wins wars—and gets in *Who's Who*—is set opposite a nice quiet chap who stays home and putters around the garden. Auden has always obviously imagined himself in the latter role, as man or poet.

In the new volume the verse center is apt to be a quiet occasion or offhand remark. The title poem for example seems to have been given its start when Auden's godson Philip Spender scribbled in a guestbook, "Thank God for boozy godfathers" (the poem is a meditation about what boozy godfathers who are poets ought to do with themselves to be either good poets or good godfathers, now that the world has gone to hell). Another poem is directed toward a doctor-friend on the occasion of his retirement; a third takes off from that crucial daily event, martini-time; and a fourth begins with an article about bacteria in *Scientific American*. As a whole the ornamentation is less extensive, less vigorous than in the earlier Auden, and where it surfaces most obviously it is in verbal play rather than analogy or image; Auden would seem to have been living with a large dictionary by his bedside recently, for he finds delight in harnessing to his poetic wagon such oddities as lipids and guddling. He even has a pleasant little "lexical exercise" for us entitled "A Bad Night," in which he says of the hero,

> *Far he must hirple,*
> *Clumsied by cold,*
> *Buffeted often*
> *By blouts of hail*
> *Or pirries of rain,*
> *On stolchy paths*
> *Over glunch clouds,*

*Where infrequent shepherds,*
*Sloomy of face,*
*Snudge of spirit,*
*Snoachy of speech,*
*With scaddle dogs*
*Tend a few scrawny*
*Cag-mag sheep*

To which one can best reply mildly, Wow. There's a good bit of such playfulness in the volume, and many very slight pieces indeed, which may be taken as further evidence of Auden's movement shelfward. It does begin to appear now that we are not going to have many more big, extended efforts from him; the sere and yellow leaf impresses him as a time for tapering off rather than rising to epic final profundities. Nor will he be likely, I'd guess, to rise to final angers either; he will instead go gentle into the good night because his is essentially a gentle and also genteel sensibility, and, perhaps more importantly, because he has found himself surrounded by the ungentle and has reacted, has made a sort of career of *not* being what *they* are.

Which may be why most of the students I now teach have never heard of Auden. It isn't that he is too academic, for he has never set himself up seriously as a teacher-poet, or gone in for poetry and criticism as a way to general enlightenment (enlightenment for Auden comes if it comes at all from puttering rather than from muscular pedagogical and intellectual efforts); it is that he is so detached and so quiet an observer of the human scene that the younger generations— which he is occasionally petulant about—simply aren't hearing him over their own noise. I don't know that they will ever hear him, yet I can't believe he is permanently out of play, though at the moment unfashionable. At least *if* poetry manages to persist at all in the future as, among other things, a high order of rational discourse, Auden should remain with us, he being preeminently a poet with a good and orderly bean whose decibels of feeling are not impressive but who emerges consistently as a gracious and well-slippered seer. I could wish here for more of the vivacity of early Auden, as in the immense letter to Lord Byron in *Letters from Iceland*, or in the early ballads (there's a ballad in the new volume, but it's a subdued affair), but that would be to wish against some natural law like gravity, and if Auden is didactic about anything it is that we must respect and accept what we have, like gravity, and not lament what we haven't. Since we have now an aging Auden we shouldn't ask him to turn somersaults but should continue to be grateful not only for his enormous wisdom but also for his kindly, well modulated and always slightly surprising presence.

1972

# End of the
# Old Vaudeville

THE HUMAN SEASON:
SELECTED POEMS 1926-1972
*by Archibald MacLeish;*

COMPLETE POEMS 1913-1962
*by E. E. Cummings;*

THE OLD DOG BARKS BACKWARDS
*by Ogden Nash*

T hree good poets out of the past have suddenly been stirred up by three good publishers who may be behind a plot to steal poetry back from the guitar players. I hope they succeed. First, Archibald MacLeish.

MacLeish at 80, putting his affairs in order, has produced a selection of his poems consisting of a large sampling of short poems dating back to the twenties plus excerpts from longer works like *Conquistador, J.B.* and *The Hamlet of A. MacLeish.* He has also done a bit of editing here and there—knocking off the last stanza of "Memorial Rain," for example—and has devised seven general topic headings to classify his poems by, thereby bolixing up the academicians who want poets to be helpful and arrange everything chronologically. Thus he puts under the heading *Autobiography and Omens* some of his best known early poems—"Eleven," "The End of the World," "You, Andrew Marvell," "Epistle to be Left in the Earth"—but he also includes work out of his old age. The same procedure is followed under *Actors and Scenes, Strange Thing . . . to be an American, The Art* and so on, and except for *The Art,* which is predictably about poets being poets and includes his old conundrum about how a poem should not mean but be, the categories do not make much sense, at least to me. I was pleased though to find the old order of MacLeishian events disrupted even for dubious categories. MacLeish has long labored under the cloud of a bad press for being an opportunist, latching on to fads, lacking a center of his own, and he does now need to be looked at as one walking breathing distinct and unborrowed being without reference to his "phases." Edmund Wilson's "Omelet of A. MacLeish" did much of the original damage in the late thirties when MacLeish was busy drumming up trade for a kind of national poetry that went against both the twenties expatriate notions of an artist's proper (*i.e.*, detached) relationship to his country and the thirties Marxism. Wilson asserted that MacLeish was simply a man trying to get on who would do absolutely anything to *get* on, and the attribution stuck. MacLeish's new volume may at last help—if anyone really reads it as a unit, which is always hard to do with disparate short pieces—to lift the Wilson curse and present MacLeish as a poet with his own homemade character, a poet perhaps misunderstood as the other poets to be reviewed here were not.

MacLeish always worried about the poet's role as a citizen of the world, and so made gestures outward from poetry's private sensibility cliques and claques that annoyed insiders. The new volume renders nearly invisible all that early fuss, and shows us a MacLeish who like many others of his literary generation—and I would here include prose writers like Hemingway and Gertrude Stein—was indeed after all a private sensibility, and therefore obsessed like the rest with finding and perfecting an individual style, a distinctive manner, preferably untraditional and spanking new. Unlike some of the others, however, he failed to find and settle on a simple oddity clearly his own, but in his search indulged in frequent rhetorical excesses—he was for example terribly wordy at times about the unimportance of words. Much of the excess is eliminated in the new volume, with the happy result that his distinctiveness now appears as genuine, a consistent part of his poetic being, rather than the bundle of contrivings Wilson thought it was. The distinctiveness is not easily detected in lower-case "i's" or exotically bad rhymes, but is nonetheless pervasive and clearly present; to me it appears as a cluster of mannerisms adding up to a working esthetics of immediacy. Like Pound and Eliot and F.M. Ford he always insisted upon "rendering" rather than "talking *about*," but his renderings were his own in that they had his own infallibly MacLeishian personae speaking a bit breathlessly and privately while at the same time struggling to be rather stagey and generalized, men speaking among men, universal persons addressing multitudes. I do think that nobody except MacLeish has ever quite done it the way he did it and furthermore that this curious mixture of public and private rhetoric—sometimes ringing quite false, but standing up well in the carefully pared-down new volume—is a genuine part both of his speaking manner and of his so often defeated hopes for the art of poetry itself, hopes for the art that his contemporaries mostly did not share, hopes for it as a medium for more than the private life, something beyond Prufrock speaking to himself under water.

If Cummings were alive now he would be 78. He has been dead ten years, yet this new edition gives us nothing that was not publicly published before except one dirty poem of little consequence for which earlier editions left a coy blank page. Oh, and somebody has helpfully added an index of first lines. Cummings was down on editors and editing processes; he wanted poems printed precisely as he wrote them, to the last tiny item of spacing, and he wanted them printed without comment in the order in which he had written them. So we find no revising and rearranging here even 10 years after the death; in fact we are allowed to witness no editorial hand at all—no introduction, no footnotes. I suppose that somebody eventually will come along and say who Joe Gould was and what city park filled up with

6
twirls of do
gsh
it m
uch f
ilt
h
y slus
h & h
ideou
s3m
aybe

o
nce V
o
ices

but for the moment we are spared, though I personally don't want to be. The best edition of Cummings is, I think, Harcourt's own paperback (Harvest No. 92), which came out in 1965 and has at least a worthy short introduction by Horace Gregory, though little comment on individual poems. We could use more comment now, and fewer poems, with an unfussy scholar violating the no-hunting signs Cummings put up on his territory, signs his wife continued to enforce for him until her death last year. I certainly don't think Cummings' reputation is helped by the persistent preservation, inviolate, of the 739 poems in the new edition; for his was a narrow art: he repeated himself shamelessly and went through practically no development of theme or method once he had settled into his niche. If poems were paintings the 739 could be bought and sold and hung with joy in 739 individual parlors, but since they are not paintings they huddle together uncomfortably in this heavyweight volume and represent him as a heavyweight poet, which he was not; he was a gloriously special poet who could do what he could do.

Particularly since he prided himself on uniqueness—and in fact thought of any act of creation as primarily an individual's assertion of uniqueness—it seems a mistake to have the 739 wandering around forever in a lump. He deserves a slimmer, brighter image, for he remains a delight for youth. It doesn't matter that while he tells youth not to pay any attention to the syntax of things he is himself infatuated by the syntax of things; he comes over loud and clear as an indefatigable promoter of spring, love and the private life, and an equally indefatigable condemner of most of our faceless modernity.

Unfortunately he also emerges to me in my non-youth, finally, as an extraordinarily isolated man with fixed and unchanging social opinions that if triumphant would leave us with no society at all. His limitations don't dismay his fans though, and I still try to be one.

If we are to measure poets by their distinctiveness—and for better or worse the achieving of distinctiveness is the *raison d'etre* for most 20th-century American poetry—it simply won't do to think of Ogden Nash as a minor figure. He is as distinctive as Cummings, and will perhaps be around as long as Cummings. He was slightly younger but not much, and his death in 1971 left us with a clear—maybe too clear— vision of how the art of light verse should be perpetrated. He created a body of work that went triumphantly against the prevailing aesthetic of poetry as a lofty, Sextus-Propertius affair, and he stuck with his creation for nearly forever, thereby becoming the chief poetic practitioner of the grand mundane in our country's most successful literary magazine, *The New Yorker*. *The New Yorker* has published good and important works by most of America's most highly thought-of sobersides, but it would nonetheless have been a nothing venture without its comedians. Nash was, forever, its chief verse comedian. Nash was the one who kept reminding *New Yorker* readers—who might otherwise have been scared away by the flavor of compressed elegance characteristic of the "serious" poetry its editors favored—that verse could be relaxed and topical. In other words Nash was the one who practically singlehandedly kept the verse department of the magazine in the business that the rest of the magazine was in, of commenting with intelligence, wit and asperity upon the contemporary American scene—its fads and fashions, its promotional and rhetorical excesses, its varied social and cultural crises. His contributions were too often on the cute side, and one could argue that a greater satirical severity toward America's multitudinous morasses—in a magazine that has always had after all the most serious of literary and critical aspirations—would have been in order; but Nash could hardly have been expected to carry the whole burden here. What he did he did well, and in so doing he not only kept American verse more open and various in its aims and interests than it otherwise would have been, but also kept *The New Yorker* on a track from which its artier verse contributors constantly wished to remove it.

Nash's new volume is work from the last three or four years of his life. Some of it is not particularly good Nash; all of it wears thin, as does Cummings' work, if read in big hunks; but it is all sufficiently sharp and sufficiently attuned to contemporary occasions to suggest that Nash's feel for the here and now did not diminish in old age. Nor did his wit. There are even some surprising brief pieces in which he abandons his lifelong pose of Look-I-Can-Write-Worse-Verse-Than-You-Can, and easily qualifies as a *good* comic poet.

So there they are, three poets of a nearly common age that I, a couple of decades younger, grew up with. All's changed now, as another poet I grew up with once said, but a terrible beauty has not as a result been born. We are in a verse hole, I'd say, speaking from the dubious heights of my own upbringing—dubious because things may be worse than they were *because* of what they were. I mean that the poets who are now finally subsiding—I think of Pound and Eliot as the chief architects of the early century's poetry, but would include my three poets here, and a few others, as significant attendant lords— managed to destroy the poetic past *they* inherited, with the result that poets now have to take starting-from-scratch as poetry's way of life. They are pushed into being primitives by the culture's climate, a climate that would deny its own primitive past. Pound's and Eliot's contributions to the new condition are large but beyond my province here, but it can be said that MacLeish emulated and enforced them in his search for immediacies that would supplant old narrative and descriptive conventions, and that Cummings and Nash in their turn also did irremediable damage to the prosodic staples they were brought up with. Who for instance damaged the sonnet (though he loved it) more than Cummings? And who damaged rhyme (though he loved it) more than Nash? It is not that these staples did not need to be damaged, it is merely that they were; a make-it-new wave passed slowly but always noisily over our verse culture for several decades, with the result that finally its force took effect and nobody was left who could lisp in numbers or do any of the other fine old vaudeville stuff of the Great Tradition. The irony is that of course all the old rebels *could* lisp by the numbers; they just didn't want to.

So now the old rebels are mostly gone. There have been many kinds of verse rebels in this century—it has been a century of miscellaneous rebellions, so many that the little magazines and publishing houses that brought them forth are almost unindexable— but each of the three poets here has in his own way earned the title to rebel more than most, and each has also been more fortunate than most, in that he has had talent as well as aversions. Another publishing autumn is not likely to produce such a harvest of autumnal figures from what is perhaps the last era of poetry having a tradition even to *complain* about. English departments should take note; their occupations may be nearly gone. Poets should take note too; their occupation's not gone but nobody can figure out what it is.

1972

# *Ezra Pound*
# *1885—1972*

F or most Americans Ezra Pound is a dim avant-garde expatriate, but for a few hundred sympathizers he is a major literary figure. For those few the recent critical biography, *The Pound Era,* by Hugh Kenner is appropriately entitled; they think there *was* a Pound era and that it began in London around 1912 when Pound began shipping poems and instructions about poetry to Harriet Monroe in Chicago. To find out what the era consisted of, think the few, one merely takes in college any course that is called, or used to be called, modern poetry. Modern poetry is, or was, Pound—Pound mixed in with Eliot, Yeats and a half dozen others.

I was brought up as one of the few, and so must speak personally. I was too young to know about the early days of the era except as history—and unquestionably the early days were *the* days—but in 1939 I did meet the big red-bearded mythological person in the flesh in New Haven, where he was my family's guest for one night and stuffed all my mother's best towels, wet, under his bed before coming into the living room to read his copy of Li Po before us and inform us that it was "restful." There was also in that year his extraordinary contribution to the first issue of a poetry magazine that my roommate at Yale and I had just begun, *Furioso.* The contribution was a one-page "Introductory Textbook" in economics, consisting of four short quotations from John Adams, Thomas Jefferson, Abraham Lincoln and George Washington that he generously supplied us rather than the important poem we had been expecting. For later issues of *Furioso* he did give us some poems—such as the unremarkable "lesson no school book teaches:/Women's bums are often/Too big for their breeches"—but he did not grace our pages with important Pound until the death of Ford Madox Ford, when we succeeded in extracting from him an obituary. His first words there could now stand, with a change of month, as the kernel of his own obit: "There passed from us this June a very gallant combatant for those things of the mind and letters which have been in our time too little prized. There passed a man who took in his time more punishment of one sort and another than I have seen meted out to anyone else. . . ."

*Gallant combatant,* yes. Surely Pound was thinking of himself, and most characteristically, when he wrote those words about Ford. Early in Pound's own verse is to be found "The Goodly Fere," that describes Christ as a good fighting man, not one of your namby-pamby lamb types. That image—of the savior and himself—never deserted him. He became a sort of art-tiger raging around in Western culture, knocking off mediocrity, usury, shoddiness, iambic. My guess is that Pound will be remembered for his fighting longer than for his poetry. Pound was the one who should have been the pugilist, not Hemingway.

*Things of the mind and letters . . . too little prized.* Yes again. Things too little prized are what he fought *for,* against those partly imaginary enemies, the bourgeoisie and their institutions, from *The Saturday Evening Post* to the University of Pennsylvania. He fought for the well-made line, the clean image, the unpropagandized perception. He fought, as he says in one of his best poems, for a few broken statues and battered books. He fought for a world where the best would preside, and though he was so egotistical that he kept finding the best being made or remade in his own neighborhood, he was right quite often. Sometimes he fought with despairing irony, as in the Mauberly poems; and sometimes he fought hotly and openly, as in his many angry letters. But he always fought, and fought for his notion of the best.

*Who took in his time more punishment . . .* yes. His punishment began before his incarceration at Pisa and did not end when he was released from St. Elizabeth's Hospital. He was punished by the judges and by the doctors, who may have been right, but he was also punished by himself. He had large expectations of and for himself as an artist, expectations that remained unfulfilled. That great poem that his Cantos were to be did not become, finally, a great poem but only a collection of occasionally great lyric fragments. Nor did any of his high plans for the improvement of society and art ever descend from the mountains and take hold except among a few, as at Black Mountain. Late photographs of him show us a face of darkness, of losses for which there is no consoling.

He has been dead as a creator for a number of years but he is dead now, at 88, in the books, and spread around—as Auden put it about Yeats—among his admirers. His admirers will continue to think of him as a gallant combatant for the prized things, and will be right; and the rest of the world will think of him—if they think of him at all—as an exotic eccentric, and will be right too. He was unique, one of America's strangest emanations. His era, if it was an era, is over.

# T.S. Eliot
# 1888-1965

In a better world than this one I might have been able to write these words before reading T.S. Eliot's obituary in the *Times*. But the *Times* in its orderly way has been lying in wait for the man for years; so too have a great many teachers and scholars who have sensed dimly for more than a decade that they had on their hands perhaps a major poet, perhaps a minor poet, but certainly a dead poet, and therefore fair game. Even Mr. Eliot himself seemed to have this sense of himself a few years back when he delivered a lecture about "The Waste Land" with the detachment of a Martian. All our literary morticians have had their say. Perhaps he has earned a few years of simple silence.

Yet (always the "yet," followed by pages and pages), for anyone who grew up between the big wars thinking of "Prufrock" and the rest as somehow of the essence of poetry, it is difficult even to meditate in silence about this poet's death without as it were employing some of the poet's own "terms." I am saying that in a sense he now lives on, for his admirers, in the quotation-ridden thoughts they entertain about his death, they having learned a good deal of what they know and feel about death from him, learned of growing old with their trousers rolled, of dying with a little patience, of shoring fragments against their ruin, of dancers gone under the sea, houses gone under the sea, of captains, bankers and eminent men of letters fading off into the dark. It is not just the words and phrases that contain the death preachment; the preachment is also lodged in the tone and manner, in the basic intellectual and emotional stance that the poems project, a stance that the admirers, having picked up, now live with.

Meanwhile it is this stance that Eliot's detractors have also picked up, but only to mock him. In the word "stance"—an unfortunate one— lies their complaint: the man consciously and with insufferable deliberation and detachment adopted, cultivated, rigged up a way of poetry that produced poetry which was not merely not good poetry on the subject of death but nearly managed to be the death *of* poetry.

These lines have been long drawn, but now the man is dead. As a reluctant long-time admirer I can only see a great and abiding consistency in his controversial stance, a stance that seems to me now to have been surely no stance at all in the bad sense, but just a way of looking at things, a considerate way. Partly of course the way was bred into him by all the immediate social and cultural circumstances the positivists have always been eager to cite; but of course it was also more than that, it was a way that has always been bred into all considerate poetry. A poetry of death like his is no more a stance in the bad sense than the surge of the sea may be said to be a stance, the sea to which, to paraphrase the man, there is no end, no beginning—and certainly at the heart of it no contriving. To his admirers Eliot was a great poet of that sea.

But how unsealike and unseaworthy is *this* poem, *this* stance: "Twit twit twit . . . so rudely forced."

# The Poet as
# Effete Snob

My subject is the poet as effete snob, which means that sometimes I will be writing self-indulgently about me. I also want to give you a short history of poetry, that is, modern poetry. I've decided to start with Erasmus. Some of my colleagues think I should have gone back further—and actually I *will* refer to Moses—but Erasmus is the best starting point. The progression is from Erasmus to T.S. Eliot to me.

Erasmus was not a poet but a very early Humanities man, a man of letters among priests, but himself a priest. He lived with and loathed clerical fanaticism, Catholic and Protestant. I think we prize his memory chiefly because he was one of the great prizers of intellectual independence. As a thinker he insisted on being a loner.

Yet he is reported also to have been gregarious—not at all introspective, no more persuaded of the solipsistic authority of the self than of clerical authority. It was he who led the way in the Renaissance to finding, in classical literature, an instrument of liberation from both church *and* self.

What was the Renaissance anyway. It was a renewal of faith in the mind, the independent mind. So much for Erasmus.

As a young man T.S. Eliot set himself up as something of a modern humanist of the Erasmus sort, in an essay now too famous to be read except in outlines for tests. "Tradition and the Individual Talent" was written in 1917, between "Prufrock" and "The Waste Land." In it Eliot observed that the poet extinguishes his private sensibility in a poem; he becomes a "finely perfected medium" through which experience passes and comes out pure on the other side.

What a marvelous idea, extinguishing the poet's sensibility. Making him a filter. Some people think that if only the poet's poetry were extinguished too, the world would be saved. What Eliot was trying to do, though, was not extinguish poetry but liberate it from the pressures of the sentimental self, the self so familiar in bad romantic poetry, the self that can't see the world through its own tears.

In other words Eliot, with his friend Pound, and with a number of other interesting persons that courses in modern literature now begin with, were trying to start their own Renaissance; and aside from independence from the bleeding-heart self he was seeking independence, as Erasmus had, from surrounding cultural pressures. The Greek and Latin classics were no longer the powerful instrument in this effort that they had been for Erasmus, and though Eliot obviously was learned in them he sometimes had to skate up and down many other cultural ages for refuge from the present. Those of you who have read him know how far he skated, only to come back to the Church of England. I don't think he made it to a new intellectual Renaissance—and perhaps this was because somebody had decreed that Renaissances in the 20th century would not be run by Men of Letters—but certainly he tried hard; and the poems, especially the early poems, are a reflection of the effort.

"Prufrock" is very much a self poem, about an effete snob. I wouldn't give ten cents for the difference between the sentiments of the persona Prufrock and his creator. I'd say that "The Waste Land" is also very much a self poem* but I'm not going to talk here about these old classroom warhorses. Later, in his *Four Quartets,* Eliot gave up being a filter and spoke more directly. To be selfless was not the idea anyway, despite the filter propaganda. No, the Erasmus idea, and then the Eliot idea, was to be a discriminatory self guided by one's own senses and a wise selection of man's literature and thought. A loner yes, but not a solipsistic loner. So much for Eliot.

Now me. I was definitely a solipsistic loner when I became a poet. My yearning for independence from the authorities around me may have had one per cent honest selflessness in it (that is, I think I eventually wanted to develop my powers for God, country and Yale *as well as me*), but I was 15 at the time so can't be sure.

At 15 the profession of literature is like muscle building. You build the muscles because, as Charles Atlas has always said, someone has kicked sand in your face. You want to grow strong and kick sand

---

*Eliot makes fun of Prufrock the way his teacher Irving Babbitt ridicules romantic melancholics—and sometimes I think the model for Prufrock must have come out of *Rousseau and Romanticism*—but he also sympathizes with all of Prufrock's feelings about the parlor. Identifies, as we say. Similarly Eliot identifies with the various patrician loners in "The Waste Land" who make up the poem's composite voice—including Tiresias, God, The Fisher King and a number of aristocrats.

back—on muscle beach or in a scandalous best seller. My first literary work was begun at prep school because the school was kicking sand in my face. I badly needed to get strong on my terms, not its. I needed something to satisfy *me*, something the school couldn't measure and flunk me in like solid geometry. One thing I could do was typewrite. So at the age of 15 I sat down to typewrite a novel. I typewrote three single-spaced chapters, discovered there was more to novels than typing, and ran away from school.

I came back. A teacher persuaded me of the existence of poetry. I shuttled between Vachel Lindsay and A.E. Housman, and wrote my first poem. It was a mystical poem of deep understatement and might have persuaded me that poetry was something I couldn't do like solid geometry, except for encouragement from the same teacher. I went on, and by virtue of this early writing I surmounted a great big barrier in my development so that forever after, whenever I flunked in class or on the rifle range, at least I could sit down at my desk and do my thing. Doing it like Erasmus and Eliot was another matter.

Between the aloneness of alienation such as mine in prep school (a mild case), and the independence of the mature humanist there is only a fine line. Both have to set themselves up as outsiders to do their work. One may be self-centered, the other selfless and modest; one may be orderly, clear and perceptive, the other erratic and blind to all but his own neurotic visions; but both will have as a basic preliminary mission in life escaping or at least getting beyond the orthodoxy. And, for both, sitting down alone at a desk with a pencil can be a good start. Many influences converge on that desk, but at least the loner is there trying manfully to reckon with them in his own way. In this sense he is never neutral, never a filter. He may try to deal directly with the stubborn rock of objective reality, but he will also display his own up-to-the-minute complex of attitudes *toward* the rock. In revealing the rock he will also reveal, or perhaps find, himself.

Writing is inevitably an identity-finding operation in some measure; and poetry in its original impulse is largely this, whether the poet be 15 or 50. So even if a poem comes to have a veneer of impersonality it is also in its hidden recesses a self document. It is a revealing, a discovering, even a creating of self. As Yeats once put it, the poem is the poet making his soul. What a great idea. Imagine constructing one's own soul at one's own desk, with dirty old tennis shoes on in the dawn's early light. Asking one's soul, What will I be today?

I failed to create a very good me in that prep school novel, and so I ran away to create still another one. As I ran I thought of myself as a wild Russian anarchist escaping through Siberia to freedom; but all I actually did was take a bus from Massachusetts to New York, and when I got to New York I felt I'd already gone too far. I was a moderate revolutionary after all. When I came spookily home, and was in due course returned to the school, I said no revolutionary words to anyone. I did not condemn the school, the system or the world. I did not have a confrontation with my parents. I just cried. Ever after, as I have sat at my desk creating myself, my creating has been limited by my awareness of is-ness of me (an is-ness that does not include me as a wild Russian anarchist), and also by an awareness of the is-ness of a reality outside me that does include solid geometry. Yet within these limits I still do like to go about my creating and recreating of me; and each new creation has a little bit of the anti-orthodox that I have pridefully here based all Humanism on. So much for me.

No, not really. But there will be an interlude now. Orthodoxy descended rapidly upon the Humanities about thirty seconds after the death of Erasmus, and it has been with them since. The humanist ideal remains, however, that of the intelligent, relatively selfless loner, whether poet or scholar. Our universities would have followed a quite different course without faith in the exotic properties of a library carrel, just as our literature would have been profoundly different without faith in the evocative powers of Tintern Abbey. The spirit of lonerism has been strong in us. Yeats particularly has a number of marvelous images for it, and the one I like best is in his Irish airman poem:

> *Nor law nor duty bade him fight,*
> *Nor public man,. nor cheering crowds.*
> *A lonely impulse of delight*
> *Drove to this tumult in the clouds.*

That's an image of the poet perhaps, not the scholar. Delight is not the scholar's bag much, though it should be. Delight was what was too frequently missing in the kind of literary scholarship to which I was bred up, a kind that had a good Erasmus flavor that should have pleased both scholar and poet—except for the delight. The delight was noticeably missing from the main line of the New Criticism; otherwise it was, before it became an orthodoxy, a criticism tailormade for loner poets and loner readers. By its principles both poet and reader are to try to come at a poem with a minimum of outside interference. The poet's obligation is to see and report the world and himself with an unpropagandized eye. The reader's obligation is to come to the poem with no controlling preconceptions. In other words the New Criticism, like Humanism itself, is partly antibehavioral. Its theme song: to understand human behavior clearly one has to stand apart from it. Otherwise, the most evil of fates will descend: one will, like a Skinner rat, give a stock response to incoming stimuli. A form of orthodoxy.

If there is one thing an effete snob doesn't want to be it is a Skinner rat, but it's a lifetime's work not being one. Thoreau was a great loner; he didn't want to be caught rattily responding with the hoi polloi of Concord. Yet he took the culture of Concord and Europe *with* him when he went out to Walden. Fortunately he knew how tough escape was; he worked and worked on it.

Now we are machined. Escape seems easier, but is tougher. I turn on the TV and I find that the country is having a big new commercial romance with lonerism. Heroes on motorcycles on lonely roads (where did those lonely roads come from?) flash across the screen between commercials; and the commercials themselves show muscular loners drinking beer on mountain tops. In popular literature Bob Dylan and Rod McKuen have made it big as professional loners. Erasmus, here we come—or do we?

One of the early prophets of the new loner fashions was Jack Kerouac—in his book *On the Road*, in the mid-fifties. Another was James Dean at about the same time, in the movies.

Kerouac subsided slowly into unhappiness and sickness. But James Dean died violently in his prime in the way motorcycle loners die. His impulse seems to have been rather like those of Yeats' Irish airman, and like the airman it drove him into the wide open spaces. But think of the Yeats lines again:

> *Nor law nor duty bade him fight,*
> *Nor public men, nor cheering crowds.*

It all applies to Dean except the cheering crowds. What is a loner doing with cheering crowds?

The poet Frank O'Hara asked that question, and wrote a poem about James Dean, an elegy in which he blamed the modern Hollywood gods of fame and fortune for the death. It was *they*, he said, who sucked this talented young actor into a life unnatural and deceiving. A familiar American story.

The number of cheap enticements we confront each day is incredible. They will lead us to fortune, love, high office, fame, above all, fame. Fame comes in different shapes and sizes, but there are chiefly the Hollywood kind and the heavenly kind. The Hollywood kind we all know; the heavenly kind is described in Milton's "Lycidas":

> *Fame is no plant that grows on mortal soil . . .*
> *But lives and spreads aloft by those pure eyes*
> *And perfect witness of all-judging Jove.*

The Hollywood kind is the cheapest and the most obviously destructive; certainly no loner can afford to put up with cheering crowds long. The crowds are as dangerous as any dictator to the independence he prizes. The whole art of the film, as well as the lives of those who practice the art, have been muddied by the presence of the crowds. Poetry on the other hand has traditionally tended to follow the Milton line and look for the approval of Jove rather than cheering crowds and box office. Many poets have thus *positively* dissented from popularity, have been the most absolute effete snobs on the subject—to preserve their independence. And because there is frequently no one around to listen to poems *except* Jove, the snobbery has been easy. Yet in the fifties there was another case, not unlike the James Dean case, in poetry: the case of Dylan Thomas. He died of too much booze in a New York hotel during a poetry-reading tour of our country; and, in an elegy for Thomas, Kenneth Rexroth blamed not only the Hollywood gods but all the American gods for his death, the gods of commerce, science, war, culture, all. Rexroth went further than O'Hara; he even used the word "murder" to describe what America had done to Thomas.

Let me throw in two other cases. Years ago the conservative literary critic Yvor Winters, in an extraordinary essay on Hart Crane and Romanticism, blamed the hypocritically romantic teachers of American literature for Crane's suicide.

And much further back there was poor old John Keats, knocked off by the *Edinburgh Review*.

Other cases could be cited. I'd like also to cite cases where Jove rather than Hollywood was responsible, for heavenly fame is a goal with dangers too. But the nice thing about Jove is that he isn't around much, or if he is he isn't somebody we go around blaming; blaming Jove went out with King Lear. Anyway I am not concerned here with *who* gets blamed, or what, but with the blaming process, and with the depressing fact that being a loner turns out not to be as easy in life as on TV.

I go back to that lone Irish airman who took his life *in his own hands* in the Yeats poem—or thought he did. Maybe his thoughts were wrong; maybe he imagined he was independently making a decision when it was sociologically being made for him by the absentee British landlords of Ireland. Causes are always to be found; blame outside the self can always be assigned—and the assignings may be hard to refute. Yet the more of a life (or death) we explain away with absentee landlords or cheering crowds, the less there is left of life (or death) in the hands of the poor soul trying to live it or die it.

The loner at his desk or in the library carrel, trying to escape his assignments, trying to spring himself from the orthodoxies of life and death for at least a few slim moments, is always surrounded by busy bees constructing a non-loner existence for him, making him out as a helpless victim, an innocent, a sensitive plant in a meatgrinder. One is not alone in the best Erasmian sense if in a meatgrinder.

If I had been Dylan Thomas I'd have been offended by Rexroth's efforts to surround me with a meatgrinder. In Thomas's own poetry we see him as a fatalist of a quite different order from Rexroth. On the merciless orthodoxy of time and death Thomas was marvelous:— "Time held me green and dying/Though I sang in my chains like the sea;"—"After the first death is no other"—but he was seldom angry at people. When he is angry, he is angry at victimization, as in his great line, "Do not go gentle into that good night." There he is speaking to his father, imploring him to rage against the inevitable, fight to stay alive to the end—but not, as it were, bitching about anybody or anything. And when he himself went into the good night he did not go gentle (he seems to have asserted his independence by *speeding* his own death), and he wasn't to my knowledge blaming anybody for it. So what he might have said to Rexroth is, for God's sake leave me make my own death my own.

Which is not to say that Rexroth was wholly wrong. Or that doctors who think of alcoholics as victims are wholly wrong. It seems hard to deny that the loner, far from being the tower of personal strength that Erasmus and I would like him to be, is weak, susceptible, frequently in need of outside help. Modern psychological pictures of loners are especially derogatory (in the sweet kindly way that psychology can be derogatory), but not thereby false. Psychology gives us the loner as abnormal, as a misfit, and sometimes as homosexual, sadistic, perverted, off his rocker, poor thing. It was a loner who killed those nine nurses in Chicago, wasn't it? Frankenstein was a loner (poor thing). Milton's Satan, my god, was a loner. And except that loners are sometimes terribly strong and wicked they are weak and need special care, special protection from forces like Hollywood, martinis and the *Edinburgh Review*. You know what they specially need?—*They need not to be left alone.*

What Satan needed was a real pal. So did Ahab. Beelzebub and Satan, Ahab and Starbuck weren't really intimates. And Hamlet, if only he'd *married* Ophelia.

Satan, Ahab and Hamlet are the most famous fictional loners I can think of (except God himself, and he's on the side of orthodoxy). They are famous, and they are also extremist, great romantic loners, imaginative projections of the possibilities and dangers of lonerism. Add Faust. All heroic figures, and all dangerous.

But lonerism in its extreme forms has always been dangerous. Once it was satanic, now it's abnormal. Up to recently, however, its dangers have been balanced by possibility, usually the sort of possibility to be found in the funny old Arts and Humanities, a possibility beyond the behavioral. Maybe there *is* nothing beyond the behavioral, but the Arts and Humanities have developed on the opposite assumption, and the loner, good or bad, strong or weak, dangerous or benign, has persistently been at the center of it all. The loner *away* from the cheering crowds. The loner with his loner mind erratically idling someplace. Unprogrammed.

Not always unprogrammed. There *was* Moses, alone and idling in the bulrushes—but programmed from birth. And where was Moses when the lights went out? Alone, but programmed.

It's a lucky thing that most of us are less programmatic than these men. When our mind idles it really idles. There's where the freedom begins. For example, the creators of Hamlet, Ahab and Satan had diverse other interests. Satan was an infirmity of Milton's noble mind—a great infirmity, but not the whole thing. Ahab was matched by Bartleby the Scrivener in Melville's, Hamlet by Bottom in Shakespeare's. Sometimes I think our psychologists treat us as if we had been programmed the way characters in fictions are programmed, just to do one thing in one play. There's a famous test, the Minnesota multiphasic test, used all over the place as in effect a test for normalcy—used by employers to make sure they won't get any Ahabs. My untutored impression of the exam is that although it's described as multiphasic it is mostly concerned with just two "phases" of personality—innerdirectedness (lonerism) and other-directedness (groupism). The test has been a great practical success, and I am overstating its trouble; I don't think I'd like to hire anybody who said that when he is with people he is bothered by hearing very queer things, or denies that he ever gets angry, or denies that he ever puts off to tomorrow what he ought to do today, or says he always tells the truth. The test has its uses, but when the personalities of difficult and talented people are judged by its terms, the test seems foolish and patronizing. Can you imagine asking Hamlet or his creator to say true or false to the assertion, Nobody understands me?

The fact is I don't know *any* questions or statements that can begin to plumb the behavioral mysteries of the intelligently idling, unprogrammed mind.

If you are too young to have had insomnia, you haven't spent ages living with a conscious but idling mind. At 3 a.m. the mere *fact* of consciousness is enormous and obscure, like something out of Milton. Your mind chugs gloomily along on its own while your body lies there, and you wonder how you could possibly be *it*, but you are. At 3 a.m. you are both; you are a doubleness. You are a behavioral machine, but you are also a serene bag of something like marshmallow.

The marshmallow is the mind. The Arts and Humanities are all about the mind, which comes, I note, in ones: a basic loner construction. Pavlov didn't like the word 'mind'—he expunged it from his dog reports—but I like it: the mind, an anti-behavioral marshmallow acting snobbish about the reflexive system it sits on top of.

For it *is* above it.

And its premise is: *it is free.*

1970

# Checks & Balances:
# The Poet in the Bank

A teacher for 20 years, I have sometimes felt incapable of teaching anyone anything. A poet for the same depressing period, I have sometimes felt like a Powerful Pedagogue. Yet when I play teacher I work reasonably hard at trying to teach, and when I play poet I mostly try not to teach. The disparity between what I set out to do and what I do worries me. I wish it would also worry educators and people concerned about the arts.

When the school bell rings at 9 am the teacher stands before his students, frowns, and begins to teach—or so the system would have him perform when he is not on strike. But when the poet steps before an audience at 8:30 pm, and frowns, he begins not to teach but to read—or so the system would have him do when he is sober. In both cases the audience, which may be the same audience, is a passive partner to the proceedings, but in the first instance it is supposed to receive a lesson, while in the second it is supposed to receive an experience. A lesson is somehow smaller than an experience; hence a poet who provides only a lesson is sometimes said not to understand art. But an experience is somehow fuzzier than a lesson; hence a teacher who provides an experience is sometimes said to be undisciplined, not minding his p's and q's.

Now all teachers and all poets know the audience responses can't be cubbyholed in this fashion; but the system doesn't know. The system is blind, deaf and dumb; it hires its teachers to do one thing and its artists another, without regard for what in fact they can do. Put the schools on one side of the street, the museum on the other. Have education from nine to three weekdays, have art at night and on weekends.

Doubtless the system will never be substantially changed, perhaps it shouldn't be. Not only would the system fall apart without its categories, but we who live within the system might fall apart too. Despite many assertions to the contrary, it seems unlikely that any of us can be whole men and also sane. We need to specialize, to concentrate, to avoid peace so we can have war, art so we can have science, and so on; otherwise, in trying to do and be everything simultaneously, our minds would spread out like melted butter and quietly fry.

On the other hand we need to know that we are specializing when we do so, and we need to know that the specializing is a convenience, an arbitrary man-made arrangement, not a natural or god-given order of things with which there is no disputing and from which there is no deviating. To know that the order is our own creation is the first step in changing the order.

The cubbyholes for art and education, it is thought in some cubbyholes, are undergoing drastic remodeling. Much talk of educational and artistic innovation fills the air. But I'm a pessimist; I think the freeze is still on. In their separate ways both art and education remain, like culture (to which both of them are supposed to contribute), frozen out of the action, out of play, out of the social center of things, just as the mindless system would have them. Education is for those not yet old enough to work. Art, theoretically for everybody, is for them after they get out of work. And though these arrangements have nothing at all to do with how, or why, an artist or teacher makes it with the citizenry, they are arrangements so firm and settled that they have come actually to define the character of art and pedagogy. The character of art and pedagogy is in other words being determined by the times of the day they "occur," and the situations they "occur" in.

I get strong philistine feelings about art, education and culture—that frozen triumvirate—nearly every time I read of some big new cultural project. I want to walk away from it, *not* be enlightened and etherealized by it. In these feelings I am hardly alone; the world of art and literature seems to be dominated now by establishment wreckers who would put a moustache on the Mona Lisa, dress the Cleveland Symphony in blue jeans, and write poetry that is anti-poetry. The difference between these rebels and me is that I am more philistine than they are; I don't want a new art so much as an engaged art. I want to change the time and place of art; I want to get it into the working day. In my more stirring moments I sound a bit like *Pravda*.

No art in America in our time—or at least no art that we brag about as an art—really makes it into the working day, the prime time. Establishment art and anti-establishment art are equally removed from prime time, and their common removal is an important reason why it is so easy for safe and solid patrons of art to look venturesome. Whether they put their money on a symphony orchestra or a used-car sculpture they affirm the same safe patronage principle: keep art out of government, business, the professions, war, and the paying of taxes. Keep it where it won't cause any trouble. If it can't be kept clean, at least it can be kept alienated, and therefore ineffectual. (Sometimes the ineffectual is called the non-political. To a man the patrons of art want art to be non-political.)

What depresses me most is that our artists are almost unanimous in reinforcing the patrons' principle here. For years, for example, anti-establishment artists have deplored and ridiculed safe art, conventional art, museum art, Metropolitan Opera Art, garden club art, poetry circle art, landscape art. But in their opposition to safe art they have not challenged the basic system-function of art or artist at all. The artist may produce a decorative object for a dowager's neck, or an obscenity to be wrestled with by the court; but in either case he remains by his own choice and the system's an outsider. Benign or malicious, he is an eccentric whose mind and spirit can be safely patronized by powers public or private—patronized but not consulted, not recognized, not thought to have serious opinions about anything but his art.

There are significant recent exceptions. A good many literary Blacks have harnessed their artistic talents, in their writings and as teachers of literature and drama, to the Black revolution; and a good many artists of all kinds have found their lives as artists and their lives as pacifists tending to merge as the anti-war movement grows in political power. Possibly these two important political movements will make the art of the late sixties look rather like that of the thirties. So far, however, the art has not kept up with the sentiments of the artists. The artists continue to agree to step outside art to become engaged.

Such separation in function is produced in part by the genres and conventions of art, which remain genres and conventions of alienation (stories and poems are not news, paintings are not social science, and so on). But I suspect the genres would change rapidly if the lives and convictions of the artists changed. Our artists are choosing their forms of alienation and defending their choice because these forms suit their lives, lives largely conditioned to be out of play. If an artist is not in education (and I have already carefully put education out of play), he is apt to have no public role except that of artist. He will not be in business or government; he will not be in science or social science; he will not be in any of those funny new collectivities like Urban Affairs or Systems Analysis; he will not be anyplace where there is a concentration of political, social, or economic power. Or if he is in such a place he is a rare artist, a part-time artist, a divided artist; he will perhaps have an ordinary true-blue bourgeois job, but the job will be his daytime life, the art reserved for his nights and vacations.

Most American artists deny vehemently that any real artistic accommodation to such jobs can be made. They say the jobs are irremediably alien to art, and destructive of artistic talent and integrity, hence necessarily jobs to be put aside when the artistic act occurs. Maybe so. Maybe this *is* what we have come to, that is, to a life of endlessly boring, dishonest, and uncreative primary functions that automatically put the artist's functions outside the primary ones. But the fact of this condition, if indeed it is a fact, is more readily and frequently asserted than demonstrated; worse, all our artistic energy and money keep being spent to reinforce the fact, if it is a fact, rather than to investigate it or, better, to undermine it. The artist wants to get away, so the patron gives him money to get away; the artist wants to be free of the social whatnot, so the patron gives him money to be free of it. Is anybody experimenting with staying home trapped?

If I were an independent, immeasurably wealthy patron of artists, I think I would put at least half my unlimited capital into some good solid artistic enslavement. Ezra Pound spent a lot of time and energy getting T.S. Eliot out of a bank; I'd put him back in. The Guggenheim people keep sending our novelists to Rome; I'd put them in the Post Office Department. I'd immerse our artists in the depressing responsibilities of the journalist, businessman, bureaucrat, and technician.

I'd do this with half my money. The other half I'd spend conventionally, lest I appear extremist.

Thirty years after the waning of the Marxist impulse for artistic engagement in this country we seem to be coming around again to some version of that much-maligned ideal, but our disillusion with Russian practice still runs so deep that no discussion of engagement can take place without someone's seeing red. As a result, though revolutions surround us on our campuses, in our slums, and in our artistic communities, the principle of artistic *dis*engagement remains relatively unchallenged. Even an artist calling for violent revolutionary social change nonetheless tends to hang in there with Ezra Pound, intent on getting the poet out of the bank. He may read and approve a radical tract such as Frantz Fanon's *Wretched of the Earth*; he may give nearly full assent to the principle that the last shall be first. He will generally reserve, however, the status quo for himself, the artist. He will elide or delete the strong passages in revolutionary theory against bourgeois individualism when those passages apply to art. His careful omissions make him an odd figure of a revolutionary.

I am not a revolutionary, so it may be tactless of me to go about giving tips on effective revolutionary practice. I am sufficiently persuaded of the possibility of living with the bank that I do not see why the poet has to destroy the bank or be destroyed by it. I can imagine (naively?) the poet actually working at the bank and contributing some small measure of light and humanity to it, while incidentally learning something about banking. It is my moderateness that my fellow artists find most radical. They can readily imagine revolution; they can propose various forms of civil disobedience, such as not paying their income taxes; but they can't imagine giving up their bourgeois individualism as artists. Be they Southern patricians or black-power advocates, their insistent individualism automatically reduces, I believe, their effectiveness as political *and* artistic beings. (But of course, radical or conservative, they are eminently eligible for an establishment grant.)

The artist's plight is one thing, the patron's another. I should like to imagine that an honest and idealistic patron looking about for worthy projects and worthy talents would worry less about the possible immediate political consequences of encouraging artistic engagement than about the current anomalies in our artistic practices, that is, the *long-term* political and social consequences of removing a whole community of talented persons from circulation. Pound talked about the waste of Eliot's talent in the bank, yet would *The Waste Land* have been birthed without the bank experience? Furthermore, while saving Eliot from the bank seems a worthy venture, saving the bank from artists does not. And must not a patron assess the bank's problem as well as the poet's if he is to do his job intelligently? The patron ought to weigh the social need with the artistic need, and not merely accept the easy piety that the artist serves civilization best by being put out in the woods.

The practical patron should, I think, consider where and when he may go against the fashionable wheres and whens of artistic patronage. If the patron's Eliot needs to be removed from the bank, fine; but perhaps the patron knows an artist not looking for removal but looking instead for a job, a daytime job, a job where he can engage his talents *on* the job (as Eliot apparently could not). There are such artists, and there are such jobs, but current artistic notions do not encourage the search for them.

When that old cynic Thorstein Veblen looked at art patronage, he saw it as just one more manifestation of conspicuous consumption on the part of the powers that be. By implication the artist was, like all the earth's disinherited, simply another person exploited by those powers.

Now those powers are in deep trouble, and so the patron of art, inevitably aligned with them, is also in trouble. If he wishes to exploit the artist in the Veblen way by commissioning golden statues of General Westmoreland, he may; if he wishes to exploit the artist by giving him a job in a bank (I would be the first to acknowledge that job patronage is potentially a great device for exploitation), he may do that, too. But if he is *not* trying to exploit the artist but help him, and if he is also concerned with opposing the revolutionary conviction that everything those who are first do for those who are last *is* exploitation, then his duties change drastically. Then in looking for a job for an artist he will in fact be looking for a socially relevant place for that artist. He will want the place to be a place where the artist's *artist* talents will be of service to the place, and he will want the place to be ruled by powers amenable to giving the artist powers in the place.

This last is especially important. Without giving power away, patronage *will* turn into exploitation. Like welfare, it will introduce all the contempt that welfare breeds on both sides into art patronage. A danger.

There are other dangers too, specifically those which caused the revulsion against artistic engagement in the thirties: party-line art, suppression of deviation from the line, subordination of the imaginative life to the material life, and so on. The dangers are real enough, but they are at least the dangers of an art that is a force in society, the dangers accruing to artistic power, not weakness. In our country the present dangers are the reverse.

That art is too weak in our time to affect the destinies of a bank may be of little concern, but that art has no role and no voice in any of our public affairs except education seems to me bad for both art and public affairs. The humanities, too, have opted out, leaving not a vacuum but a bunch of the enemy, or the potential enemy, in their place. I'll conclude by enumerating the staff of just one important intellectual organization, the Rand Corporation: 145 engineers, 82 economists, 75 mathematicians, 60 physicists, 51 computer programmers, 32 political scientists, 22 operations analysts and, as the corporation's last annual report put it, "57 *specialists* in such fields as meteorology, history, psychology, linguistics, physical chemistry and sociology." So history made it as a specialty, but otherwise the dear old arts and humanities didn't make the scene at all. They could have.

1968

# TV &
# JOURNALISM

*Of all the assignments I struggled with at TNR the TV columns I wrote under the pseudonym of Sedulus were the easiest. I'd lie in front of the tube being irresponsible and suddenly I'd have a topic, suddenly my piece would be done, and suddenly I'd be happy.*

*And Gilbert Harrison was happy too. He liked Sedulus and was convinced that TNR should jump into TV with both feet. But he came to disagree with me about what Sedulus should focus on. He wanted me to stick to specific shows and to the politics of TV as it kept being enacted at the FCC down the street, while I turned slowly into a fanatic about TV conditioning—and media conditioning in general—and started to issue blasts against The System. Maybe he was right that I should have let The System stew in its own juice, but at this distance The System pieces have at least the merit of being less dated than were the columns about specific programs. In the twelve short columns printed here I reach out only rarely for events of the moment—one of the events being the press's handling of Senator Eagleton during the presidential campaign of 1972, when he was discovered to have had electric shock treatment at the Mayo Clinic.*

*Following the TV columns I include a previously unprinted essay on journalistic coverage of the Teapot Dome scandal—a small historical venture in which I try to suggest that while the journalists then could be yellow journalists or journalists of integrity just as now, they weren't quite as* pushy *then.*

# Little Rascals

**R**ecently I was sick a-bed and out of my mind and had several other sound reasons for watching TV in the afternoon. The show was one of the old "Little Rascals" films containing a wild scene on a Pullman, a sleeping car with firecrackers and upper-berth athletics. I had already seen it ten times, and it was just as funny as ever. I lay there giggling like an idiot.

My children giggle like idiots at the Little Rascals too, so my sentimental recollections seem not to be the sole cause of my giggle. Mack Sennett is the cause, being funny no matter what generation is watching; and he seems to be a specially valuable aesthetic commodity right now. His films exude an innocence social, technical and ideological that is at once devastating to lose and impossible to recapture. Modern attempts at equivalence on TV turn out to be deliberate and phony camp.

Maybe the trouble with TV is that it never had an age of innocence. Even its earliest days, on small screens filled with snow, inherited the whole Hollywood experience of cameras and corn, plus the radio experience of commercials and electronic stagemanship. Because of its inheritance TV burst on us fully grown, that is, fully conditioned to a variety of conventional techniques, customs, manners; and this conditioning took effect at both the sending and receiving ends. Only the instrument itself was new. What we expected and what was delivered were old in the worst way—old in spirit.

And the oldness grows apace; even the shows for children (I think particularly of the present generation of cartoons) are sick-old. Nor is commercialism the chief trouble. Mack Sennett was commercial too, and knew how to overdo a good thing—but he somehow avoided being slick, smooth, sophisticated, machine-like in his productions. Partly it was his technical simplicity that leaves us now with the sense that he was at one with his rascals (and the dog with the circle around his right eye should be included here with the kids; he always looked intelligent enough to run a camera); but partly it was his plain humanity—for example, his interest in children's faces and in genuinely sentimental children's events.

Another word for "old" in this context (I am searching for the opposite of Mack Sennett) is professional. From its infancy TV has been run by professionals who were first learned in the ways of Hollywood and radio, then learned in the ways of TV itself—and who were never accordingly blessed with the kind of devil-may-care feelings that were behind "Little Rascals." The only place I can think of on TV where amateurism has had any play has been in educational TV, with miserable results. Amateurism on educational TV has meant not the "Little Rascals" but up-tight teachers lecturing in front of the camera as if they were in class but had lost their students and didn't know where to find them (and in fact such teachers *have* lost their students every time on TV except when it's closed-circuit TV, programmed TV within school course arrangements). Quite properly the recent big investments in educational TV by the Corporation for Public Broadcasting, the Ford Foundation and others have been aimed at making educational TV professional, and therefore competitive with the commercial stuff. That is fine and dandy—educational TV must be competitive to survive—yet its new sophistication is one more blow against the amateur spirit. And though the amateur spirit has to my knowledge produced only bad TV shows so far—except for legacies like "Little Rascals"—we do need to preserve amateurism *somewhere* on the tube if we are ever to achieve a measure of genuinely public broadcasting.

Remember that the public, though conditioned to professional TV, is itself incurably amateur; it will therefore never be able to make of TV a participatory sport unless room can be made, and a suitable format found, for people to appear who are not professionals. (And an audience trained to watch them.) Take politics for instance. We armchair reformers can talk up a storm about giving prime time to dissenters, to minority groups, to consumer defenders, representatives of youth, all those the air waves obviously ought to be open to if they are to be regarded as truly public; but our proposals are merely utopian if we can't at the same time propose practical measures for making the *climate* of the medium more inviting to the amateur spirit than it now is. Not everybody who appears on TV can afford, like our presidents, a crash course in TV performing.

The medium may of course simply not be amenable to

amateurism, in which case it will not, I would guess, remain a superpower very long. Perhaps in twenty years the professionals will have killed it dead; nobody will believe a word or smile it emits, so won't turn it on.

But since a bad actor of a fat boy chased by a bad actor of a mustachioed cop can still slay me, I refuse to believe that the tube's public and amateur potential has been thoroughly explored.

1970

# Wormy Norms

**H**alf the literates of the country will be annoyed by the recent standard for literacy promulgated by Louis Harris and Associates, namely, the capacity to fill out correctly "applications for a personal bank loan, a driver's license, a Social Security number, welfare aid and Medicare."

Why did Mr. Harris not first ask if the model forms were themselves literate? Since when do befuddled bureaucrats determine the course of language? And by what shenanigans was Louis Harris granted $40,000 by the National Reading Council to produce such nonsense? But the Harris impulse, exasperating as it may be to purists who think the bloody country is going to the dogs *because* its norms for literacy and everything else are established by devils, fools and machines with club feet—the Harris impulse is undoubtedly sound: if I can't make it with the Medicare commissariat I am a "functional" illiterate—and will probably starve—even though I can read Shakespeare at nine different levels.

Perhaps a new academic discipline needs to be created, in which the intellectual, spiritual and ethical merits of prevailing social norms are continuously investigated. What do the demands of the insane norms do to our tender private souls? If literacy is determined by Medicare, mathematical and economic competence determined by IRS, and standards of right and wrong by George Gallup and Mannix, where are we?—a discouraging discipline it would be.

Among its most discouraging areas of concern would be the good old tube. We don't, I think, understand the tube's norms well—the cynics dismiss TV as establishing a ten-year-old norm, the boosters deny its conditioning properties entirely—but we live with these norms far more intimately than with Medicare forms. TV's norms surround us like the weather. To put it differently, TV is one of a comparatively small number of windows opening out on the American's world. The issues of free speech, private enterprise, equal time and all of the rest are continuing distractions from the crucial facts of the tube's enormous *presence,* and its manipulability (in most windows the view is just there). If St. George's dragon were with us now we could call for St. George; but with the basiliskish tube staring at us we seem only to be able to think of ways of feeding and currying it.

Procter & Gamble, Bristol-Myers—all the big sponsors—turn their sales problems over to Mad Ave; Mad Ave hires dozens of scholars like Louis Harris to ferret out and tame significant public norms; and the tube people themselves feel the popular pulse with the tenderness of a specialist waiting on a queen. All the lovely characters who manipulate the tube's world view thus deny that they are manipulators; they are merely 'umble servants of something (freedom or a buck) or someone (a divinely average someone; a norm). Nobody is in charge as the TV window fills with lies, with grotesque and simplistic images of middle-class life, with phony cuteness. Nobody is in charge, yet the nobody is insatiably preoccupied with chasing (and therefore creating) the faddish relevance that keeps half of America continuously thinking about the same things in the same way at the same time.

Our anarchist soul, stashed away in New York City (in Wall Street, in publishing and the press, in advertising and TV) demands the grand freedoms yet is constantly chained down to social and economic imperatives of the lowest order. We are fearful of open, above-board regulation, so allow ourselves to be regulated instead by cruel blind forces we have ourselves created.

We have substituted functional norms (like those for literacy discovered by Louis Harris) for the traditional and ideological norms of grandpappy, and the new norms are controlling us.

TV's problems are the country's, but TV, intelligently controlled could be a force running counter to the controlling norms, a force for freedom. Agnew is not wrong here, folksies, what is wrong is letting conservative politicans with blood in their eyes control the dimensions and character of the ideal image of control.

1970

# Equal Brainwash Time

TV has *again* been discovered as the great brainwasher, and everybody wants equal wash time. The democratic way: spread the evil around.

I'd rather listen to Fulbright than Nixon, and I wish somebody would win a few rounds against the Executive Branch, but making an issue of equal time seems to me a distraction from the main issues of brainwash. We should seek to reduce it, not spread it. We don't want fair play so much as free minds. Equal time is important, especially in election year, but it should have no status as an independent issue. The President, the Congress, the cigaret people and anti-cigaret people, the networks and their reformer foes are equal parts of the wash. We can't beat the wash one hankie at a time.

We need to get back down to elementals like the infinitely repeatable one-minute commercial. We need to understand how that commercial works, and then we need legislation to keep it from working so well. We need to understand the impact of regular programming too. What happens to the frontal lobes of an average moron watching McHale's Navy every night for two years? How many ulcers are there per hundred news addicts—as compared with the ulcers of the non-news set? Do children who spend Saturday mornings with cartoons ever go out in the big world and get jobs? Is it true that color TV is largely the possession of Republicans? And can a senator compete with Bonanza?—We need less talk and more information about what the tube and the other media are doing to us, but particularly we need to understand how the tube's salesmanship (starting with the one-minute commercial and working up to Nixon's appearances) works. My impression is that our reformers think the process is a rational one. Every mature brainwasher knows better.

The reformers, for example, have recently been high-tailing it after the deceptive advertising of drugs, breakfast foods, cars and the like. This is worthy of them, but deception by fact and reason is a relatively trivial factor on the wash scene. Our eight-year-olds know the ads are frauds and they (like us) keep buying the snake oil. Rational? Furthermore most of the fraudulence is not factual at all, that is, not assessable in terms of claims made for products; it is atmospheric fraudulence, hoked-up circumstances and verbiage rather than facts. My favorite ad at the moment, for a dry-skin remedy, brings us a scholarly, bespectacled geezer who takes a medical book from his five-foot shelf, sits down at a dignified desk, recites a gentle melodious patter about the ailment and the remedy (with no claims at all), and then launches into his key testimonial line: "X provides ephemeral relief in mild cases."

X PROVIDES EPHEMERAL RELIEF IN MILD CASES! It could be said of dirty crankcase oil. I am reminded of P.T. Barnum's come-on under the big tent: "This way to the Egress." Ain't no court gonna find fraud here—we are, suh, playing a fine old American game. Some of this selling is even truthful (heavens to Betsy), and innocent as pie— except that it comes at us ten times an hour. With none of it are we persuaded by argument; we simply slowly drown in product awareness.

Selling is the vice that lays the golden eggs in America; it is the true national pastime, perhaps the last vice we will ever give up (after the Bomb there will be someone left selling Unguentine). It is also one of our more attractive vices. A high-powered salesman or politician in our mythology is not a villain but a Mark Twain or W.C. Fields figure, someone we may not be able to trust but can certainly live with. And live with him we have, throughout America's growing up. Now the reformers themselves emulate him; they have discovered that reform needs P.T. Barnum too, and so we have Nader and his new breed carrying the ball with shock-effect promotion schemes, repetition, facile expertise, the whole bag. Why not? Equal time.

There's just one catch. When many parties play the game, and seek to solve the country's ills by a sort of grand competition in selling, then salesmanship becomes the *whole* game. Products and issues cease to matter.

We are, I think, approaching such a condition now, and the seller is becoming as much a dupe of the process as the buyer. I can imagine the head of Bristol Myers actually taking Excedrin for a headache (W.C. Fields would have known better), and the Congress coming to think that it has a prime-time message for the people simply because the time itself has been provided. These are the conditions of true wash that we need to fear—wash that goes beyond true-false, right-wrong, and puts things in our heads as arbitrarily and mechanically as a robot spoon stuffing a goose.

With commercials the only kind of legislation I can imagine that would effectively reduce wash would limit the frequency of their appearance. By law Pepsi-Cola could hit me no more than once a day on any one channel; by law Winston could give me only one chorus of its bloody song, etc. The law would be in effect an anti-assault law, and once we get around to acknowledging that the tube has unlimited assault potential, the law would not, I think, seem as exotic and frivolous as it does now. The law would start by limiting commercials and then move out to limiting the politicos, the newsmen, all those who in innocence or guile, deliberately or by chance, have a measure of control over our intake. It would be a negative law, saving us from concentrated, long-term assaults, yet keeping no single claim, position, argument, product from us no matter how crumby.

But we first have to take the knowledge step, that is, assess the tube's wash powers. Then perhaps we'll start thinking rather than competing—thinking of how to save us.

1970

# Boston Pops

**A**rthur Fiedler, the handsome white-haired leader of the Boston Pops Orchestra, wound up a series of concerts for National Educational Television recently with a program of powerfully odoriferous oldies, up to and including *Auld Lang Syne*. He proved that he was the king of corn, and he even produced a barbershop quartet while the audience sang, rocked back and forth, clapped and drank beer (there was also a quick camera vision of what looked like martinis). At the end the announcer briefly recapitulated the programs in the series—which had included a fine round of *Peter and the Wolf*—and signed off ambiguously, seeming to suggest that another series was unlikely.

On the off chance that the moguls are looking for audience response, here's one: let's have more, more. Fiedler's corn is mostly precise, professional and eloquent—though when he tries jazz it sounds like an elephant tapdancing—and the camera work is great. I don't think I'd want to see and hear a Pops concert on a 27-incher with tweeters—then it would seem pretentious and *frightfully* boojwah— but on my portable with its two inch speaker the reception was great. I and my family liked the corn, and my three-year-old daughter danced the corn. More, I say.

Music on NET—at least on the Washington, D.C. station—has been extraordinarily good for the past year or so, from Pete Seeger and rock concerts to gold-plated symphonies. I have no dope on the ratings for non-commercial musical programs, and don't know if the amount of music to be broadcast in the coming year will be greater or less than last. But for what has already been done, bully.

The commercial people on the other hand have been dreadful; they can imagine music only as reinforcement for melodrama—this is the Hollywood tradition—or as part of variety shows, with each number lasting three minutes. What a daring innovation it has been for the NET people to let the music roll without interruption (such is the state of this blastedly artificial medium that letting it roll *is* an innovation). The leisure of not meeting 3-minute deadlines is balanced by the nice intensities engendered by slow development. The whole medium, during a good music program, seems even potentially *sane*. Obviously the TV merchandiser-experts can have had little to do with this extraordinary development.

1970

# Media Fads

A television set sits at my left hand, a window at my right—which shall I look at and out? The TV, obviously. I am paid munificently by this noble rag to watch the tube and its vision of life, not the yellowing leaves and the blue sky. Nature's programs change slowly; except for occasional storms they offer no challenge to the journalistic mind. And nature's art is excessively subtle; it knows not the world bludgeons. No, the journalist must stick with his tube—and of course his newspapers.

Yet I confess that I am shamed by the demands of my profession, that I worry for the world if it be left long in our hands, and that, sitting between the window and the tube I dream of starting a vast anti-journalist, anti-tube movement; of stumping the country preaching the dangers of being With It.

The tube and the newspaper do have with-itness in common; they reinforce each other in our daily lives, leaving us with less and less time for the window, or less and less mind for the window—which comes to the same thing. The window has become the equivalent of a vacuum for us; when we look out it we are unemployed. Tube and paper, on the other hand, wake us from our dull tree-gazings and idiotic communings with the universe, to give us—what?

For one thing they give us news, for which I am each year more dubiously grateful.

For another, they give us cartoons. On the tube the big cartoon day is Saturday; in the newspaper it is Sunday—but both media have their cartoons gloriously daily too—such a surfeit of gags and dumb fancies as history has never before known.

And, for a third thing, tube and newspaper give us without let-up the multitudinous currencies of our greedy capitalism (hah), a system that would immerse each of us in boiling detergents if there were profit in so doing.

To live thoughtfully for an extended period with paper and tube—

as they keep struggling to search out or manufacture the top ten in fads and vices—is to wish helplessly for almost any revolution, anything to free us in some measure from the blind economic agents conditioning us to violence, sex, drugs, chaos, sports-chauvinism, law-and-order, and deodorants.

The sad maple tree out my window speaks to me and says the emphasis is all wrong—and that I myself am witlessly one of the emphasizers. Am I not one of those *paid* to be With It?

Most of us who are paid to be With It live in Washington and New York. We are neither notably wise nor notably observant. Most of us never look out the window at all, and our notions of how to be With It are drastically molded by our machined surroundings. Importance, in our value systems, is merely that which we have been *assigned*. Thus we are the pawns of the robot assigners, and in turn the public is our pawn. We serve the public by laboring mightily to *distract* it from looking out its window. There, my pals, is dear old media capitalism in a nutshell—and so long as it prevails, so long as the media offer more hotsy-totsy attractions than the views out our real windows, America will be full of fatheads.

And now I must hurry to watch *Hee Haw.*

1970

# Two Immodest Proposals

The science of hypnosis is not my science, but as one who must play guinea pig to some of its most eminent practioners I feel I have a right to speak anyway. All advertisers would like to hypnotise me; so would many TV producers, the ones who borrow advertising techniques to sell me their dramatic or journalistic wares. Let me start with a basic instance: a Pepsi-Cola ad. At the rate of 30 or so substantively different images a minute (the producers are capable of stepping it up to several a second), a composite view of the American scene flashes at me, with famous faces mixed in with mothers, children, muscles, bosoms, beaches, and naturally Pepsi. My eyes take most of these shots in as discrete entities, but my poor old mind does not; there they all mush together like different ice cream flavors in a thawing freezer, a mushing hastened by the celebrated Pepsi musical theme, with its quiet beginning and intense, screechy end. My mind is left with a mud in which Pepsi is so firmly imbedded that America the Beautiful seems, for the period of the hypnotic condition, merely a Pepsi bottle.

There are hundred of ads like the Pepsi ad; it is a sort of archetype. It defies, as far as I know, legal action against it. The company will never be persuaded that the ad tells a fib about Pepsi. And though the ad does tell a monstrous and continuing fib about Pepsi, by suggesting that hundreds of intimate, meaningful alliances exist between life (energy, beauty, love) and that insipid drink, I can't imagine the FCC or any regulatory agency taking action aginst the fib—it is the fib that launches a thousand commercial ships.

Anyway one could argue that the fib, as practiced by Pepsi, is a white fib; and while I am not persuaded of its whiteness I will agree that it is less black than a good many extant fibs—for example, those emanating from the PR section of the Pentagon. So what to do? My point is that we should get after the Pepsi people and their kind by devising measures to control their advertising *techniques*, rather than (or in addition to) trying to make honest the substance of their propositions. One could ban, for example, or limit quantitatively, the "flicker" technique in the Pepsi ad.

Many and diverse are the ways of hypnosis, but they can all be described as deliberate attempts to take over somebody's mind, and are therefore, among other things, acts against the freedom of that mind. To the objection that the mind can always change the channel the answer is that the hypnotist does all he can, with such resources as the "flicker" technique, to keep the mind pinned there—and while a strong mind can resist, even strong minds are at their weakest lounging in front of the tube. Also, my impression is that the most hypnotic techniques are directed less at strong Miltonic adults than at children; think, for example, of the interminable speedy flickering in cartoons.

The fine, swinging numbers game on "Sesame Street" is unfortunately a powerful instance too. Indeed the instances are numerous and from the best and worst TV shows, which makes the problem difficult but not, I think, dismissable. Education and enlightenment by hypnosis? Is this the way to bring independence?

If a thousand bearded experts think it is I'll subside, but in the meantime I *don't* think it is. Hence, Proposal One: I propose that the FCC gather together a lofty panel to analyze TV's techniques for persuasion (or should I say possession?) and try to work pragmatically toward a system of assessing safe levels of hypnosis. My rationale? I would like to have somebody estimate for me, before I die, whether it is safer for me to receive thirty units of imagery from the tube per minute than to receive so and so many milligrams of mercury from my tunafish per lunch. Let the experts speak to this point, please.

Proposal Two is simpler, and may for all I know have been proposed, plotted and rejected a thousand times: let's persuade Consumers Union to go on the air and tell all.

The precedents for some such program are beginning to be with us. There was Ralph Nader's series on PBS, and now there is "The Great American Dream Machine" on the same network. Also, the fear on the commercial networks of mentioning brand names when something goes wrong with the brands seems to be diminishing. Frank Pollock, the executive assistant to the director of Consumers Union reported recently to *The New Republic's* Managing Editor some experiences CU had had in trying to publicize, on the tube, news about dangerous toys. I quote from the editor's report:

*In one instance Norris Kaplan, a CU official, had been invited to appear on a WABC (New York) program called the "AM Show." He'd been told in advance that he could identify the dangerous toys by name but when he got to the studio he saw that the toys he planned to display were covered with masking tape obscuring their names. The production crew cited "legal problems" and would not dispense with the tape until Kaplan threatened to walk out on the show just as it was about to begin. He was able to identify the toys and hence warn people of their dangers.*

*WABC-TV, on a news program, ran an item about CU's attempts to get stronger enforcement of the Toy Safety Act, and an interview with a representative of Consumers Union, but omitted mention of the specific toys CU had found to be hazardous.*

*"The Today Show," broadcast nationally on NBC, invited Mr. Kaplan to appear to discuss toy safety, but cancelled out when informed that he intended to single out brands. Subsequently the show's producers said the appearance had been cancelled because the subject had been so well covered elsewhere.*

*Oddly enough CU had no such problems on other shows. The NBC Nightly News, WNBC News, NBC's Monitor, WCBS News, and WABC-FM all ran stories in which toy names were named.*

I see no reason why CU's name-calling and analytical methods in its magazine could not be practiced with success and impunity on the tube. Perhaps the magazine procedure would need to be jazzed up (slightly); certainly there would be tedium connected with peering into fifty stoves, shall we say, and comparing, one by one, their lighting fixtures. There would also be an indexing problem: why should I be obliged to hear about nasal sprays for twenty minutes when my nose is all right, but I badly need help on pre-mixed dry martinis? But tedium and delay could be minimized by intelligent direction, and are at any rate minor frailties that TV already fears too much. If there is to be solid information there is to be tedium (my motto for the week).

With the consumer movement now approaching high tide, the tube should begin to play its part. And once again, the job would seem to fall to PBS. Some of the commercial people are getting braver, but not enough braver to take on the advertisers.

1971

# 1983

*This Sedulus column is so dated in one respect—projecting the
continuance of Agnew into our distant political future—that
it has gained a charm it didn't have in the first place. And if
for Agnew some other name were to be substituted maybe it
could still be timely too, except for the reference to Roy Chalk
who was retired from D.C. busing soon after the piece was
written (and I cheated once by omitting a paragraph on the
Vietnam war).*

This is 1983. President Agnew has been in office for six years and
gives a fireside chat for an hour of prime time every Thursday.
Otherwise life in America is much the same. The bus line in the
District of Columbia is still in the hands of Roy Chalk, who has cut the
service in half and claims that he will be insolvent in ten days if the fare
is not raised to $3.75. The dollar is worth seven cents on the 1972 scale
in the average food market. The minimum wage is only $2.50 though
the poverty level has been raised statistically to $20,000 a year, with
the result that sixty million persons are being fed breakfast by the
Black Panthers. Also it is hard to get anything fixed: plumbers for
example charge a minimum of $100 a visit, and it costs three times as
much to install an air conditioner as to buy one. Not that many people
are buying air conditioners; power companies shut down at noon on
hot days. But President Agnew has declared that the water ration
must be doubled on hot days, so it comes out even and everybody is
content except on *cold* days, when the oil, gas, wood and power
shortages drive most people back under covers.

Walking along an average American street in 1983 offers little
novelty to anyone over forty. Most store windows are boarded up.
Sidewalks are safe to walk on at noon and the rates for all kinds of
crime except disloyalty are up only slightly (the new federal gun law
makes it a misdemeanor for anybody under 14 to be in possession of
firearms without parental permission). Newsstands are emptier, girlie
magazines having been banned, but only the aged miss *The New York
Times* whose editors were hanged for sedition after a six year trial.
Movie houses are closed but their marquees still look lively with their

constantly changing advertisements for joining the Marine Corps. Doctors' offices are still filled with Muzak, but in most of them the secretary requires a $20 deposit from each patient before he may sit in the waiting room.

The average American automobile is no longer powered by a gasoline combustion engine but by an atomic powered steam engine perfected by Ford in 1977. Shielding made the motor an extremely heavy device in the early models, but now a 900 hp model weighs no more than its much less powerful gasoline counterpart, and takes about the same space. A car is refueled once a year, then sealed and locked; nothing can go wrong with it, it has never been known to explode or turn into a cloud, and in six years it has virtually replaced the gasoline car, a fact that delighted ecologists, conservationists and concerned citizens until only a few months ago when an outbreak of an odd kind of viral pneumonia in New York during a muggy period was traced to invisible exhalations from what is known as the hot-coil system of the car, necessitating instant banning of all atomic models from the roads of America until further notice. Gasoline cars have been reduced in numbers by 90 percent since the late '70s, and now it is difficult to buy gasoline even if you have a gasoline car; so people are walking mostly.

I might add that no books are being published but that is of little consequence because there are, in 1983, in the average American town, 58 available TV channels of which two are classified as educational and have programs against the Middle East War, the middle class, the profit motive, pollution, poverty, malnutrition, inadequate medical care, inequitable taxation, segregation, deceptive advertising, high interest rates, shoddy merchandise and bad schools. All such subversive matter is preceded by a statement, required by law, to the effect that what follows is the truth the whole truth and nothing but the truth, that it doesn't necessarily represent the views of the station and may be hazardous to health. Regular TV in the meantime is going well: the number of commercials per hour has been doubled, unnecessary regulations hedging in advertisers having been abolished, and cartoons are available 19 hours a day. NBC has taken over financial control of the major baseball and football leagues, CBS owns Hollywood and gold and ABC, and the enormous CATV conglomerate that blossomed in the late seventies has become part of the AT & T—ITT complex. In short, things are going a lot better than some of the pessimists imagined. Meanwhile there *have* been unpleasant reports of the state of mind of regular tube viewers. A characteristic case was reported by a young social worker in Chicago who was canvassing a block near the University for a computerized social science firm. She knocked at the half-open door of a third-floor apartment, and when no one replied she looked in and saw, behind the door and seated in such a way as to be looking directly at the door, a small plain female of uncertain age with *TV Guide* in her lap. The social worker apologized for the intrusion and asked the woman timidly if she had voted in the last election. No answer. Did she know what the Electoral College was? No answer. Would she say that there were more or less Republicans than Democrats in her building? Did she share bathroom facilities with another family? Had she moved her place of residence in the last year? Did she believe in national health insurance? Did she plan to watch the upcoming elections on TV?—To none of these questions did the woman reply, but when TV was mentioned she began to thumb through *TV Guide*. The social worker, now noticing that the woman's TV set was behind the door, realized that the woman had mistaken her for a program. The following conversation ensued:

> Social worker: *I'm not on TV, Ma'am. I'm conducting a survey.*
> Woman: *If you are real why are you asking such questions?*
> SW: *I represent . . . (and here the SW supplied the name of her firm).*
> W: *Are you sure you aren't on Channel 11?*
> SW: *I have nothing to do with Channel 11.*
> W: *Then you must be real. Could you take me somewhere where there are real people?*

Needless to say the social worker took the woman to a psychiatric clinic where her case was treated with the latest group-therapy techniques. These have proved effective in combatting TV withdrawal, and in six months the woman had been rehabilitated though the doctors warned her against ever watching TV for stretches of more than six hours again.

The new Center for Audio Visual Diseases in Houston estimates that at least 10,000 new cases of TV withdrawal are now developing annually, and while this figure indicates that the disease is still a long way from reaching epidemic proportions its presence has become a matter of national concern. Dr. Edmund (Ben) Casey of the Houston Center has recommended three basic steps: 1) that all TV stations be required to go off the air simultaneously for five minutes of each hour; 2) that information about simple home remedies for "TV fix" be widely disseminated—rolling the eyes to the window for example, or playing "lookie-feelie" with a fellow sufferer; and 3) that the schools institute a program in the primary grades to develop children's awareness of the three-dimensional world. Dr. Casey says that at present there is no cause for alarm, but he does caution against the large-scale development and production of whole-wall TV, an invention now being pushed by some of the larger manufacturers.

# *Eagleton*

The destruction of Tom Eagleton by the press was instructive. I watched three channels and read three newspapers sporadically during the crucial days of the killing, and it seemed to me like a mob scene out of Shakespeare. Shakespeare, remember, didn't like mobs, calling them the mutable, rank-scented many.

A *Washington Star-News* reporter covering Eagleton in Hawaii noted innocently that Eagleton wanted to talk about other things than electric-shock treatment, but that *people* kept wanting to talk about electric-shock treatment. People hell, it was journalists who wanted to talk about electric-shock treatment, and did, until finally a few of the more sensitive ones began to realize that what they were doing collectively was rank-scented. In San Francisco, for example, an interviewer asked Eagleton if he minded the *hysteria* of the press. Eagleton was disarmingly nice, but both he and the reporter seemed to agree that 'hysteria' was a good word. It was. In fact only by calling it hysteria can we escape calling it worse; the difference between first and second degree murder is that one is premeditated.

Right in the middle of the fuss Supreme Court Justice William Douglas stopped the Ellsberg trial pending the resolution of a wire-tap complaint from the defense. Douglas's particular point has no bearing here but he took a whack at the feds *en passant*, observing that "the ear of government . . . these days seeks to learn more and more of the affairs of men." Yes, and of course the press has been extremely militant of late about the ear of the government. But what of the ear of the press?

Bad-tempered Charles Dickens visited our country in 1842 and was impressed by our jails and hospitals but distressed by our newspapers and politicos. His sour concluding remarks included these gems: "You [Americans] carry jealousy and distrust into every transaction of public life. By repelling worthy men from your legislative assemblies it has bred up a class of candidates for the

suffrage who . . . disgrace your institutions and your people's choice.
. . . For you no sooner set up an idol firmly than you are sure to pull it
down and dash it into fragments. . . . Any man who attains a high place
among you, from the president downward, may date his downfall
from that moment: for any printed lie that any notorious villain pens
. . . appeals at once to your distrust and is believed. . . . Is this well,
think you, or likely to elevate the character of governors or the
governed among you?"

Dickens found a few good journals amidst the "licentious press,"
but he felt they were helpless against "the moral poison of the bad."
The bad he described as a "monster of depravity" against which no
"private excellence" was safe from attack. He added that the "press has
its evil eye in every house, and its black hand in every appointment in
the state."

One might of course ask Charles Dickens to stick to the facts; he
did have a penchant for editorializing. The interesting point here,
however, is not that he editorialized but that he editorialized against
what he thought of as positive, deliberate villainy, whereas what we
have before us for editorializing about in the case of Senator Eagleton
would seem to be instead a sort of mischance-factor built into our
competitive system, a factor that sends hundreds of reporters,
cameramen, technicians and all manner of self-appointed instant wise
men chasing without malice (mostly) after political candidates as if on
a foxhunt.

The Agnew-Nixon-Clay Whithead school of thought about the
press is still Dickensian, with the Eastern Establishment vaguely cast
in the role of villain. I respect and wholeheartedly sympathize with the
defensiveness that has developed at the White House in the face of the
press's enormous presence, but I do think the White House has found
the wrong cause for its trouble. From the high-falutin James Reston
right on down to Jack (Scoop) Anderson I don't see villainy, and though
I confess that Anderson's notions of how to be competitive strike me
as wholly contemptible I think of him as an agent of our media chaos,
not in himself a cause. In other words the media *system* has become the
cause (the medium is not the message but the tyrant), a system that
demands of journalists caught in the system that they traipse around
in clusters, like army ants, after the big story. Yes, hysteria is the word
rather than villainy.

Yet we can probably distinguish, if only impressionistically,
between malicious and neutral coverage of such an event. In the

Washington papers it was the *Star-News* surprisingly that seemed chiefly to have the knife out for Eagleton, with loaded bannerheads for the whole week and with the columnist Mary McGrory casting forth heavy ironies about Eagleton's and McGovern's bad judgment. I say the *Star*'s role was surprising because the *Post* is now normally Washington's loaded newspaper, an expensively capitalist manifestation of the New Journalism, with hardly a reporter on its enormous staff deigning to play a story straight like in the dear old dead gone days. But in this instance the *Post* front page, in headline and copy, was relatively straight-faced about Eagleton, though the editorial page took out after him.

On the tube it was NBC's John Chancellor who was the objective one. He has a fine detachment of manner anyway; there is no malice when he speaks. The other networks were consistently more aggressive, especially CBS, which has developed a more inquisitorial mode of interviewing (did it all begin with Mike Wallace?) than the others. The inquisition technique was especially evident on a Sunday talk show "Face the Nation" where Eagleton and columnist Anderson confronted each other and where CBS's George Herman managed to dig in like a Jewish mother who suspects her son of lying; he started one question by saying, "Senator, you sound very decisive and confident," and later became so nosy about the skeletons in Eagleton's closet that Eagleton had to joke that he had "given up pickpocketing for a living," at which point Herman said, "No, I don't mean it as a joke, because you must know you're under very strict scrutiny." Indeed.

Unfortunately it doesn't seem to matter much whether the reportage is aggressive or neutral, so long as it is there for a week or so, propping up before a billion eyes doubts about the candidate's character. Just having the reportage there, with or without malice, is enough to kill him off. Or, to go back to Dickens, the results are the same whether villainy or hysteria runs the show. In either case a politician is destroyed—and destroyed in the Eagleton instance with such thoroughness and dispatch that even Dickens's rhetoric would have had trouble rising to the occasion.

All in all what impressed me throughout the proceedings was the dazzling insensitivity of the press to their power role. Mary McGrory observed, for example, in a witty but aggressively judgmental piece following Eagleton's "resignation" that an execution had taken place and that the executioner was—you guess—George McGovern. She didn't mention the press. And in a *New York Times* follow-up there was detailed coverage of the McGovern staff's day-by-day changes of opinion about what the great Eagleton affair signified, yet no attention was paid to who created the significance.

For what it's worth I'm undecided about the merits of removing Eagleton from the ticket; his case is a complicated one that will be a good conversation piece for politicos, historians, psychologists and even ordinary people for a long time. But I do think it is important here to separate the Eagleton case from those who moved in to settle the case, and to ask by what particular dispensation from God or Jefferson or even the Democratic party they did so. For it does seem apparent that in this case we have a stunning contemporary instance of how the press has come to display all the tyrannous powers that our country has traditionally feared to have vested in the hands of government. The journalists have set *themselves* up as the appropriate makers and unmakers of a presidential candidate, though candidate-choosing is conventionally thought to be a matter for our political parties and the citizenry as a whole, a matter that the press is expected merely to report on. We do not, I think, have the bad will around us that Dickens attributed to journalists in the 1840s, but if journalists should in the future continue to have the rope to run things as they ran Eagleton, they may well produce the bad will. Then Dickens's loaded words below may come to seem thoroughly appropriate again:

> *It is the game of these men and of their profligate organs to make the strife of politics so fierce and brutal, and so destructive of all self-respect in worthy men, that sensitive and delicate-minded persons shall be kept aloof . . . and thus the lowest of all scrambling fights goes on, and they who in other countries would, from their intelligence and station, most aspire to make the laws, do here recoil the furthest from that degradation.*

1972

# The Aspirin Conspiracy

Getting advertisers to cease and desist saying that such and such a drug will put more iron in a citizen's oversoul takes years, and by the time the cease and desist order is effective the advertising campaign is over anyway and the same drug is being sold as a correction for nearsightedness. You can't beat the money men with random pot shots, and if there is anything the late unlamented election tells us it is that the money men will be with us a while. But let us take a significant instance, drugs and TV—what does the entrenchment here mean? A couple of weeks ago the National Council of Churches held a well-publicized conference on drug advertising in which the fat companies were shot at, not randomly but with a big fusillade, for spending four times as much on promotion ($2 billion) as on research. Senator Gaylord Nelson roasted them for their activities with the doctors, claiming that $5000 per doctor "is spent annually to persuade him to prescribe drugs" (there by golly is a case of the entrenched speaking to the entrenched). And Nicholas Johnson and others roasted them for their TV advertising, with Johnson recommending a ban on advertising *all* over-the-counter drugs. What will come of these roasts? Nothing, I assume. Not only did the drug companies cooperate beautifully with the President's reelection committee—we will be hearing more about those campaign contributions for months to come—but their advertising has already been so successful that despite the constant revelations about overcharging, misrepresentation, and behind-doors deals their image remains one of integrity; they are among the pillars of our society.

It is hard not to be cynical about this most cynical of industries, where human lives and the great American buck keep being given equal time. Until there's a change in the social heart about these particular fat cats the social heart is, I'd say, not ready to be changed about other industries either. And yet for the reformers to be indignant and righteous about drug advertising is probably not very smart; the reformers should learn from McGovern the fate of the righteous. Take Nick Johnson's righteousness for example at the church conference. I admire Johnson very much but hear this: he complained about pushing beer and wine on TV, and he managed even to be upset because drunks were portrayed sympathetically in TV comedies. Now I *have* heard that alcoholism is a drug problem *too*, but I don't think we will hasten the millenium by suggesting that we should legislate out of existence the vices themselves. The spirit of prohibition (of drugs and drinks and smokes) has been in the reformist air for sometime, and it's a false spirit, I think, one that needs to be kept from tainting sensible efforts to control the promoters. In other words the reformers should set before themselves aphorisms like "before setting world on fire, buy matches" (Charlie Chan?), and not rush about trying to bring mankind back to the Garden in the age of Watergate.

Yet even the loosest live-and-let-live philosophy can produce a reasonably good case against the drug and liquor *promoters*, so perhaps we should not despair. In behalf of their own self-interest they set out every morning deliberately to persuade the public to imbibe the available poisons, an action we have accepted as their right—but is it? To persuade the public to imbibe the stuff is a very different thing from just making the stuff available and letting the public do the choosing. The promoters are after all our official brainwashers and proud of it. Their job *is* to influence choice; hence they are mixed up kids in this land of the free when they, as washers of brains, oppose, as they always do, regulation. They wish not to be regulated in their own lives and businesses yet insist upon their right to move others. Now I'd say this latter right is not a right at all by any construction of our Constitution, and, because it is not, most of the drug and alcohol promotion on the tube is suspect; it could, I'd say, be banned from the air waves with much greater justice than we ban prayer from our public schools. Furthermore the banning or close supervision of such promotion could take place without touching the products themselves or the rights of consumers to consume them. The banning of promotions would not even threaten those light comedies that Nick Johnson is annoyed by—the ones that display drunks sympathetically—so long as the comedies themselves have not been purchased or created by Old Rotgut. In other words, in the area of advertising there would seem to be some possible legal occasion for regulations to *preserve* freedom, and to preserve it not for the advertiser but for the consumer whose free choice the advertiser is always trying to take over.

Take one current brainwash ad as an instance of what we ought to be trying to move against: a plain old Bayer commercial, the kind to be seen on NBC News almost any night. A no-nonsense young matron steps forward from her no-nonsense daily business to tell us that if there's one thing she wants to be sure about for *her* family it's *medicine*. Then she holds up a pamphlet turned out by Bayer saying why Bayer is best. All we see is the outside of the pamphlet but that's enough. She then retreats efficiently back to her family and poses with them—a sort of benign still—for fade-out. What this ad tries to persuade us of, with no documentation and with no suggestion that anything is to be argued, is that Bayer aspirin is more than a headache pill; it is also a strong and loyal ally of that family, a family moreover that represents the very best features of American familiness, being close-knit, sensible, well-dressed, hard-working, well-off—watch the ad and supply your own adjectives. Now I submit that the background fluff for that ad—and the ad is all background, really—is characteristic modern American brainwash of the most insidious kind, and of a kind that can be gotten at by attacking the techniques and intentions of the advertiser. He has smuggled articles of faith into the ad that inhibit the citizenry's free choice of both faith and medicine. Get him. I submit, at least, that going after such noxious promotion is preferable to, and potentially more effective than, trying to eliminate the noxious vices themselves.

1972

# Shakespeare and CBS

I found myself a few nights ago at Washington's Folger Shakespeare Library for a preview of CBS's three-hour Shakespeare special, Joseph Papp's *Much Ado About Nothing* (which appeared for real over CBS in prime time for three hours on February 2). There were murky moments in the first two acts when the pairings of the lovers lost me, and a great many mere Shakespearean words didn't enter my inner ear—but in general it *was* understandable.

Papp is one of the great anybody-can-appreciate-it practitioners, but ironically his practice shows he doesn't believe anybody *can* appreciate it. He acknowledges a wide cultural gap between Shakespeare and us by making great stage efforts to bridge it. Furthermore his method of bridging seems to me the least promising. He wants to be faithful to the original, and at the same time hep, that is, accommodating to the demands of a modern and not-up-to-the-original audience; hence, rather than revising the original he puts a second play on top of it. In the present TV production, which I am told is a very straight transmutation to film of the stage version now playing in New York, Papp provides setting and clothing out of the Gay Nineties—this being a temporal removal the audience *has* been educated up to—and imports music and conventions from early film melodrama; but he leaves Shakespeare's script intact, so that the villain doesn't say "curses," but what Shakespearean villains say. The result is two plays, with the Shakespearean play rendered hysterical by its competitor.

Shakespeare's medium was words. Here the words compete with bright busy images and a sophisticated musical score. The Shakespeare part of the play would have been more "visible," I submit, on radio. Only when the screen medium achieves a rare quiet moment do the words manage to dominate the pictures. Such domination occurred chiefly in Act III, the play's high moment when Benedick soliloquizes comically in a canoe, and listens in on comments about himself and Beatrice. Here the words matter; they are audible and well paced, and are effectively reinforced but not supplanted by the clever canoe business. More typical, however, is the handling of Dogberry, Shakespeare's malaprop constable, where the words are so slurred that the word-play is rarely evident, being replaced by vaudevillean pushing and shoving.

The hysteria I refer to comes from having both plays—or perhaps I should say both the media—going at full speed at once. Instead of a light comedy and the appropriate emotional levels for light comedy, we are treated to a big, loud, indiscriminate bundle of farce, tragedy, melodrama and fairy tale. The play on top of the Shakespeare play creates the indiscriminateness; it is a play of effects rather than unities; it moves from scene to scene doing what seems best to give horsepower to each, rather than trying to enforce the singular old conventional verbal-comic mode.

There is not only the hysteria of too much and too often, but also the final fatigue of too long. Two plays on top of each other don't take quite twice as long as one, but the abundance of stage business must add at least half to three-quarters of an hour to a straight reading of the play. And the play is damnably long anyway for a modern audience. Richard Jencks, vice president of CBS, introducing it at the Folger to a small audience of congressmen, journalists and media people, said he hoped 20 million would be watching it on February 2, or more than had watched *Much Ado* in all the years since its first staging. I wondered, after sitting through five acts handsomely visible on the Folger's good big screen, how many of the 20 million would hang in there in their living rooms, in front of a 12-incher, for three hours.

This is CBS's big season for specials, and it is with the specials that, as I see it, the industry will find its way. The specials can be at once experimental and saleable, being one-shot affairs that the curious will turn on for at least a piece of. To experiment with how long an audience not watching the Miami Dolphins will sit there for *Much Ado* is a worthy and daring venture, though it fails.

Ah Shakespeare if thou wert living at this hour, wouldst thou not like a one-hour slot? And wouldst thou not like to *merge* those two plays, to meet the new demands of the medium and the Kulch? I think so. I think we could makest thou into a good media man after just one sitting at the Folger.

1973

# Mickey Mouse Slouches Toward Bethlehem

When I was a young, tame radical in college Walt Disney received an honorary degree from that college. The citation, written by a very famous English prof, William Lyon Phelps, contained the line, "he laboured like a mountain and brought forth a mouse," which went over the nation's wires and amused everybody, even radical me. I was not amused, though, by the award itself. I had been brought up on Disney shorts, and had enjoyed them unreservedly like the rest of the world; but at the time of the honorary degree Disney was suffering a change of life, being deep in the production of full-length films— *Bambi, Snow White* and the like—that seemed to me and my radical friends to be wholly decadent, though they were obviously profitable outlets for the Disney entrepreneurial energy. Some French or classical voice in us whispered that a genre had been villainously encouraged to jump its bounds, with the result that a mouse had brought forth a mountain. And *that* was wrong.

Last week my family and I stumbled for the first time through the new Disney World in Florida—we have never been near the California establishment—and my old feelings swept over me again, though my radicalism was asleep. My family agreed. We found the whole show a rip-off. As we saw it the Disney interests had out-Barnumed Barnum; they had figured out a way to persuade half the country to travel tremendous distances to be relieved of significant sums; theirs was a triumph in the converting of people into sheep. We left early without using all our tickets.

Since our visit we have been quizzing citizens on street corners about the merits of Disney World, and the responses have been largely positive, a fact we are trying to live with. True, a garage man acknowledged that though he liked Disney World he liked it for the wrong reasons; that is, he had been privileged to see the "inside," all sorts of operational detail that the sheep miss. But the bulk of affirmation was unquestionably from the happy sheep themselves. They *enjoyed* it.

Now why should I knock pleasure? I shouldn't, I won't, I think pleasure is pleasurable. But I must stand firm and say that I don't think Disney World can be let off as a simple pleasure dome. Just as Walt Disney's original move from shorts to full-length cartoons violated, in the days before World War II, the natural and healthy pleasures of the original cartoon genre, similarly the new Floridian monstrosity violates the simplicities it celebrates; it is much more than a monument to the joys of Mickey, Minnie and Donald; it emerges as a sort of cultural, mebbe spiritual, shrine.

I grant that my first hint at being in the presence of holiness occurred before we actually arrived at Disney World. We spent the night at a clip joint nearby, paying more for minimal accommodations in the middle of a cold nowhere than we had spent each night the previous week for pleasant rooms with kitchenette on the beach at Palm Beach. But hotel gods are minor deities and it was evident that these particular itchy Mammons were clustering in central Florida because there was a higher god, a true determiner of price. Sure enough we came into his august presence in the Mickey Mouse Theater the next morning.

First we were herded into a stand-up auditorium and treated to a short pious history of Mickey Mouse cartoons. Then we were herded into a sitdown puppet theater (the two-auditorium arrangement was a logistical triumph, since it speeded the flow *through* the show), where a concert by characters out of the whole Disney heaven took place for perhaps 20 minutes, with Mickey himself as the orchestra conductor. He and his orchestra rose from the pit at the beginning, and played a tune through in a mock symphonic manner borrowed from *Fantasia;* then the orchestra gave way to specialty numbers by Snow White, Donald Duck and so on for a few minutes, after which the whole cast was exposed for a grand finale that ended with Mickey turning around and bowing to us, the sheep.

Remember, the Disney characters were all presented as puppets. They were in constant motion during the show, doing their respective things, and they were programmed very precisely so that their mouths opened and their arms wiggled for just the right musical notes (I pictured behind the scene a complicated version of an oldtime player-piano roll), so that one could have said of the show—had one been disposed to defend it as pleasure merely—that it was merely a puppet show and a rather good one. But my point is that when Mickey turned to us and bowed, it seemed absolutely plain that he had graduated from his modest "merely" roles; he was no longer a simple fantasy figure from a smart artist's pen, but the central idol of a $400 million church. Certainly as he bowed he gave us sheep a moment of genuine confusion about what we were in the presence of. As a herd we clapped, ever so briefly, then stopped, embarrassed.

After all, what were we applauding? The player-piano machine? The engineers who built it? The entrepreneurs who financed it? Or the great imago, Mickey himself?

The embarrassment came, I think, from the sudden realization that we *were* applauding a puppet, and a computerized puppet at that, a puppet that had gone through its whole performance untouched by human hand. Furthermore it was an absurd puppet, a mouse puppet— nothing with a long beard and high forehead like a sage, but a plump round thing with large round ears that had nonetheless been presented as more than that, with the result that we sheep were confused about what we had experienced, and about the intentions behind the production—justifiably because the confusion was central. If that performance had been originally constructed as a serious satire on the capacity of human sheep to find huge, and hugely ridiculous, imagos for worship, not a single change would have been needed in the "script."

Pieties abound elsewhere at Disney World. Perhaps the central piety—which is behind the imago fascination of Mickey himself but controls as well the mythology propagated by the entire enterprise—is a faith in the simple virtues of children and childhood. But as those virtues get filtered through the American money machine they become, as all know, drippy sentimental. This they of course do at Disney World. Even the cutie corn of Winnie-the-Pooh has been incorporated. Furthermore many of the peripheral characters and myths that the Disney interests have appropriated over the years have been gimcracked to death, so that they have none of their original integrity. As my wife observed, Mickey Mouse is in some respects the only authentic figure on the grounds. Now I submit, Mr. Bentham, that when half the country is busy flying, driving and pedaling down to Fla. to be infantile—and infantile as well in the worship of gods that are false, and that drip—then there is at work here more than a pleasure principle.

I have just seen this phenomenon, and though I thought I was too old and experienced in the ways of my country to be shocked by anything, the experience did shock me. We are being *taken*, ladies and gentlemen, taken in a big way. We sheep weren't there just for pleasure, just for laughs. We were there for something higher, something ineffably cultural, an important life-experience, and perhaps more than that, an *ultimate* experience; at any rate something to fill the vacuums of our lives. The mouse knew our need.

And TV? (I have not forgotten that this is a TV column.) The precedent at Disney World shows us how far a country that lives in a social and ideological vacuum can be betrayed by a vacuum-ideology. I doubt if we can find in the history of the world a better example of the worship of a false god than now, west of Orlando; in our national emptiness we are, it has been convincingly demonstrated, open to *anything*. So the question immediately comes up: what will the next anything be?

If *The Wizard of Oz* were not a teensie weensie bit passé I would suggest that somebody build a $500 million empire based upon it in the Arizona desert. For would not the Wizard make another perfect non-god for eventual serious worship? (The film is halfway there already.) Aside from the Wizard my inclination is to look to the tube for the next big imago breakthrough, and while I don't know which tube celebrity to put money on—Lucy in the Everglades? Archie Bunker in the Tetons?—my heart sinks when I contemplate the tube's potential to follow the Disney path.

Yet so far, happily, the big TV money has been devoted to the production of simple pleasure shows, as in the early days of Disney and of the movies as a whole. I see little to fear from Lucy and the like as they now exist, and it seems to me shortsighted of the idealistic reformers of TV to keep proposing that TV perform somehow more significant functions. In a society that can make a god of Mickey Mouse the chief danger is probably not that TV *fail* to raise its sights, but rather that it do so and raise them toward the wrong targets, letting significance be created arbitrarily, created by unscrupulous entrepreneurs.

Do I mean that TV would do best simply to avoid "worthy" social and educational ventures? Of course not. I mean that TV's functions, whatever they are or may become, should be modestly conceived and performed; tube operators with high and churchy notions should be emphatically discouraged. In reverse, the talents of those still devoted to keeping the tube lowbrow and light should not be scorned. We could be in the hands of darker forces, and probably will be.

1973

N.B.: After the appearance of this article I was informed that a Wizard of Oz empire (of modest dimensions) was already in existence, not in Arizona but North Carolina.

# The Big Sell

On the Saturday afternoon that Apollo 14 prepared to return to earth, I watched, without stirring, ice skating, skiing, bobsledding, bowling, basketball, golf, and moon circling. Some of the world's great capitalists at NBC, ABC, CBS, Gillette, General Motors, General Foods, United Airlines, Bristol Myers and NASA (my apologies to those I have inadvertently failed to acknowledge) had not only sweated forth all this testimony to man's vigor, but also mashed it into neat units for my edification. Hawaii and the moon were in conjunction. The lush and the barren. Cameras zoomed busily in and out of craters and sand traps. Arnold Palmer made a crucial 20-foot birdie putt, Alan Shepard made a hard dock. On the previous day Shepard had taken a practice, six-iron swing in the Fra Mauro Highlands. Would Palmer then soon be gathering moon rocks?

One thing was clear: all these good sports belonged to the same spiritual country club. It didn't matter much what country. It mattered less what sport. Play up, play the game—and the subsidiary increments would roll in. Horatio Alger forever.

Remember Horatio? He was a nice, hard-working boy who started at around 10 cents a week. Worked his way up. Saved his pennies. But as Frederick Lewis Allen once pointed out, Horatio didn't actually make it to "up" by working or saving pennies. He made it by windfalls—from grateful bystanders, distant relatives, gold doubloons in old caves.

The same kind of economic and moral madness applies to our modern Saturday afternoon sports types; they look as if they're doing one thing—chipping the ball cleanly out of a bunker, twirling daintily on the ice, donning their pretty space suits, playing governor of Texas—but look again; the real action is elsewhere, the money is in Tang and Bufferin, the windfall is waiting slyly in the alley next to the success story—waiting to jump out like a Neapolitan pimp and offer "up."

TV's juxtapositions of the capitalistic reality (windfalls) and the capitalistic dream (save your pennies) are unprecedentedly crude. Remember those coy characters in Henry James who couldn't bring themselves to mention their sources of moolah? Now, on TV, they can't bring themselves not to. Golf is particularly adaptable to the merchants' designs upon it because its action is continuous and spread around; and so, come to think of it, is mooning. In football and basketball the commercials have to be sandwiched into the timeouts; but golf and mooning can be sandwiched between the commercials.

Anyway it gets harder and harder to distinguish game from commercial, so it soon won't matter who is sandwiching whom. Bufferin has its own moon-shot sequences. Gillette its own golf shots. United Airlines plants stewardesses along the runways—oops, fairways—and all the advertisers hire sports heroes by the gross to hop joyously back and forth between playing field and product.

One can hardly be surprised that the seventies have brought a rash of stories, in the Meggysey vein, of what the dollar is doing to our athletes. The dollar has the athletes well in hand, thank you, and on TV the connections are visible as never before. Tobacco company heads may indignantly deny that they plan to sneak cigaret promotion onto the tube by financing sports events named after their brands, but their defensiveness is a minor anomaly on the big-money scene. Elsewhere big money is buying up sports wholesale as if that were the most natural thing in the world for big money to do. Remember the bloated capitalist of socialist cartoons? He had knife and fork in hand, and his napkin was tied around his neck. The world and its people were spread before him on his groaning table, and he was busy, busy a-gobbling. Well, nowhere has that caricature been more truly brought to life than in TV sports. I'm fifty, and have kept my cool watching the selling of expensive individual souls to Absorbine Jr., Wheaties and the like for most of that time, but the new TV sell-scene is getting to me. The big boys are buying and selling whole games, whole sports in wholesale lots, bringing everything except maybe checkers into their sleazy, pyramidal, holding-company syndrome. I guess I'm a bad sport, for I find it unsporting.

1971

# A Bit of Nostalgia for the Oldtime Corruption

T eapot Dome has been a steady point of reference throughout the recent Washington scandals, and there is no lack of ancient footage in books and magazines about it, mostly tending to show that what could happen in public office that shouldn't happen in public office did happen in public office, and happened pretty much the way it has happened up here in our current briar patch. But there remains an instructive side to Teapot Dome that has not—or not to my knowledge—been discussed much in relation to Watergate, the CIA's trouble and the rest, and that is the role of the Press in the earlier scandal. The oilman Harry Sinclair, one of those scandalized in the twenties, was convinced, like Agnew and Nixon in the seventies, that it was largely the Press that did him in; but he had a rather special reason: he had been blackmailed by the owner of the *Denver Post*. What modern entrepreneur can make that statement?

Let us begin with the *New York Times*, saving the *Denver Post* for the climax. Essentially the *Times* in the twenties was a dutiful nonadversary paper that took its feed from institutional handouts and Congressional hearings. Its reporting of Teapot Dome was thorough and complete during the big moments of the scandal, but the reporting was of the kind that left the investigatory initiative to others. Such passivity was probably more representative of journalistic practice at the time than the curious maneuverings of the *Denver Post*.

Thus when Secretary of the Interior Albert Fall began his quiet skulduggery in 1921, working toward the leasing of government oil holdings in Wyoming to private interests, there was nothing in the *Times* about what he was doing until the following year when Fall himself began a little campaign to sell the public on the virtue of such leasing. On April 8, 1922, Fall gave out a release to the effect that government oil policy, which was then in the hands of the Navy Department, had failed to preserve government holdings from leakage and loss. The *Times* duly reported his concern, and a week or so later reported as well the concern of a Senator named McKendrick about the trustworthiness of Fall (McKendrick asked for an oil lease report), but the *Times* did not itself display any concern, sending no reporters out, writing no editorials. When, three days later, it found itself printing an announcement from the Department of the Interior of "the opening of naval oil reserves in Wyoming to private enterprise. . .to assure the Navy permanent storage of fuel oil above ground," it decided to do the printing in the back in the financial pages. There was nothing in its straightforward article to explain or even to question how the Department of the Interior had come to be entrusted with the opening of the Naval oil reserves (of course that unusual power shift was to become a scandalous affair in its own right later, implicating even President Harding). In the financial pages of the *Times* the opening looked to be an ordinary business arrangement for public as well as private betterment. Only Senators were disturbed.

After Senator McKendrick it was Senator LaFollette who was disturbed. On April 22, 1922, he could be heard asking for facts, and by April 29 he apparently had facts, or thought he had, since he put Teapot Dome on the *Times* front page for the first time by blasting away against Fall, accusing him of sacrificing government and country to private interests. On April 30, with LaFollette's needling, the Senate (so reported the *Times*) laid plans for an oil inquiry.

But journalistically the oil-inquiry announcement simply crippled the story, which thereupon retreated to the back pages for another half year. The story stayed there even when the Marines were called out (it is true that not *many* Marines were called out, that is, five) to eject what were referred to in the reports as squatters on Teapot Dome land. The "squatters" turned out to be representatives of an oil company that had claimed legal rights to a few acres in the neighborhood of Teapot Dome but had not made the deals with Fall that Sinclair and a man named Doheny had made. The Governor of Wyoming telegraphed to President Harding to protest the "squatters" being ejected by force rather than brought to court, but his protest was ineffectual—as well as hidden in a tiny squib at the end of the *Times* financial section. The ejection of the "squatters" thereupon proceeded while other more interesting stories made the front page: Henry Ford had been caught speeding, a poison pie had been analyzed and found truly poisoned.

When the Congressional oil inquiry (the first of a number of inquiries) began in January 1923 the *Times* kept it successfully bottled up in the financial section for several days and might have kept it there forever if Harry Sinclair, upon being put on the stand, had not refused to turn over his records to the investigators. His refusal, together with senatorial annoyance, did then make page one, but only for one working day. When Sinclair appeared again before the investigators he changed his tactics and bowled them over with warmth and frankness, producing a pleasantly archaic headline:

SINCLAIR SATISFIES SENATE COMMITTEE.
ANSWERS ALL QUESTIONS ABOUT OIL,
DISAPPOINTING SENSATION SEEKERS.

Frank About Income Tax

He Admits That He Saved A Good Deal
By Not Carrying All Mammoth Stock
In His Name

Good Humor Prevailing On Every Hand

Meanwhile back at the Department of the Interior Secretary Fall had announced his resignation, but that was passively taken by the *Times* to be merely an indication that Fall did not have the ear of President Harding. In the only editorial on Fall or Teapot Dome that was to appear in the *Times* for yet another year, the *Times* gently patted Fall on the back and concluded, danglingly, "As a private citizen again, everybody will wish him well."

It was the next January before sparks flew once more, and this time as before they were stirred up by an investigative Senator rather than a reporter. Senator Thomas Walsh began prying into the matter of a mysterious $100,000 with which Fall had fixed up his ranch in New Mexico. When queried about the money, Fall first claimed that his friend Ned McLean (a rich man with a richer wife who owned, among other papers, the *Washington Post*, then an innocuous journal known to the light-minded as the "Court Journal") had loaned him the money. But when Walsh began his investigation, McLean testified that, though he had given checks adding up to that amount to Fall, Fall had returned them uncashed. On January 12, 1924, the *Times* then reported (on page 3) that Walsh had passed on McLean's testimony by letter to Fall in a hotel, and Fall had replied that he had received the money from another source making the McLean loan unnecessary. Fall added, "The source from which I obtained the money which I used (to pay back taxes and restore the ranch) was in no way connected with Mr. Sinclair or in any way involved in any connection regarding the Teapot Dome or any oil concerns."

It was at this point that for the first time the *Times* became snoopy, but only momentarily. It planted a reporter or a reporter's agent in the hotel in Palm Beach where Fall was staying, with the result that it could report on January 13, on the basis of its own small investigation, that Fall was staying in a room not registered in his name, and that he had refused to answer any questions about the $100,000, calling the money his "own private affair."

The reportorial snooping angered Fall briefly but was not continued, and the whole Teapot Dome story then lapsed for another week until another break occurred, again a break produced by senatorial activity. At the Walsh oil hearing a Roosevelt in the oil business grew alarmed and preached:

> ARCHIE ROOSEVELT, QUITTING OIL
> COMPANY, TELLS SENATORS SINCLAIR'S
> SECRETARY REPORTED $68,000 PAID
> TO FALL'S FOREMAN

That confession made first page, as did rapid subsequent developments for the next two weeks (interfered with somewhat by the death of Woodrow Wilson). The best scandal headline of all was probably the one of January 25:

> DOHENY LENT FALL $100,000 IN CASH
> SENT IN BAG, NO INTEREST, NO SECURITY:
> ALL FOR FRIENDSHIP, NOT OIL, HE SAYS.

Following that revelation Mr. Fall, still in Palm Beach, was reported to have stayed in bed all day, and the *Times* at last rose to editorial indignation. The affair, it said, was a "national disgrace," and there was "danger of unsettling confidence in the integrity of public men. . .Fall was not jealous for the purity of his office. . .not guided every day by the determination to avoid even the appearance of evil, and he lightly tossed away a precious jewel of trust." As for the rich man Doheny who had given Fall the $100,000 in the black bag, yes, he too was to be censured: "We must pursue corruption relentlessly into its last lurking place."

From this point on the number of those implicated in payoffs increased rapidly; the scandal radiated outward and became everybody's province. Yet even with the case wide open the Press could be seen following rather than leading in the investigation. For example, on the very day of the *Times* editorial (January 27) President Coolidge was reported, in a banner headline, to have stepped in with a "midnight statement" that he was going to move quickly and decisively in prosecuting those involved in the oil leases. Where did he get the sudden notion to issue a *midnight* statement? From learning of the still secret intention of the Walsh committee to demand such a statement from him. How did he learn? Not from the Press. Two days later Senator Walsh and his committee were reported furious because their plan had been "leaked" directly to the President!

In other words in those fine pastoral days the Press was a tardy participant in the leakage system.

But the *Denver Post* was not like the *Times*, and its actions were instructive in a different way. On February 9, when it looked as if everybody connected with Teapot Dome had been exposed, and there was nothing left but interminable legal processing, suddenly one Frederick Bonfils made the *Times* front page:

> DENVER EDITOR TELLS OF $250,000
> PAID BY SINCLAIR FOR RIGHTS
> IN TEAPOT DOME.

And the next day Bonfils made page one again, but this time as defendant rather than accuser:

> BONFILS ACCUSED IN ONE MILLION
> DOLLAR OIL DEAL
>
> Bonfils is Ashen as He Denies
> Charges of Corruption

Bonfils as it turned out had a theory of journalism that is seldom recommended anymore, at least openly, in the enlightened air of our country's newsrooms. He believed that the news a paper picked up should be converted to currency. He had bought the *Denver Post* in 1895 and for more than two decades had alternately printed slander to destroy his enemies and not printed it so that the enemies would pay him for not being destroyed.

Or so at least his practices were said to be, in a lively book about him and his partner Harry Tammen that appeared in the thirties, *Timber Line* by Gene Fowler. Fowler rather enjoyed the two men's theory of journalism, being persuaded with them that what the American public really wanted from a newspaper was a circus. He also enjoyed the oldtime high rhetoric of journalism and was himself a practitioner. In describing an occasion when Horace Greeley nearly drowned in a mountain stream he wrote:

> Uncle Horace plunged in and began to buffet the torrent. He was washed from the back of his palfrey. The awestruck settlers saw the mule emerge and the white hat go sailing down stream. The celebrated maestro of the quill was nowhere in sight. Finally, the Westerners espied editorial bubbles rising to the surface, and then the almost albino noggin of the learned writer.
>
> Now a boat-hook is one of the rarest of utensils in Colorado family life, yet someone appeared with a boat-hook and made thrusts at the floundering leader of the Fourth Estate. It so happened that the rescuer's boat-hook got a purchase in the seat of Horace's trousers. But no matter, he was drawn ashore, half drowned but gaspingly grateful.

It was natural that a writer of such prose should be drawn to Bonfils and Tammen. Fowler lovingly described their shenanigans, making it clear that the P.T. Barnum way of newspapering was the true American way. He even managed to glorify, and perhaps exaggerate, Bonfils' practice of ruining reputations by a mixture of investigative reporting and plain bombast. One instance he dwelt on involved Bonfils' chief early journalistic enemy, the editor of the *Denver Evening Times*. Fowler quoted at length from one of Bonfils' attacks:

> From an organ of public trust (The Evening Times) has degenerated into a paid hireling of the political corporations, and the discriminating reader looks askance upon its opinions even when they happen to be right. Inane, hysterical, a poor suffering creature, that is blown hither and yon by every passing breeze, it is reaching that pitiable stage when neither excuse nor apology will justify its further existence. The poison has gone to the marrow, and it is now not a question of months but of weeks, when the Times will turn up its shrivelled toes to the daisies, and the haunts that once knew it will know it no more. (pg. 146)

Another instance was Bonfils' handling of Senator Thomas Paterson of Colorado, also a newspaper competitor. Bonfils personally struck Paterson on the head in a park, reported Fowler, and then beat

him while he was down, because Paterson had accused Bonfils of
blackmail. Paterson thereupon took the attack to court and listed a
goodly number of specific cases in which advertisers in Bonfils' *Post* had
been maligned in the *Post*'s pages upon withdrawing their advertising,
then restored to grace upon resuming the ads. At the end of the court
session Bonfils was fined the large sum of $50 for his crimes, but the
judge must have sensed that the fine did not come up to the crimes as
he felt obliged to give a lecture as well:

> *The truth is that the* Post *is daily a disgrace to journalism. Its
> policy is for the corruption of the morals of the state. It has
> raised the black flag of the buccaneer concealed beneath the
> folds of the American flag.*

It was this buccaneer then, with his concealed black flag, who
seems to have almost singlehandedly played the investigative
journalistic role for Teapot Dome, while the other publishers left the
investigating to Senators. Upon receiving a casual tip from an ex-
secretary of Fall's Bonfils sent a reporter down to Fall's New Mexico
ranch. When that reporter snooped briefly in the ranch's environs he
discovered that Fall had been thought by his neighbors to be
completely broke just before the handing out of the oil leases; he also
discovered that before the leases the ranch itself had been "run down,
the house dilapidated, the roads hazardous, the stock and equipment
depleted," and the taxes on the property had not been paid in ten years.
Then suddenly more than $100,000 had been expended: the reporter
saw a thriving ranch property with a private railroad car belonging to
an oil tycoon sitting on the ranch's siding.

The reporter went back to Bonfils with his news. It was big news,
it was hot news; and what did Bonfils do with it? He didn't print it.

Instead he launched a series of highminded editorials against the
oil leases in general, as contrary to the public interest. He then
distributed the editorials widely among Washington legislators and
made Harry Sinclair nervous. Sinclair had a meeting with Bonfils.
Meanwhile Bonfils had quickly moved into oil himself and was
working with another oil man by the name of Stack who had lost out in
the race for oil leases. Stack and Bonfils proposed to Sinclair that they
would *not* sue him for depriving them of their oil lease rights, and
would *not* bug him further in the pages of the *Denver Post*, if he would
simply give them a million dollars.

As Samuel Adams says of this episode, Sinclair, having "a distaste for blackmail. . .balked." Thereupon Bonfils returned to writing his lofty editorials, Sinclair thereupon stopped balking and paid the first installment of the million—about $250,000—and the editorials thereupon ceased. According to the evidence presented in the oil inquiry of 1924 (as reported by Fowler) "no article reflecting on Mr. Sinclair or the oil leases. . .appeared for a year" after that moment. So much for investigative reporting of the 1920s.

In passing it should be mentioned that there was one other Colorado newspaperman who became involved in Teapot Dome, John Schaffer, who ran the competing *Rocky Mountain News* and was delighted when the oil inquiry people put the finger on Bonfils. Unfortunately Schaffer himself was soon shown to have profited from Teapot Dome by nearly a hundred thousand dollars. He did so, the astounded Samuel Adams reported, not by developing information, not by threatening suit, not apparently by doing anything except to look as if he might do something. As Adams put it, "one is left to surmise that they made him a gift of love for his beaux yeux."

Though the Teapot Dome story was nearly endless—it was still percolating in 1929—the chief journalistic ploys in the handling of it were probably those described above; and from this distance neither the passivity of the *New York Times* nor the misuse of journalistic power by the *Denver Post* would seem—since we are now so much improved in grace—to point to anything the Fourth Estate need now worry about. We have—have we not?—reduced the decibels of the tendentious high rhetoric that once passed for editorial eloquence (though we are now saddled instead with the tendentious as well as confusing opening paragraphs of the New Journalism where it is fashionable to plant a Significant Anecdote and thereby hide the news completely from sight), and we have become vastly serious and uplifting about the functions of journalism, never allowing sordid matters of power and profit to intrude upon our constantly announced integrity as watchdogs of the public interest. Gene Fowler would be too bored with us to write us up.

Furthermore there is still so much corruption to be investigated, and the senatorial investigators are so thoroughly folded and spindled from Watergate and now the CIA, that the country obviously needs the journalists to stay up front, continuing to play a positive investigatory role. Yes?

Maybe "maybe" would be better. Money and power are still available to investigative journalists for performing their functions in ways that produce results damaging to individuals. The money and power may now be more apt to come from book publication than from black bags, yet the world is not even yet done with black bags. There is no reason whatsoever to doubt that in some new scandal there will be some new journalist who will be tempted and who will toss away "a precious jewel of trust," and even raise "the black flag of the buccaneer."

The modesty of the older *Times* remains therefore something to put up on a shelf and look at; and even the callousness of Bonfils remains something to look at. Despite the success of the Watergate exposures the Press is not yet quite ready to pass through the Pearly Gates. Who will volunteer to begin, dollar by dollar and source by source, the investigative reporting of *it*?

# THE KULCH

Ezra Pound talked about the Kulch more than about Culture because he was contemptuous of it, whatever it was, so wanted it spelled in the manner of Krispy Krunchies or Krazy Kat to make it philistine and American. He had his own lofty idea of what a culture would be if its values were set by persons of his stripe rather than by the middle-class conformists he saw and hated around him—academics with no respect for talent, politicians with no respect for truth, poets with no sense of a poetic line with the sea-surge (rather than the tum-te-tum) in it. And journalists he particularly disliked because they were, he believed, the supreme conformists, dishing out what the people wanted rather than offering, or seeking, leadership. Ezra had a great-man theory of leadership; he looked back on history the way Carlyle did and found that the good times in history were the times of true leadership, wise men at the tiller, thinkers, great artists. With his theories wrapped around him he became an apologist for Mussolini and thus found himself declared a traitor to his country in World War II; but a more characteristic working out of his theorizing occurred early in his career when he began a little society that he called **Le Bel Esprit**. He was going to save the world with that society—he started it shortly after World War I—by liberating certain talented artists from menial, uncreative jobs. His first candidate for help was T.S. Eliot who was working in a bank. The way to save civilization was to get T.S. out of that bank (see "The Poet in the Bank," p. 77), which was a much more modest enterprise than persuading the United States of America to abandon usury and find a strong man like Mussolini.

There was no one ever quite like Ezra but most of the artists of his generation did share with him, though with less fury and urgency, his views of the Kulch. The literary expatriates of the twenties shared them. Not to look down the nose at the society of Sauk Center or Kansas City or Hollywood then was to be a nonconformist of the wrong kind. And for the expatriate set the journalists were the leaders in cultural villainy. Between the serious artist and the journalist flowed a deep river that even the journalist acknowledged. When the journalist had artistic yearnings of his own he knew better than to imagine that he could work them out within his profession. He had to leave his profession, just as Eliot had to leave the bank, to be a true writer; he had to go out in the woods and consult the birds and his soul, or he had to go to Paris and be poor.

The heyday of Ezra's kind of expatriate was fifty years ago. Now the journalists have become so high and mighty that they threaten to take over literature, threaten so hard that the smart operators of literature like Norman Mailer have moved away from birds and souls into the news game. If there is any new truth with us—that is, any truth that has come upon us in our time, a product of the time, a big new cultural manifestation that sits in the daddy chairs of our parlors—it is that truths are not immortal, not forever, but daily. Going back with Ezra to Confucius and Malatesta and the rest is an archaic game. Away with history, tradition. On with the front page.

I am personally full of history and tradition, so can still indulge in the old familiar literary complaints against journalism and the social sciences. (See particularly the brief pieces in this section "A Prejudiced View of the Social Sciences" and "Sweet Violins in the Word House".) But I am also fatigued with the evasions of my colleagues, evasions of the new front-page truth that sits with us. In the essays in this section my antagonism goes out to my colleagues perhaps more than to the conventional unliterary enemy. I mean particularly the two-part essay on English departments and the extended essay on literary dropouts during the Vietnam war ("The Writer as Runaway.")

# A Prejudiced View of the Social Sciences

THE BEHAVIORAL AND SOCIAL SCIENCES
OUTLOOK AND NEEDS
by the National Academy of Sciences
and Social Sciences Research Council

As a Humanities man I carry with me an image of the Social Sciences out of science fiction: an organism resembling jello that keeps expanding, filling up rooms and continents. Its opponents, while being absorbed, are able to say nothing, or merely "glub glub."

I want to say more than "glub glub." The volume before me has the look of a school text but is in fact a high level survey of the Social Sciences as a whole, together with a modest plan for world conquest. It tends to confirm my reactionary Humanities view. Social and behavioral scientists are ambitious and expansionist. They see *their* revolution coming, and rub their hands:

> The broad application of their knowledge to human problems
> necessarily entails a change in our conception of ourselves and
> how we should live together, work and govern ourselves, teach
> and learn, talk and listen. Instead of offering a piece of
> technology to fix a specific problem, the behavioral sciences may
> suggest ways for men to organize their relationships more
> satisfactorily and to improve the adaptive process itself. There
> can be no higher ambition for a science and none more humane.

Just reading that passage gives me a sense of the invading jello. The passage is well and deftly expressed, not an example of old-time, big-word sociological jargon; but its easy manipulation of grand problems and processes makes me wish there *were* a piece of technology in it, something that didn't quiver. Whoever its author is— it is a committee production—he has already been revolutionized rhetorically. He has none of the word difficulties early social scientists had in describing composite beings, average beings, beings who had been "ized."

He (the author) is none other than the Behavioral and Social Sciences Survey Committee, which was sponsored by the Committee on Science and Public Policy of the National Academy of Sciences and the Committee on Problems and Policy of the Social Science Research Council (note how the invading jello occupies even this reviewing space). The book contains a good many recommendations, major and minor, for moving toward the proposed revolution, but its first proposal is the key to the whole: the development of "a system of social indicators."

We can already measure economic values in dollars, the committee tells us, but "there is no corresponding unit of value to measure the quality of life." Well gosh all hemlock, let's get one. First, we will need a "national data system" and then we will need a new federal agency to protect us from the national data system. Then we will have to expand the amount of social science research, and then we will need new schools to be called graduate schools of applied behavioral science. All these needs will be hard to satisfy, but, gosh, the social sciences "are our best hope, in the long run, for understanding our problems in depth and for providing new means of lessening tensions and improving our common life."

Only a few months ago I was sitting unprofitably in my office not improving our common life when I received a call from a not-to-be-named social scientist who wanted help in organizing a meeting to establish some decent evaluation procedures in literature and the arts. I was the only literary man he had called, and after his call I sickened rapidly and lost touch. I would have lost touch anyway. I see every reason to believe that literary criticism and aesthetics will be listed among the social sciences in a year or two, joining language and history. All these disciplines need to be shaped up if they are to help in the building of the quality-of-life indicator, and only true social scientists can shape them.

Some of my best friends are social scientists (and some of my worst enemies are literary critics). I am not anxious to be, or be called, a Luddite. Yet behind this book's facade of moderate, plodding committee reasonableness, I see the unreason of a conquering idea. It is evident in the passage already quoted; it is evident in the proposal for the giant indicator; and it is evident unobstrusively in the attitude *behind* many of the book's statements (I supply the emphasis in Roman):

> —*Shakespeare described life as a play; others have thought of it as a game. It remained for von Neumann and Morgenstern, a mathematician and an economist, to take the game notion* seriously . . .

> —*Human behavior, even in complex social situations,* begins *to be understandable in terms of the capabilities for remembering, learning and responding that are being revealed by research on simple human tasks in the psychological laboratory* . . .

> —*Nation building is* now *a fascinating problem for political scientists.*

Let the quotations stop. A sympathetic reviewer would point out that the book is full of cautionary qualifications; further, that its proposed revolution is still far away. Yes, but what impresses me is the extent to which revolution has already occurred: the book seems scholarly and inoffensive because we've already *had* it. Where once each person thought of himself first by name he now thinks first of his race, class, persuasion, blood type, bracket. The experimenters who comprise the experiment have been influencing us for so long and so effectively that we don't even feel the influence. An abstraction *can* walk down Main Street; thinking will make it (him) so.

The Committee claims that the fears that the social and behavioral sciences will mechanize us are "not well founded." Gosh all hemlock!

1969

# Sweet Violins in the Word House

## A DISRUPTED HISTORY: THE NEW LEFT AND THE NEW CAPITALISM
### by Greg Calvert and Carol Neiman

Right after World War II George Orwell published an essay, *Politics and the English Language*, that has been much prized by English teachers ever since, and largely ignored by everyone else. In it he took out after imprecision, staleness of imagery, pretentious diction, and other common characteristics of the language of our political leaders, famous scientists and even English professors, characteristics produced by foolish thoughts and in turn productive of foolish thoughts. What Orwell didn't quite say was that it was largely his political enemies who were producing the foolishness. He tried hard to find *all* political writing bad, but he concluded that exceptions to the badness were to be found where "the writer is some sort of rebel, expressing his private opinions and not a 'party line.'" Orwell was himself such a rebel, and so his discovery that party lines cause the trouble may be taken as sour grapes by those who know and dislike his political history. Yet what he said in the mid-forties that was then peculiarly applicable to the Old Left seems still so true in the early seventies of the New Left that perhaps his political prejudices can now be discounted: political writing *is* as bad as ever, and it is particularly bad when it is radical party-line writing. Just as in Orwell's time, when one turns to the language of the revolutionary Left "one often has a curious feeling that one is not watching a live human being but some kind of dummy."

My text for today is a New Left document whose authors, aware of what they describe as the "vulgar mechanistic Marxism" in the Left's past, try to be independent of party rhetoric, and fail. What is interesting to me, admittedly a sort of liberal and therefore one of the enemy, is that the authors' strong reaction against some of the verbal and ideological machinery of both the Old and New Left has produced merely more of what they profess to be reacting against. Where the leftist politicos of Orwell's time talked of *bestial atrocities, iron heel, bloodstained tyranny,* and *free peoples of the world,* Greg Calvert and Carol Neiman talk of the *military-industrial complex, American fascism, revolutionary consciousness, meaningful relationships* and the rest with a thoughtless verbal glibness that is not redeemed by their prefatory "note on language" in which they reject such conventional terms as *anarchist* and *socialist* and aspire politically to a "community in which each individual could say: 'I am a lover in a society of friends.'" Orwell might have been rendered momentarily speechless by that verbal gambit but he would have found himself in familiar territory as soon as the book begins. It professes to be a history, but contains hardly a page of exposition of any actual event. Instead we are treated to stretches of theory sandwiched between editorials against the system. In an unusually touching passage near the end the authors describe with annoyance an SDS convention full of interminable "debating about a lot of paper resolutions," but the sad thing is that they are themselves full of debate and paper resoluting rather than matter. They argue against liberalism on the one hand, and against the "Leninist-Maoist cadres" on the other, but their words and thoughts seldom touch the ground. Here is a characteristic sentence:

> *The disastrous consequences of this Leninist opposition to libertarian ideals became most apparent in the neocapitalist period when the increasingly totalitarian nature of social control made the powerlessness of the great majority of men a fertile ground for fascist ideology.*

I count eleven abstract nouns here, with about the same number of grandly cloudy adjectives modifying them, and the whole works gummed together—the phrase is Orwell's—by no less than seven prepositions. It is just the sort of sentence Orwell couldn't stand, "long strips of words which have already been set in order by somebody else." The antidote for it (not the "anecdote," as the authors aver, on page 17) would seem to be the living and loving they recommend rather than the theoretical politicking they indulge in.

Another common result of their theorizing is a sentence composed of a two-sie, or even several two-sies. A two-sie is held together by "either-or," "both-and" or some other dialectically souled connective, and it tends to be quite grand, like: "The basis of revolutionary movement is the instinct to live—Eros—as against the instinct to die—Thanatos." It also tends to be trite: "In the civil rights movement, the deep contradiction between the rhetoric of American freedom and the reality of American oppression was laid bare." And always it is vaguely euphonious, since as Orwell pointed out a common source of verbal imprecision is not wanting to let a sentence drop, suddenly, with a bump. Phineas T. Barnum himself would have been proud of the musically balanced padding of two-sies in the following sentence:

> The realization that the New Left was not an isolated phenomenon unique to the United States, but rather a specific historical movement common to all capitalist societies, was forced on us by the independent but similar development of student movements from Berkeley to Berlin and from Paris to Tokyo.

When words get rolling along good like that, neither speaker nor listener needs to think much. The sound is pleasant, familiar, reassuring (snooze snooze), and before one knows it the day, or the book, is over. I read on and on in *A Disrupted History* lazily anticipating specificity, and suddenly I was at the end and nothing had happened; the authors' program for the New Left was of a piece with their prose: it turned into soft music and went out the window. A long term program must be developed—but what program? Campus struggles must be linked "organically rather than mechanically to other sectors of society"—but by what organs? And the New Left "must begin to make its vision of the liberated human community explicit"—in the *next* book? These are not solutions but lyrics, and while solutions admittedly come hard, imagining non-solutions to *be* solutions will only make them come harder. The authors are full of a sadness, which seems justified, for what is happening to the New Left, and they retain a faith, which is admirable in its earnestness, in our capacity as a nation to renew the radical surge that has slithered off recently; but they are too full of the fuzzy ideological music that surrounds them to do a lick of work in the building of the future community they envisage, or even, for that matter, to spend any time envisaging it. Did not the Lord give us eyes to *see*? Nothing is seen here. There is no imagery, nothing solid, nothing tangible. Truly theirs is a revolution for some country none of us knows, a country not made of earth and sticks and people, but of hundreds of gummy abstractions.

1971

# Climbing the Wall

## I.

I've been sitting regularly now for nearly three years in a pleasant *New Republic* office in Washington where, every weekday, the mailman deposits a sackful of review copies of new books. We have not achieved women's lib in the office yet, so Diannne each morning opens the sack and opens the book bundles and spreads the day's loot out on a large table for me and other high functionaries to inspect. I usually pick out three or four for a close look, and cart them over to my desk and sit down with them; the rest lie on the table until sundown, when Dianne places them on the lower shelf of the great Review Copy Wall. The Review Copy Wall will hold perhaps five hundred books when it is full, and it frequently is. Nineteen of 20 books received are never reviewed but deposited on the Wall, where they slowly ascend to the top two shelves. Books on the top two shelves have been in the office a month or two. A truck arrives, takes books away—and for a day or two the top shelves are empty.

Herman Melville could have made a mighty allegory out of this. At least his speculations would have been mighty as to why the books keep rising to the ceiling rather than descending to the floor; but what impresses me is not the majestic meaning of the process but the ease with which we who work in that office arrived at the process. When we began we had no system and no notion of a system. We had an untrained room that had a bookcase in it; and when the world's publishers were told to send their wares to that room rather than to a room in New York where my predecessor had received them (for all I know his books had moved sideways out the window) the books began to come in and we haphazardly put them on the big table, haphazardly put them on the lower shelves, haphazardly began pushing them up as they disqualified themselves. Yet out of this mindlessness came the inexorableness.

If books were Chevrolets our inability to ride in all of them would not matter, but since they are not Chevrolets our reading problem as a nation is severe. There is nothing to keep us from reading the most defective products of the assembly line except a relative handful of reviewers who, even if they were not, as they inevitably are, motivated by friendships and other dubious relevancies, would be unable unerringly to choose books for review anyway, would be unable to read one-tenth of the books on the Wall. And so we in the literary business sit around watching the books climb the Wall. Sometimes in the middle of the night it occurs to us that somebody should *do* something.

So Dianne has a truck come and clear off the top shelves, and *The New Republic* comes out each week with its little collection of reviews; and as we do all this I stare at the waxing and waning of the book supply and remember that in my infancy the shelves I had to stare at were lined with Classics. In my grandmother's house we had Great Books, and we especially had uniform sets of about two dozen authors I didn't want to read. But one summer I found one novel (in three gorgeous blue volumes) that I did want to read: *The Count of Monte Cristo.* It sat in the midst of a uniform set of Dumas, and I proposed to take it off to camp with me. Could I? I could not. But in fear that I might be discouraged from reading forever, somebody went downtown and bought me a cheap *Count of Monte Cristo* and I read it and was saved—but not from my doubts about the motives behind bookshelves.

Maybe it is worse to have books that look cultural on the bookshelves than books that look gory, sexy and relevant, but in either case a book is a commodity, not a joy, not a fount, not a loved one. We in America have been badly led astray by the commodity philosophy of creation. We have been led astray not only by the grubbers but by many of our alleged large talents like Sinclair Lewis, Scott Fitzgerald, Philip Roth, Norman Mailer, James Dickey. The failure begins early, in the minds of every juvenile writer. His confusion is unlimited because we (professional teachers, writers, publishers) have given him the confusion that *we* have: on the one hand he seeks refuge from criticism in the myth that each little squeal from his self is somehow self-justifying, healthy, worthwhile in some psychic or spiritual sense, and on the other he will not be driven from the illusion that his little self will soon be beating other selves in the open market. At no time does he think of his writing in other-than-self terms. Always it is show-and-tell, with hopes of profit. This is what romantic expressionism has come to. And that is what fills the Wall.

Fifty years ago that great literary critic P.G. Wodehouse described two kind of poets in an amusing novel, *Leave It To Psmith,* that has just been reissued (Beagle Books, 95¢). One kind of poet was a "modern" poet, and he was sullen and self-centered and the author of such incomprehensible lines as "Across the pale parabola of joy." The other was a "nature" poet and a she, and she was wont to observe that the wisps of morning mist were the elves' bridal veils. The latter personage turned out also to be a crook. Perhaps we haven't fallen so far in 50 years. At heart the scene is the same, and is marked as much by ignorance as fraud. Whether you're a high-brow poet writing murkily about the pale parabola of joy or a lowbrow poet looking for new tropes for the dawn you are, as P.G. kept saying about poets, putting on an exhibition. Show-and-tell.

Show-and-tell is built deep into the Western art of rhetoric, so American capitalism shouldn't take all the blame; but the old forms of show-and-tell were less nakedly individualist. They existed within traditional authoritarian frameworks, so that even the most audacious sophistry had at least the intellectual demand upon it that it conform to laws and conventions of argument. Those were serious intellectual demands, learning demands; they forced the self to adopt other-than-self or beyond-self standards in the organization of a statement or statement-series, even if the matter of the statement was rooted in spleen. Not any more. The modern young writer imagines that he is a tremendous powerhouse ready to emit juice spontaneously; and this image of the poet's or novelist's function fits beautifully with his capitalist, self-made-man projections—the poet as millionaire, the novelist as tycoon.

I have written too much all my life—or at least written too much for print (there would seem to be no limit to the need to practice in private)—because I have chosen the American commodity-way. And when I think there are 50,000 others out there who have written more than I, and that many of them have done so with even fewer scruples about the sin of word-pollution, the enormity of our problem comes over me. I see us slowly being *not* asphyxiated by car fumes, and *not* drowned in oil, and *not* submerged in old tin cans, but buried intellectually, spiritually and physically by Mickey Spillane, Norman Mailer, Simenon (anyone may supply his own list here of production masters), by Doubleday, Random House (here again anyone may supply a list of the publishers with the most get-up-and-print), and by a whole fleet of journalists and the like who make their living by words. How to stop the flood? I would be personally quite willing to pay an intelligently devised *word tax,* perhaps because I am one of the lesser offenders and would be invigorated by what the tax might do to the big offenders. Thus for 10,000 newly minted and printed words in a year there would be no tax, but after that there would be a progression up to say 100,000 words, at which point the tax would be confiscatory (every red cent made on the words would be given over to the ten-billion dollar anti-word-pollution program).

But assuming that that is not a practical solution I turn to the word industrialists at the top levels, namely the publishers themselves, for aid. Of course they too are disturbed by the flood. A few years ago it seemed that the only way to get ahead in the industry was to match or outproduce or outadvance the other producers; so each aspiringly big publisher aimed at a 20 foot bookshelf of his own that he could package and sell whole. But slowly it has become apparent that there is only finite space in the world's booknooks, and that the competition for that space is murderous. So there are rumblings of change.

I was interested, for example, to read an interview with William Jovanovich of Harcourt Brace Jovanovich in the recent 100th anniversary issue of *Publishers Weekly.* Jovanovich is one of the most respected of New York's publishers. He is learned, speculative; he talks well on any publishing subject; and within the industrial context of his observations in *PW* one could not ask for more wisdom. It was pleasant to learn that his company was trying to cut back its seasonal lists to about two-thirds of what they have been for the last five years. If all the other publishers would do the same my Wall would not be affected much but I'd *feel* better. The tide would have turned, we could hope for sanity in 2100 A.D. maybe.

And yet, except for the intelligence and even-handedness of Jovanovich's remarks, I found myself finally unnerved by his vision. It was the commodity vision, inescapably and forever. It was books in terms of quantities, dollars. It was the mathematics of culture but not the culture itself. Does the culture itself exist, can it exist independently of the mathematics?—not, I think, according to our present arrangements. I found considerable irony in Jovanovich's concluding remarks about freedom; he said that book publishing was still the "best hope and last bastion of free expression and civil liberties in the United States," and yet for most of his interview he was talking like a behaviorist. It is not merely that he has been involved with B.F. Skinner and others in programmed learning projects (the projects aren't working, he says; "computer system instruction . . . is an idea waiting for its time"), but that he appears consistently to see his publishing role as that of an intelligent observer of cultural behavior patterns, who develops a feel for their directions and is thus prepared with the appropriate books at the appropriate times. This may be the prime entrepreneurial role; I am not faulting it but point out that to accept it as the lead role in the selection as distinguished from the selling of books is to accept the destinies of an outside, running-by-itself system that a Daddy Warbucks can capitalize on. This role is one that Jovanovich calls simply writing (or publishing) to the times, but it seems to me more than that; it is a submission to the philosophy of seizing the day, not of trying to make over the day. A day that as badly needs reforming as ours needs a different philosophy at the highest levels of writing or publishing. Otherwise the seized day is just going to get worse; the movement will be all downward. Yet even the university presses are seizing the day, though they are tax exempt so that they may be relieved of some of the pressures for doing so: Harvard for example is reported to be cutting its publishing program in half, eliminating those books that do not look potentially profitable! The need for improving the Harvard Press's bookkeeping and for cutting down its large annual deficit was cited; newspaper reports suggest that the need was definitely there. Yet the result of the need appears to have been a change of the press's leadership, putting the money men in charge.

Jovanovich is a modest prophet—without sounding godlike he notes that "fiction is weakening," and he personally looks to biographical and autobiographical writing for "tremendous growth" in the seventies. Very well—but that is behavioral talk; what does he say *after* that? What does anyone in publishing or writing do with the discovery, to be made daily, that in *any* of the genres, as they rise up the Wall, the cheap and tawdry are driving out the moderate, the intelligent, the long and truly felt? It was all very well in the old days to sit passively on the sidelines watching with amusement the antics of best sellerdom, while something called Serious Literature (those classics on my Gramma's wall?) went on its own separate way. But the separation, if it ever existed, has broken down, and the finitude of booknook space (as well as the finitude of mere mental space in the national head) is upon us. If the novel is in trouble (and I would agree with Jovanovich that it is) it is so very largely because of the incursion of a horde of opportunists playing around with sex and pop and other bright saleables. The same is true of biographies and autobiographies, where at one extreme we have Clifford Irving's singular contribution to literary depravity and at the other a bunch of *professed* put-ons such as the dreary and pointless new *Tarzan Alive* (by Philip José Farmer, Doubleday, $5.95), described as "A Definitive Biography of Lord Greystoke." In between are dozens of hastily pasted together accounts of prominent political and entertainment figures, all timed for particular occasions. Seizing the day.

The inexorableness of the production of the commodities on the great Wall is itself a product of the commodity *vision* of books. We may talk of the freedoms but the commodity vision tells us of Irving Wallace, who has just been offered $2.5 million for four books he has yet to write. Jovanovich did not mention Irving Wallace; his firm does not publish Irving Wallace; but these are the books that nonetheless will continue to fill up a large portion of the Wall.

To be governed finally—in writing or publishing—by what will *sell* is not, I submit, to be free to exercise one's best judgment of what is good and what is bad to write or publish; but no writer Warbucks or commercial publisher, not even one as concerned with humane values as Jovanovich, can admit this. He has to keep assuming that the commodity system somehow enforces a value system rather than constantly threatening it. He has to keep imagining that the masses in their purchases will keep sending back wisdom signals, value signals, when in fact what they send back is orders for the tawdry, and are thereby further corrupted by the tawdry, and so order more of the tawdry. Jovanovich fears totalitarianism, but the inexorableness of the commodity system deserves a little fearing too. The goddam Wall is full again.

II

A word tax might cut down on the number of books published but an equally fetching notion is that we place an upper limit on financial success from a single book, thus killing the goose that lays the golden egg. We could arrange with the IRS that when a writer's royalties and other income from a book reach a gross total of perhaps $200,000 his money machine clicks to a stop. So does the publisher's money machine. At that point the publisher may continue to sell and distribute the book at cost, and the writer may continue to be admired for his genius, but no more. All funds received after the critical point are put into an enormous kitty for the preservation of decency in success.

Of course these schemes are not exactly a part of the Democratic Platform yet; nor is the bureaucratic dream that we limit the number of titles a publisher can turn forth in a single year. But if the schemes seem ridiculous, so is what is going to happen to literature if we persist with our Adam Smithing. The Soviets have their indecencies but we have ours too, and it would be well that we look at our own seriously rather than taking refuge in the dubious and face-saving, status-quo-preserving proposition that we are better off than the Soviets. For nearly 40 years our intellectual community has raged at Soviet censorship, and at the insistent demands of party-line socialist critics that literature be judged by assessing its service to the "cause"; but while we have complained about socialist frailties we have managed at the same time to ignore or gloss over our chief frailty, which is a total inability to conceive of values except in terms of service to the self. All in all our two countries have managed to achieve in literature a sort of continuing parody of their respective ideological doctrines. Sensible things are frequently said in both places (especially about the other place) about what ought to be done to de-frail the frailties, but as usual the ought-to-be has little to do with practice. We go on with what the Soviets call our modernism—which includes incoherence, excessive subjectivity, excessive attention to style, bad reporting, nihilism and probably even halitosis—while they go on trying to prove Orwell. And to the question, What can be done in either country, there is presumably no intelligent answer except, Wait.

Yet to come back home, I would like to imagine the possible efficacy of a few at least tentative gestures over here against Adam Smithing. First there are the money proposals above. Second there are related aesthetic proposals that we could learn about with profit from the socialists. For example, at the still center of the college creative writing world a bit of "critical realism" would be a positive delight. Critical realism is that literary and social stance that a nonsocialist can grow into and thereby gain the socialist's blessing; it produces a literature of social and historical awareness (two models frequently cited are Dickens and Thomas Mann) and in the process subordinates the private life to the general welfare. I continue to be skeptical about how one gets to the general welfare in Creative Writing—some mornings one can't even find a quorum to discuss the Adam Smith poems that have not been written—but I nonetheless think something might be done, and done without having to start a Fascist youth corps, to at least make a start away from the self-indulgence we now encourage. Kenneth Koch once made a good case for encouraging young children to write up their wishes, lies and dreams, and that is fine; but I am talking about the older children now and the grown-ups, and looking for a way of turning the Koch phonograph record over and playing haves, truths and wakings. Naturalism?—I want neither real gardens nor real toads but reasonable approximations of these, *plus*— and this is the dubious socialist addition that few American writers now dream of—people, reasonably verisimilar people acting in concert, people displaying their best thoughts and instincts, people awake and even sober and rational, people at work (out of bed) serving causes, performing important and hopefully rewarding communal functions. Imagine! I have been thinking darkly of how to encourage such radical concerns among the young writers I find around me, and the other day I proposed to a talented poet heading in the direction of a collection of poems for an honors "thesis" that he regard the proposed collection as in part an assignment in *reportage* on his job in a local bar— the people there, the social-cultural milieu there, the whole bag—and that when the assignment is complete it be judged for its accuracy, adequacy and wisdom *as* report. Also that it be judged by others than me, maybe by some of the bar's denizens. Well, the poet upon hearing my whirling words remained calm and professed an interest—though there was something in his eyes suggesting that he knew I was mad— and left, and we will see what comes of the project: perhaps he will lose his job? Meanwhile I go on with my madness; as I write this I have just proposed to another writer that he try to move out of his inwardness by attending to communal matters. He was pleased and had a quick answer; he told me he was already living in a sort of commune. "Oh," I said, "then you have a ready-made scene and you can write about the farming and the washing dishes and the serving of the communal cause?" But no, the commune, he went on, was simply his pad, which he shared with two other poets. Their cause was poetry and that was that.

What have the whims and characteristic activities of struggling student poets to do with the Adam Smithing of the publishing world? In publishing as I have indicated the game is always money and the dream (of publisher and writer) is of a big money killing, while of course the student poet hasn't made a dime on his writing yet, nor has he yet developed a nose for what will make money. But he dreams too, and his dream is like his seniors' dream in that it is always—always at least as I have personally seen it among students—a dream of self-aggrandizement by self-expression. What does one write about and for, other than about and for the self?—such secondary matters, the argument seems to run, can be settled later.

"Ask not," John Kennedy might have said, "what your country can give you for writing, but what you can write for your country." The notion has a genuinely foolish sound, doesn't it? when the country is mining the waters and otherwise doing its incredible best to alienate still further nine-tenths of the citizens who have any designs upon writing. I assume therefore that any interest in the general welfare that I may manage to inculcate will not include, at least at the moment, the writing of patriotic ditties. But the stance of critical realism does not demand that of us: it demands primary attention to people and their plight, not government and its plight, and such attention can be paid even in bad times like these. But to develop such attention does entail a change—how strange that it should—in the vision that our writers grow up with of what it is to be a writer: the life, the role, the function. It involves among other things thinking of the writing act as a service to society rather than, or over and above, service to self—and nobody who dreams of being a writer in this unhappy country ever has such a thought.

Remember Horatio Alger? I submit that in the writing (and publishing) game we are confused as was Horatio. We think that we will serve society by working hard at the typewriter serving ourselves, when in fact we do not do that; we just get rich like Horatio if we are lucky—and of course the nasty money irony is that very few are lucky—while society watches wonderingly, down at the bar. Another way of putting it is that by the present arrangements we are, increasingly, serving neither self nor society well.

1972

# English Department Ills

CONFESSIONS OF
AN AMERICAN SCHOLAR
*by Simon O'Toole*

T he name Simon O'Toole is a pseudonym for an unhappy professor of English who wants to tell all—without identifying himself or his university. Telling all turns out to be a matter of "confessing" that English professors are venal *too*, that academicians in general have been cowards in recent crises, and that the truth is not hidden under every research project. Not many teachers and scholars will be startled by these revelations, and O'Toole's solutions, thrown out half-heartedly at the end, are not likely to rage through the educational system: he would, for example, have "less education instead of more;" he would replace the present singular and tedious PhD dissertation with two short (and tedious?) dissertations; and he would arrange the world so that anyone hired to teach at a college could then "assume he is a permanent member of the staff, barring insanity, wickedness, or his own desire to move on." (How *do* you arrange that?) Thus the book is a disappointment—and yet it represents a mode of statement we could use more of, and from less petulant confessors than O'Toole. Imagine our institutional life if it were peopled with modest and constructive self critics trying to reform themselves and their establishments—even to the extent of pushing for the scuttling of outworn, unworthy projects and jobs— rather than constantly holding the line, struggling to preserve and maintain the grand old regimes they began with.

English departments badly need scuttlings—there O'Toole is on the right track—and they need to have the impetus for scuttling occur from within. But what O'Toole would do (when it is clear what he would do) is scuttle indiscriminately because he has personally soured on his academic life and finds everything around him in need of scuttling. "My experience says," he says, "that American higher education is a low-grade farce." The remark befits an outsider, someone who has no commitments, and to whom throw-aways come easy. By "higher education" he seems to mean primarily graduate or research work in English—a curious equating—and he seems to think it farcical because its sabbaticals, its sieges in the British Museum, and the resultant unreadable monographs are commonly mistaken for wisdom, enlightenment, truth. Here he is, though properly annoyed by the monographs, confused. No matter how fruitless the scholarship in English may sometimes be it is only farcical when it is conducted by the confirmed cynic, the unscrupulous opportunist, or the fool. To find waste in the lives of persons one admires is not to find farce—which is to say that O'Toole's "confession" is flawed by his basic contempt for his colleagues. He would not mend their patches but dispose of them—surely an outsider's attitude. I don't know where and how he as an insider picked up his outsiderism—he gives us the impression that he made the choice himself and has devoted most of his professional career to figuring out ways of staying off campus—but I do feel, from my own not-very-far-inside experience of about a hundred years, that he has maligned his profession. The characteristic English scholar is much more apt to be honest and idealistic—and baffled and frustrated—than villainous or idiotic. Neither his life nor his work makes good farce, for the simple reason that commitment is present and evident in his affairs even when, as is common, he is dubious of the merit or profit in the commitment.

What is happening in the English profession—aside from the relatively rare profiteering in bigtime textbooks and forever grants—is worth extensive and considerate "confessing" by compassionate insiders, for what is happening is significant for all education: English as a subject, though not yet as a department, is going down the drain. The English teacher or scholar is constantly being whispered to out of the woodwork, and told that his profession's gone. Farce? Only for the uncommitted.

Journalists, social scientists, McLuhanites and a variety of outside villains can be blamed for having usurped many English department functions in recent years. And English departments themselves can be blamed for remaining extraordinarily rigid and imperceptive about objectives in English, in the face of the academic revolution we have been living through. And of course the venality of individual scholars can also be blamed, following the O'Toole line. But beyond blame—and O'Toole somehow never gets beyond blame—is the simple though obscure fact of loss. Literature as we have known it is somewhere, somehow seeping out the door. And language as we have known it has the seeps too. A linguist or social scientist can jump on me about that "we"; it makes me at best some sort of brahmin, at worst something worthy of the growl word "fascist"—but I'll let it stand. As we have known language and literature, they are vanishing.

Now these are losses beyond English departments and English scholars; so the grand scuttling that is to take place will not be speeded or slowed mightily by a few rearrangements within English departments, or by deliberate, committee-inspired revisions in the direction or scope of scholarly publications in English, though such revisionism is badly needed (published literary criticism, for example, has lost almost all general currency even within the profession in the last couple of decades; out of the hundred or so books published yearly, only a handful will be read by more than a handful). No, the changes will be made by outsiders holding purse strings, and at the registration desks for college courses, and in all those curious focal points of what "we" call illiteracy, where the language and its literature are being made into oatmeal and bludgeons. But if the English scholar or teacher cannot control very much of all this he can still, if he so wishes, brighten the corner where he is; that is, he can make local decisions (to scuttle or preserve) tending to keep the corner bright a little longer than it would be without him. O'Toole has no interest in this kind of preserving; in fact O'Toole manages to miss that whole big cultural point of loss, and imagine that literature and language will survive in a shape he can recognize if only the scholars and teachers leave them alone. They won't, and I suspect that he will be shocked and chagrined when they don't—even though at one point in his book he praises a student for asking, "What's the use of being literate?"

1970

# English Department Ills (II)

STUFF

*edited by Herbert Kohl and Victor H. Cruz*

The decade of the sixties was, among other things, a long siege of youth and romance in literature, and a good bit of that romance was tied in with Rousseauistic notions about teaching (no, not teaching—allowing, encouraging) children to write. To write creatively. Not to write as English teachers had for generations taught them to write. One of the most romantic books of the decade—and also, I must add, lest I be misunderstood, one of the best—was Herbert Kohl's *Thirty-six Children*. It was a straightforward account of Kohl's experiences as a teacher with a group of black children who had been declared in effect unteachable by "the system." He taught them by not teaching them. He encouraged them to find themselves by expressing themselves. His short-lived experiment amounted to a sort of miniature Summerhill in Harlem, and while he sadly observed at the end of the book that many of the children returned to their state of institutional incorrigibility in the year following their experience with him, the book still left with its readers the warm feeling that always attends a good man's discovery of mankind's essential goodness.

And all around the country, especially in the big cities, freewheeling writing programs and arts programs sprang up in the sixties, run mostly by young poets who had great faith in children's native, uncoached powers of expression and great contempt for the capacity of school systems to evoke those powers. Sometimes the programs were within English departments, sometimes they were separate. Sometimes they were not in schools at all, but in storefront retreats from the schools, in church basements and the like. But wherever they were they were a new force for the scholastic, academic literary world to contend with.

In general, academia contended by accepting the new force and letting the old forces continue too. Bureaucracies can never get rid of anything, never make decisions; they just keep adding on—and in this case muddling through with *all* the possibilities was probably a sound, if inadvertent, strategy; the issues at stake, not to mention the human and institutional commitments, were enormous.

Nobody yet knows which way the prevailing winds will finally blow in the teaching of writing; but certainly the Kohl kind of thing is now a force in the schools, and has put the traditionalist teachers on the defensive. Perhaps more important has been its effect on poetry itself, or at least on the image of poetry that those who use the word "poetry" in a belligerent, missionary manner carry around with them. If when the neon sign flashes "poetry," the missionaries think "sonnet," one gets, eventually, tradition, discipline, analysis, all that; but if when the sign flashes "poetry" the missionary thinks "me" or "soul," one gets native woodnotes wild. For better or worse Kohl has been an extremely important missionary for the latter.

In *Thirty-six Children*, Kohl was concerned primarily with education; in his new book *Stuff*, which is an anthology, he is after poetry itself, or the image thereof. In his introduction to *Stuff* he is not just telling us how to get children to express themselves; he is telling us what he believes the nature of poetry, at all ages, is or should be. Poetry, he is saying, is stuff: "What we [Kohl and his co-editor Victor Cruz] have come up with is a lot of stuff we like. That is the only way we knew how to do it." Using the word "stuff" is deceptively cute. This book is a poetry manifesto, a document presenting modes of expression; it gives us the child or the child-mind as the bearer of essential poetic wisdom, after the manner of early 19th-century sages.

The same could be said of the activities of another well-known teacher of writing, Kenneth Koch, in *Wishes, Lies, and Dreams*. There Koch describes many fascinating exercises for starting young poets on the road to thinking spaciously and imaginatively, but he is also, as if incidentally, writing his own ticket for the art. And several other writer-teachers could be mentioned whose pedagogy and art have similarly become closely intertwined. In the fifties it was commonplace for Rousseauistically inclined poets to complain about the effect of academia upon the divine stuff. Now in reverse Rousseau is working for control of academia.

What is being produced is very late, very with-it Rousseau. I find the selections in *Stuff* enormously uneven—sometimes full of the freshness and spontaneity the mode calls for, sometimes turgidly repetitive of the most commonplace current social complaints—but in general good enough to make a strong case for the missionaries. I was particularly taken by a poem by Alvin Curry about a stolen "tailor-made" coat that ends:

> *Now I got a 'Tailor-Made Hat'*
> *Ain't nobody gettin'*
> *Their hands on that!*

Also vivid is Alice Schilz's piece, "harvey," about a boy who, among other things doesn't brush

> *hist*
> *eeth.*

One is tempted to list the names of all the book's contributors, and cheer them on, partly for genuinely displaying the imagination and vitality that in many, many cases their regular teachers had not imagined they possessed, and partly because they need encouragement if they are to continue to explore their talents as they do in this collection. Kohl has on his hands what appears to be an enormously effective form of group therapy.

But what of those lovely old English departments, and their lovely old language and poetry?—will they survive the new Rousseauists? and does it matter?

Feeling obscurely the strange new forces at work in my own college English classes, and in the published "stuff" that passes as poetry and song where artistic fashions are made, I'd say it matters very much. One doesn't have to be strong on literature's Great Tradition or on the felicities of law and order in language to be worried by the opposite extreme moving in. And assuming, as I do, that the extremes on both sides are undesirable I still do not see at the moment what an effective compromise might come to, in either schools or poems.

The choice is not simply a theoretical one, between the romantics and the classicists, or between modern versions of these ancient dualisms, though the dualisms are still alive and kicking. Beyond theory are the advocates, and to the extent that the old world is represented by the likes of Professor O'Toole (see my review of *Confessions of an American Scholar*) one has to be with Kohl and the new world. O'Toole's sentiments are not, I think, running English yet, but certainly the profession is filled with cynicism and petty frustrations. The Kohls offer energy, warmth, hope.

But to join Stuff with the tradition *would* be hard. Where do the standards for Stuff come from? Even to mention standards is sticky in the Stuff world, but if Stuff judgment must be made it must come, as I understand Kohl, in terms of the norms in the poet's peer group. In other words the writing of Stuff is primarily a communal act, a solidarity enforcer, and only secondarily an art act, a truth act, any of that. Thus Kohl complains of the notions of poetry *he* was conditioned to in school, that they made poetry and poets separate from wherever the action was; poetry was accordingly a polite, frail, effeminate business in his adolescence whereas now, for his eager Stuff poets, it is tougher, more real, less arty—they are attracted to it apparently as an "in" thing. In the face of such observations the poets who were models in *my* adolescence would shiver.

The verse of Yeats, Eliot, Pound and others who dominated the early century was hardly effeminate—it was as much a reaction against the polite magazine verse of their time as the poetry in *Stuff* is to polite magazine verse now (if there is any polite magazine verse now)—but it was hardly an "in" verse either. To practice the art of poetry in the footsteps of Yeats, Eliot and Pound was to move out and away from what the age, as Pound kept saying, demanded; it was to fly solo or with a small group of kindred solo spirits. Call it a snobbish art if you will; certainly it achieved snobbishness, arrogance, intolerance and profoundly anti-communal statement on occasion. But it was also an art deeply committed to the loftiest ideals Western culture has had for poetry and poets—to the poet as seer and to poetry as a distillation of the best man has known. Poetry as Stuff?—the word "stuff" is the best possible word to illustrate what the old world thought poetry was not.

Now we have Stuff all over—up and down the schools and colleges, and flooding editors' desks. Also we are developing a sort of aesthetic of Stuff, an aesthetic that has been bred on the foreign soil of the social sciences and is therefore doubly annoying to the priests of the old aesthetic. The aesthetic of Stuff is of course an aesthetic of Poetry-is-Good-for-you, and Poetry-is-Relevant. To it the old says, Grrr.

I don't know how long English departments can house simultaneously, as they are now doing, these contradictory aesthetics.

Perhaps in a decade or two the social sciences will have the whole bag and there will be no contradiction. But in the meantime the first step in solving the dilemma, one way or another, would seem to be for the Kohls to recognize the enormity of the contradiction, and for the anti-Kohls to recognize how much the Kohls have done to restore life to the teaching of writing.

1970

# Black Studies in Glass Houses

AMISTAD I

*edited by John A. Williams and Charles F. Harris*

In my salad days I once enunciated a general law (which I then applied to book reviewing): that judgment is impugned to the extent that it is exercised. Here I want to discuss a second law, applicable in special situations: judgment is impugned *before* it is exercised. It is really a different kind of law, but equally meritorious; for example, a student may impugn my judgment as a teacher before I have graded a paper of his, and do so on rumors from his roommate that I eat student flesh. The case at hand is that of the white man in relation to black literature, and of course any black wishing to impugn my judgment here has plenty of evidence to bring to bear of previous bad judgment by whites, if not bad judgments by me.

This second law has important bearing on all the problems of black-white relations. Part of the new black awareness is an aggravated sensitivity to white weakness. A chance phrase, a suggestion of irony in speech tone, any small mannerism on the part of a white may quickly be taken as evidence of racism. And the racism may be there. But the concerned white, the non-racist-professing white is the one sensitive to black radar, and therefore the one who may be driven most quickly into silence.

His silence is further encouraged in the literary world in recent years by the common claim of militant blacks that a white man is not capable of judging black literature. That is a bad claim anyway, though the white can make it seem good by being a fool; and it certainly is another force discouraging amity. My impression is that many white English teachers and literary critics have felt disposed to back off from black literary affairs because to deal with them is constantly to invite confrontations. Yet not to deal with them is to invite confrontations too.

The publication of *Amistad I* is obviously an occasion when whites *should* speak. It is directed at Black Studies programs, but it also constantly invites white comment. It is the first issue of a publisher's periodical dedicated to the provision of "a systematic cohesive body of basic material for Black Studies courses." I have, of course, no way of knowing how well *Amistad I* will fare with Black Studies teachers; nor if the "basic material" in it is in any way representative of what Black Studies people as a whole would like to do with their programs, but as one white man across the hall, I must admit to not liking the prospect. I realize that for militants my dislike will be in the book's favor.

Of the essays in the anthology that seem to deal most directly with the problems of content for Black Studies programs, there is, most importantly, an essay by Vincent Harding, essentially a history of the development of Black History. Before Black History, says Harding, was Negro History. Negro History set out "to reveal the 'contributions' of blacks to the America saga," and to make the Negro a part of the American saga. Negro History aimed at objectivity; it was written by George Washington Williams, John Hope Franklin and others, and the best of it contained the seeds of the later Black History. The more obvious germinal sources of Black History, however, are DuBois and Frantz Fanon. It was Fanon who said that if the blacks were to shape their future they first had to reshape their past, a reshaping that would end the presenting of "evidence in favor of America."

Harding does not give us instances of what Black History will consist of (though we have instances elsewhere in the volume), but he does describe briefly the stage beyond Black History, namely Black Studies proper. Black Studies is the larger intellectual whole that includes History and provides for, "the search for the new land, the new society, the new being." Theology? Whatever it should be called, it will dispose of the "ancient shibboleths about detachment and objectivity"; for Black History and Black Studies are aggressively political. Not stated but implied is that they are also subjective; that is, they provide facts or truths that are exclusively manifestations of black consciousness.

A more conservative essay by C.L.R. James describes what can be done, in the area of Black History, with the old slave trade and its significance for the West. Then there are two radical essays, in which the vision of the black historian is transferred to the literary scene. Calvin C. Hernton traces the developing radicalness in the literature of James Baldwin, and notes that now black writing has gone beyond Baldwin in the sense that the new black writers "are not preoccupied with the chic, personalized trivia of their own individual hang-ups."

And in the most militant essay in the book Addison Gayle, Jr. describes how the Southern white writer, picking up his notions of slavery from the Greeks, developed a plantation literature that continues to dominate American letters. Here is a bit of the flavor of the Gayle essay:

> The southern mind was attracted to the Greek ideal partly because of a justification of slavery offered by the world's first "democracy"; it was not attracted by what Matthew Arnold called the "humane principles" handed down from the Aegean through Greece's most famous sons—principles which distinguished man by placing him at the center of the universe. To the southern mind, historically incapable of dealing with complexity, seeking a stable, ordered society free from the disruption occasioned by the intrusion of enlightened ideas, Greece offered a model of the agrarian society.

> Sometimes called "the Bible for agrarianism" I'll Take My Stand is a racist fascist document, equaled in the 20th century only by Hitler's Mein Kampf. Among its contributors are men whose names are legend in the field of American literary criticism . . .

> . . . the university, quick to move on reactionary principles, fell sway to the sophistry of the agrarians in less than two years. The teachers of English were the most culpable. Guardians of the national taste, these men of letters determined what cultured Americans will or will not read, what work of art deserves or does not deserve the National Book Award or the Pulitzer Prize, what writer will or will not receive a fellowship to work in leisure or obtain a seat at a renowned university. The control of the nation's cultural apparatus rests in the hands of English professors and critics who, more often than not, peer out upon American society with a condescension reserved for idiots and half-wits.

Gayle is an English teacher himself so he knows some of this from the inside. I gather that he would like to get rid of the plantation literature of such writers as Faulkner and Styron and Ellison, and move his own pedagogy across the hall to Black Studies.

Many whites, some of them English and History teachers, have complained about the arrogance and incompetence to be found in English teaching, the narrow prescriptive chauvinism to be found in History, and the general stuffiness of the American university. They have also complained about that ill-fated "fascist" book, I'll Take My

*Stand*, which was a favorite object of Northern liberal ridicule in the 30s. So in a sense the black writers of *Amistad I* are not saying anything new to the white world. But in another sense they are. They are shifting the blame from political or professional stupidity to simple whiteness, and they are also greatly magnifying the strenuousness of the complaints. Furthermore, what they are doing in their own backyard is genuinely new: the moves from Negro History to Black History, from James Baldwin to non "personalized" literature, and from defensive polemics to pronouncements expressing a high degree of certitude—these shifts have taken place so fast that it is very hard to keep up (and also hard to believe that the shifts have actually taken place). As I sit symbolically across the hall from it all, aging, and depressed with the profession of Humanities as now practiced, I am not sure whether I should try to keep up with Black Studies, or merely wait for it to take over or blow over. I know feelingly, though, that the attitudes expressed by militant blacks, even if they should be shallow and ephemeral (as I think they are not), are related to the attitudes expressed by thousands of white students; and that the accumulating rebellion against "ancient shibboleths about detachment and objectivity" is having an immediate and wholly inhibitory effect on the classes now being taught *outside* Black Studies. In other words, I can sit quietly, across the hall, but as a teacher I have no immunity from the rebellion.

History and English should perhaps be more ready for rebellion than they are; they are as full of revisionary theory as the sciences, or politics; and even their conservatives preach change as an element of health. Thus the reactionary villain from Columbia, Jacques Barzun, once said that "history has to be periodically rewritten," and in literature T.S. Eliot, who admired the Southern agrarians Vincent Harding raged against, notoriously observed that whenever a really new work of literature was written it changed the whole order of literary affairs in the past. Furthermore, the best white teachers in English and History would agree with Harding and Gayle at least to the extent of disapproving emphatically of much that is being taught in these subjects. In History for example, they would agree with Barzun that popular history, which is largely textbook history, "fosters national egotism and distorts the reality of human affairs" (Harding would substitute the word "white" for the word "national"). And over in English, without regard to the plight of black students in bad schools, the very best teachers are much disturbed at the ineffectiveness of English teaching that allows students to land in college vastly mature and worldly about everything except the word. So with all this acknowledgment of trouble, and with all this recognition of the need for change, one would think that the proposals of the Black Studies people would be met with enthusiasm by white reformers.

But the radical black educator is not, I deduce from the strenuous character of the accusations and proposals in *Amistad I*, looking for backing. White backing in the past has come to nothing; hence the black educator and student feel they must go it alone if they are to go it at all. The white is to look (and perhaps be shocked or shamed), but not touch. He is even expected to sympathize (if he does not he is a racist), but not touch.

But I confess that I am shocked by, and cannot sympathize with, the vision of Black Studies I see in *Amistad I*. My impression is that in both English and History the blacks are in danger of duplicating the very worst errors of the whites. Particularly their tendency to identify the truth with their racially subjective vision seems apt to destroy the whole Black Studies enterprise. Three decades ago Barzun, not thinking of black problems at all, described the difficulty well:

> We are all too familiar with histories [and I would add literature] built on an evolutionary plan which naively interprets the whole past as a mere preparation for the modern age; which systematically strains the evidence for germs of institutions or ideas which we find important, whether our ancestors found them so or not. This kind of history is pure narcissism.

It is also, I might add, the beginning of totalitarianism.

To put this differently, I would say that Black Studies, as it is conceived by the contributors to *Amistad I*, inherits the worst kind of white pedagogy. It is a pedagogy displaying always a high degree of certitude, and coming at any subject with a quick generalization and prescription. In both History and English it is the kind of education one gets in white cram courses—Henry VIII was born in 1491 and had bad table manners—except that the Black Studies student is expected to cram pleasant facts about blacks and unpleasant facts about whites.

Prescriptive pedagogy has its virtues as discipline (memorize the goddam stuff; good for you) and as a way of mastering cold turkey matters like the parts of a rifle; but there are fewer cold turkey subjects in the world than most people imagine. *No* generalizations are cold turkey.

Also, prescriptive pedagogy encourages mental passivity. A little passivity may be desirable, but with TV, overcrowded schools and prescriptive teaching surrounding us, our nation has long since passed any possibly desirable passivity *norm*. In my opinion the chief mission of a college English or History teacher is to encourage thinking and observing rather than receiving and speechifying; that is, to encourage the spirit of look and see rather than show and tell. Such a mission is subversive; to succeed, it must undermine almost everything that is happening to our pre-college students, in school and out. They come to us burdened like donkeys with prescriptions and stock speeches.

*If* our country's Black Studies programs were to come to be largely guided by the philosophy expressed in *Amistad I*, I suspect that these studies would be in need of similar subversion. I would not deny the black need "to face with courage the truth concerning the ways in which the representatives of Western power [have] totally distorted the nonwhite past" (the statement is Vincent Harding's), but I see an equal need for Black Studies people to face the possibilities of distortion in their own ranks.

1970

# Charles Lindbergh

THE WARTIME JOURNALS OF
CHARLES A. LINDBERGH

In 1938 Lindbergh moved in the highest diplomatic and military circles of London, Paris and Berlin. He also made a trip to the Soviet Union, where he was well received and given a good look at Soviet aviation; but his subsequent comments about Russia—comments distorted, he claimed, by the press—caused the Soviets later to announce that if he ever came back to see them he would be arrested. His dislike of Russia and Communism permeates these journals, as does his admiration for the Germans. Late in 1938 he tried to help prevent a European war by working to persuade the Germans to sell plane engines to the French! He admired the efficiency of the Germans, their industries and the character of their industrial and scientific leaders—but was occasionally disturbed by the Jewish thing, which he professed not to understand. He was awarded the "German Eagle" by Goering personally. The thought of a war with Germany repelled him, partly because he knew at first hand the strength of Germany and the weakness of its neighbors, and partly because he believed that "the future welfare of Western civilization depended largely upon the strength of Germany and the avoidance of a major war in Western Europe." Such statements place the book for Lindbergh haters.

Both France and Germany professed interest in his weird plane-engine project early in 1939, but suddenly the subject vanishes from his journals. He returned to the US in April, was given an Air Corps commission as colonel, toured American airfields, sat on important committees and talked with officials up to and including his favorite enemy (worse even than the Russians), FDR. When England and France declared war on Germany, Lindbergh went on the radio to declare his opposition to American entrance.

He began the year 1940 talking quietly in Cambridge with Alfred North Whitehead. He ended the year active in the America First

Committee. Nineteen forty was a critical year in his alienation from the ways of FDR's Administration. His sense of mission became grandiose; he came to feel that he was one of a dedicated few who might keep the Administration from pushing America into the war. And in 1940 he had some reason for optimism. He also had a large following.

Nineteen forty-one was the year of the locust. Lindbergh continued his activities for the America First Committee right up to Pearl Harbor, battling the war forces whose ranks, he said, included "the American government, the British government, the Jews and a major portion of the press, radio and motion picture facilities of the country." When Pearl Harbor came Lindbergh phoned General Wood of the America First Committee, and General Wood's first words were, "Well, he [Roosevelt] got us in through the back door." Apparently this was Lindbergh's sentiment too, but the issue was incidental now; he switched gears and prepared to fight for his country.

Fighting for his country proved to be harder than he had anticipated; Washington didn't want him. He had an unpleasant session with Secretary Stimson in January of 1942, during which Stimson refused to put Lindbergh "into any position of command" because of his past. So Lindbergh, who had been complaining about the Administration's war mongering now found himself complaining that he couldn't join up: "I have always believed in the past that every American citizen had the right and duty to state his opinion in peace and fight for his country in war. But the Roosevelt administration seems to think otherwise." Meanwhile his enemies the newspapers kept after him, misquoting him, turning his words into statements seeming to express continued disaffection with our participation in the war. He was now fully committed, yet he kept writing disconcerting doubts into the journals: "A Russian dominated Europe would in my belief be far worse than a German dominated Europe."

With the United States in the war, and with the Armed Services not open to him, what to do? He soon was working for Ford at Willow Run, a gadfly on the B-24 production line. The journals now throttle down on Big Think and concentrate instead on details of flying and production. His comments about flying and particular flights, and about the flying characteristics of the dozens of military and commercial planes he tested are marvelous for anyone who has been an active flyer. Sometimes the information is technical, sometimes it branches off into divine poesy, but always his descriptions are clear and well written.

He emerges as one of the most careful and deliberate of flyers—and though he is his own press agent on the point there seems little reason to doubt him, nor to doubt that during the war years he remained both one of the world's great flyers and one of aviation's true experts.

At about midpoint in Lindbergh's Willow Run life, his journal lapses for some months. When we pick up again, he is still working for Ford but planning a trip to the Pacific. In 1944 this trip comes off and we find him flying with the Navy in mid-Pacific, although he is still not in uniform. He tells us that he downed one Jap. The military life gives us Lindbergh at his best, not worrying very much about the course of civilization but doing his job and doing it well. Eventually one of the generals tells him he must stop flying missions because there would be hell to pay if Washington heard.

He returns home; there is another lapse in the journal and suddenly we are at the end of the war with Lindbergh back touring Germany at the moment the various conquerors spread through the ravaged landscape. Here, after the pleasant military calm of the Pacific we find again Lindbergh the "civilized" man. His German sympathies are so strong that he has no time for any of the other forces present in Germany; all are bad but some are worse—with the French Senegalese the worst, then the Russians, French, British and Americans. The beaten Germans, none of whom seem to be Nazis, become objects of Lindbergh's sympathy. He goes to visit his old friends like Professor Messerschmitt (Messerschmitt was imprisoned shortly after Lindbergh talked with him). All these nice civilized scientist types treat Lindbergh courteously (this is the civilized part) and begin to negotiate with him to have their affairs put in the hands of Americans instead of Russians. Lindbergh is delighted. One proposal which comes to him, for example, is that "ten of the Junkers' technical men together with their families [be taken] into the American zone." To the suggestion Lindbergh replies that he thinks the idea excellent: "The only improvement I can suggest is to try to get one hundred of them into our area instead of ten." As for the divvying up of Germany among the victorious powers, Lindbergh fears for those who are left in the hands of the Russians: "We are turning her [a young girl] and thousands of others like her over to Soviet soldiers for their sport. I feel ashamed. What responsibility has this child had for Hitler and the Nazis?"

When at the very end Lindbergh visits a Nazi prison camp and sees the two furnaces, his rationalization is as follows: "This, I realize, is not a thing confined to any nation or to any people. What the German has done to the Jew in Europe, we are doing to the Jap in the Pacific." How such an argument leads to the conclusion of the journals—that it is finally the Russians who are the world's barbarians—is never made clear.

Shortly before this book's publication Frank Mankiewicz and Tom Braden, in one of their newspaper columns, criticized publisher William Jovanovich for bringing the Lindbergh book out at this time. They described Lindbergh as a muddled racist, an apologist for the Nazis and something of an obscenity upon the political landscape. They concluded that Mr. Jovanovich had chosen a particularly bad time to publish the book: "It helps the nation decide its policy towards Israel as gasoline helps a fire. It will bring out the racists."

There is, I think, an element of truth in their remarks. The timing of the book's publication *is* curious; and of course the Lindbergh record is disturbing for those who have no time for German apologists. Yet what Mankiewicz and Braden did in their column is so characteristic of journalistic treatment of Lindbergh in general, during the years of his glory and infamy, that all of Lindbergh's hatred of journalists, and the reasons for it, are immediately brought to mind. In the first place they didn't read the book apparently, but only promotional material *about* the book; and in the second place they were thoroughly intemperate in their description of him.

At worst Lindbergh has been perhaps a snob, a sucker for old-world manners. He reminds me of some American soldiers in a marvelous story about Occupation Germany by Robie Macaulay ("A Nest of Gentlefolk") who are completely taken in by the manner and culture of a castleful of aristocrat Nazis, and therefore fail to uncover the castle's nasty secrets. But at best Lindbergh is a genuinely civilized man who, from the time of his Paris flight, has been surrounded by Yahoos and literally driven into anti-democratic isolation. There is no more depressing testimony to the brutishness of American journalism than that which Lindbergh has seen for nearly half a century—and Mankiewicz and Braden have added to the record.

It is one of Lindbergh's continuing complaints that journalists have only rarely quoted him accurately and represented his position fairly. The chances of their now representing the *Journals* fairly seem equally slim. After all, he was an isolationist and a culture vulture; he hated Roosevelt and was more than a little anti-semitic. He had enormous capitalist connections, knew the conservative Western military mind like an open book, and believed that cleanliness is next to godliness. Does this not damn him?

Yet the liberal who does not recognize in Lindbergh, beyond these qualities, an extraordinarily strong and characteristic American intelligence, and fails to see the complications of such a character behind the anti-liberal views that he displays, will never, I am afraid, understand America very well.

This is an important book. Lindbergh is an important man, with a spacious mental life that is not well represented if one takes into account only his America First connections. Much of that life is committed to the art, science and romance of flying; much more to preserving and making habitable the private life that Yahoo journalists always were anxious to turn to nightmare. And even in the parts of the *Journals* that journalists might call obscene we see less evidence of racism and the like than of the reasoning of a military specialist. He tried, after the manner of many non-fascist military thinkers, to make judgments about America's entrance into the war exclusively in terms of the military chess board in Europe. He saw narrowly perhaps, but he saw truly what he did see—a powerful Germany that would be beaten, if at all, only in a long and exhausting end game. He therefore feared that the effects of a war with Germany would not be measured in terms of victor and loser. One can certainly argue against such a position—especially after the fact—but it is nonetheless a position seriously to be reckoned with, not an obscenity.

His *Journals* are extensive, diverse, full of variety and contradiction—and great honesty and humanity.

1970

# The Soviets' Problem— or Is It Ours?

**M**y wife Helen, our 18-year-old son Ned and I flew into Moscow late last winter wearing very large boots because we knew that in winter one needed boots in Moscow to wade through the heavy snow. We also wore heavy winter coats and fur hats, but in Moscow when we arrived the weather was mild and there was no snow in the streets. The condition persisted. In two weeks in the USSR we never again wore our heavy boots. At the end we had them quietly shipped home.

Our political timing was bad too. We arrived in Moscow to be the guests of the Soviet Writers' Union—an exchange arrangement with the U.S. State Department—in the week that Solzhenitsyn appeared on the covers of both *Time* and *Newsweek* for having been booted out of the USSR, presumably at the behest of the Writers' Union. Our hosts did not wish to talk of Solzhenitsyn's exile, nor to introduce us to dissenters who might wish to talk about it. Our hosts preferred to talk about American literature. We on the other hand had an American imperative to talk about Solzhenitsyn's exile; the covers of *Time* and *Newsweek* told us to. We should have shipped our imperative home with the boots.

When our hosts did talk about Soviet literature they talked about the virtues and accomplishments of the Soviet Writers' Union, and since the West has never paid any attention to these, what they said was instructive. We were treated to a view of the nondissenting core of Soviet writing that the West chooses to ignore but is there. It is living in ordinary dailiness in Moscow, Leningrad and other cities, and though the dissent against it is reputed to be severe, the outsider who is guest of the Writers' Union can see none of this. What he sees is a steady, solid establishment determined not to flap. (At about the same time as our visit, however, the novelist Herb Gold was in Kiev under unofficial auspices, meeting and talking with dissenters and reporting that resentment of establishment repression was now firmly built into all Soviet intellectual life.)

The Writers' Union in Moscow is the nucleus of an organization of 7,000 writers who man a network of publications and translation projects, as well as performing their own diverse writing chores. The magnitude of the publications and projects is impressive and insisted upon, but the headquarters of the Writers' Union is modest. It was once the stables for a great mansion that figured in Tolstoy's *War and Peace*. It is a drab one-story U-shaped building with many small offices and a dining hall. The largest office I saw was occupied not by a writer but an economist.

This economist has been many things besides an economist—an ambassador even—but economics rather than literature is his profession and must have brought him the big office. He has received wide recognition as a scholar—even in our country he has honorary degrees, from Harvard and Illinois—but he is obviously more than a scholar; he is a leader, a presence, a man accustomed to command. He is ironic and witty; he likes to bait his conversational opponents— particularly, one would guess, Americans—and he is good at it, but he displayed no malice in my presence. He told me that English was harder to learn than Chinese, and we agreed—in English not Chinese—that American ineptitude at languages was a national vice. He treated me with efficient grace, escorted me from his good office and I did not see him again. He is Nikolai Fedorenko, secretary-general of the Writers' Union.

The rest of the Moscow establishment that we met was more writerly. Among those we saw frequently were two poets—Mikhail Lukonin and Sergei Narovchatov—and a kindly, mild-mannered translator, Valentin Kotkin, who has done John Cheever and Agatha Christie and now wants to take on the next Arthur Hailey. We also had a number of sessions with a variety of scholars learned in American literature, all of whom had impressive titles. But it was Nikolai Fedorenko with nothing on his calling card but "USSR"—and·with the same apparently repeated on the back in Chinese—who seemed to be in charge.

Another important personage in the Moscow establishment was Freda Lurie, interpreter and guide, of whom Lukonin said admiringly, "a real professional." He was speaking of her skills as interpreter but she was literary too, and of high standing in the union. Friendly and outgoing, she liked to try out her American slang on us. She was quick to catch innuendos, sense trouble in corners. She mothered us, fussing over our cars, planes, trains, pulling strings to get us seats for ballet and circus, worrying about our finances. When I think of the Writers' Union I think of her first and then the Union seems a kindly wayside inn where intellectuals talk without rancor and the sky is kept cloudless by planned good will.

The intellectuals also drink and eat at the Writers' Union. There was a lot of that. On our first full day in Moscow our decks were washed steadily with vodka and wine for two hours in mid-afternoon. Then I was carted off to a seminar room to read poems and talk learnedly about my country. I was very learned. Poet Lukonin presided at this first feast and he kept pouring our vodka into our wine glasses rather than the smaller vodka glasses. He had a story to go with the vodka pouring about an aged arthritic vodka drinker whose hand was unable to close on small glasses. He had many stories, many toasts. On this first day I was pleased that he seemed pleased with my drinking. I was also pleased that I did not have to be carried home.

We were hurried off on the night train to Leningrad as I harbored this pleasure. We stayed in Leningrad four days, flew to Georgia for four days, then flew back to Moscow for a final three. In all, when I was not toasting or being toasted, I read poetry and talked about American poetry and America in front of ten or twelve audiences, of which the biggest were English-speaking audiences at the universities of Moscow, Leningrad and Tbilisi. The students at these universities were anxious to be up to date on things American, and their questions were themselves instructive. For example: What do you think of the songs of Simon and Garfunkel? What about the *really new* names? Do you in the United States distinguish between the poetry of the white and the poetry of the black? What is your attitude toward Marxism? Could you please tell us if Faulkner fits your idea of modernism? Please say what you can about Ogden Nash. How about Edgar Allan Poe's influence on contemporary American literature? Will you ask your son to sing songs? (I asked. Ned sang.)

In Tbilisi the university audience knew perhaps less English than the classes in the north and was more subdued, but their preoccupation with American jazz made up for the language block. A student jazz band played ten-year-old rock-and-roll for us as we left, with its amplifiers blurry but deafening. The band's female singer was a hefty disciple of Aretha Franklin.

When not addressing students I spoke around tables to experts on

Faulkner, Hemingway, little magazines, what not. I was quizzed on the mechanics of applying for a grant from the National Endowment for the Arts, queried about how a young aspiring American writer could break into print, asked to suggest contemporary poets worthy of translation, and questioned with great exactitude about details in the life of William Carlos Williams. These specialist audiences varied in their capacity to speak English but were uniformly knowledgeable about American letters—and uniformly anxious to display how up to date their knowledge was.

But some of our hosts were writers and editors without special American assignments. These had as little English as we had Russian. We were therefore always accompanied by a young woman with a leopard coat and yellow boots named Tanya. She guided us through the wilderness. She read menus and directions to us. She translated toasts for us, and solved other basic survival problems. She even found out for us, when we arrived by train in Leningrad, that the photographers on the station platform were taking pictures not of us but of Raul Castro and his entourage who had been on the same train. It was stupid but we simply could not learn to say, "How do you do" or "Where is the bathroom?" How absurd not to know the Russian alphabet, not to be able to read a host's name, syllable by syllable. Many of our hosts, to be sure, had equal trouble with English but the fault—since *we* had come to *them*—seemed ours. There, particularly, was I, walking about their country as a characteristically dissenting American literary intellectual, talking glibly of the importance of the American dissent tradition, professing to be broadminded—and all the time feeling irredeemably American, incapable of breaking away for an instant from our language, money, hamburgers.

If we were stupid about the limitations of our dissent they were silent about theirs. I would mention Solzhenitsyn, Mandelstam, Brodsky, the forbidden names, and there would be no follow-up, the names would not be mentioned back. Even Yevtushenko wasn't mentioned back. We had a fine lunch at the poet Narovchatov's, the conversation seemed warm and open; but after the party I learned that Narovchatov had spoken out publicly—and presumably officially— against Yevtushenko in a letter to the *Literary Gazette* (circulation 1.5 million) just that week. Why at the private lunch could he not have mentioned the public letter?

But I was learning how little I knew. The littleness began, I think, in Leningrad with the Castro experience and radiated out. Not that we made no friends and learned nothing in Leningrad. There was even a party there for us at the home of the editor of *Aurora* (circulation 150,000) where we learned about dirty jokes on the Armenian radio and drank so much that I cannot now say whether or not we discussed Solzhenitsyn, but I know that our host read a long poem of mine out loud in Russian and it sounded well, and Ned played his guitar and it sounded well, and everything sounded well and there was obviously no chasm between the Russians and the Americans. Then, too, the fiction editor of *Aurora*, a very large man, kept drinking two vodkas to everyone else's one and saying his two English words, "Let's go!" That party was instructive, as was a friendly session at Leningrad University, a moving trip to the Leningrad cemetery with a shy doctor-poet, and a long tour through Leningrad's great art museum, The Hermitage, where we again met Raul. There was all this instruction, yet the ignorance crept over us anyway.

I had thought for example that I knew something about Socialist Realism. I had read the English Marxist critic Arnold Kettle and I had worked hard over the book on Socialist Realism most widely circulated in the United States, Georg Lukacs' *Realism in Our Time*. I knew that though Lukacs had had trouble with the Soviet regime (if he had not he would never have been well-read in the United States), his stand against capitalism and its literary offshoot, modernism, was firm and stern—equal in firmness, I assumed, to Lukonin's and Narovchatov's. In modernism Lukacs found only *Angst*, chaos, uncontrolled subjectivity, and an unhealthy preoccupation with form and style that militated against the kind of literature of which he approved, an Aristotelian literature as he put it, a literature that dealt with man as *zoon politikon*. Lukacs asserted that any modern writer with perspective was a writer with Socialist perspective. He insisted that realism itself consisted of recognizing the Marxist "objective" historical view of society and social change. With all this anti-capitalism built into him I did not think that I could go far astray in my talks if I mentioned him, especially since I had myself found him sufficiently perceptive about modernist literature that I could be honest in praising him. Yet as soon as I mentioned him in Leningrad at the university the professor of the class I had been invited to broke in to chide me for being *behind the times*. I should read Christopher Caudwell, he said, or Ralph Fox.

What was the professor telling me? I had skimmed through Caudwell once, and pictured him as a sort of British Stalinist of the 1930's who would hardly be an "advance" over Lukacs. As for Fox I had never heard of him, but when his name was mentioned by the professor the whole class laughed. What did *that* mean? Whom were they laughing at?—at the professor for hewing too close to some current party directive?—at me for simple ignorance? I never found out. What I did find out was that I would have had to spend much more time than we had available with that class before I would have been able to catch its particular Leningradian nuances, and would also have had to spend much more time than we had available in the Soviet Union as a whole before I would know with any assurance whether Socialist Realism even really still *existed* there as practical daily aesthetic doctrine, and if so in what form. Reading the likes of Lukacs in a lounge chair in the United States would never tell me. Nonetheless, after the Leningrad class I did go back to my Lukacs volume, and did find what could be construed as subversion:

> *The motives of the modernists' opposition to Stalinist dogmatists' rejection of formalism are likewise mixed. Defense of extreme modernism goes hand in hand with a— justified—rejection of the dogmatists' oversimplifications about subject matter and style of realism, and of their tendency to suppress the contradictions existing in Socialist society, their reduction of the "Socialist perspective" to childish happy endings.*

That was a start perhaps. From that I could at least deduce a Lukacs who had troubled authority, perhaps by specific reference to specific "oversimplifiers." Yet I still did not understand the Leningrad professor. The most complicated construction to be put on his chiding was that he was really not chiding at all, but telling me indirectly in his Caudwell-Fox code that the Soviet Union had *again* retreated into Stalinism, was *again* in a period of "oversimplification." But I didn't know that he intended any such confession. I was over my head. I had no way of discovering what might or might not at that moment constitute "oversimplification" for a loyal union member.

It was not only that the practical working side of Socialist Realism could not be understood in meaningful detail by an outsider only conversant with theory; it was also that the very much not-dead Czarist past kept showing up and competing with Socialist doctrine, muddying the waters. Why was it that Solzhenitsyn was a menace and Peter the Great was not, except that the latter could no longer speak up? Leningrad seemed—from the point of view of a visiting American—to be one great big Russian Williamsburg sitting on top of the revolutionary Socialist state, a handsome but ridiculous anomaly. Peter had made it all in one tyrannical swoop, and now the progressive Socialists were bending every civic back to restore or preserve what he, their ancient enemy, had done. How odd, that they should physically restore a past more despicable than capitalism. Yet the same oddness that restored the buildings could be found lurking also in their artistic doctrine. Soviet art was weighted down to the ground with traditionalist sentiment antedating socialism. The Russian Revolution had simply not made it to the "make-it-new" artistic revolution of the early century in the West. It was, therefore, wasn't it, a big mistake to think that Soviet objections to modernism were exclusively or even primarily Socialist objections? They had to be equally the objections of stern Mother-Russia traditionalists who did not like to see old forms and conventions violated, and who thought that the make-it-new doctrine was itself, without regard for its decadent following, erroneous. Chamber of Commerce views of modernism in the United States are much the same.

In Leningrad the traditionalism is stronger than in Moscow, perhaps because Leningrad hates Moscow and so seeks ways of asserting its difference; but Moscow is crammed full of the past too, the Kremlin itself being a giant monument to grim old centuries. As for Georgia, in Georgia we found the traditionalism fiercer yet. In Georgia we did nothing but look at medieval Christian churches and icons, and be advised of the marvels of Georgia's ancient triple rhymes. Since in our country we now have trouble with single rhymes I did in Georgia begin to feel very revolutionary. And when I thought not only of Russia's modernist literary exiles but also of Chagall and Kandinsky and how their paintings at Leningrad's Hermitage are hidden away in the cellar because they are socially unhealthy, I began to conceive that these artists' ill health proceeded not from their modernist subjectivism or perhaps their rootless cosmopolitanism, but from their simple repudiation of the old formal holies of traditionalist Western art. If that was so, then Socialist Realism was not at all what had put them in the cellar but Mother Russia herself, wanting the past preserved, the old pictures on the mantel. My knowledge of Socialist Realism grew dimmer and dimmer.

Then there was one morning when I did not talk to an audience at all but listened and became more ignorant. I had expected to talk to an audience because I woke up every morning expecting to talk to an audience, and since on this morning we were programmed to visit an elementary school where they specialized in English-language training I prepared myself, over breakfast tea, to tell the nice little children in their neat suits and dresses about William Carlos Williams' red wheelbarrow. But I never did. When we arrived at the school we were taken to the principal's office and it was the principal who talked. He talked for an hour about the school system, then led us upstairs and pushed us in and out of several classes, in each of which we had brief indoctrination in Soviet language-teaching methods and resources. At the end we were walked to the school's treasure, a small room described as a museum that had, pinned to the walls, a number of simple student-made exhibits of the life and accomplishments of a certain Soviet hero by the name of Richard Sorge. Their most famous spy. We were then made to sit in the museum for twenty minutes while Sorge and his spying and his eventual execution by the Japanese were explained to us by a doctrinaire female pedagogue of great earnestness. As this woman concluded her address to us she brought forth her most dramatic assertion, which she had been saving: the students themselves had *spontaneously* and on their own hook decided to start the school museum in his honor, and to name the school after him. (The school, we then learned, *had* been so named, as had five other schools in the USSR.) So I spoke not a word that morning but went away wondering if we in the United States had any schools named after Allen Dulles or Gary Powers. Also, why had the Leningradians programmed *us* to listen to the heroic-spy lecture? The children at the school were indeed very good in English.

Never out of my mind after I had achieved ignorance was the question of how much the West, and particularly the United States by its long-term top-to-bottom denial of all things Soviet, had managed to shape and strengthen the Russian defensive postures we were constantly and uncomfortably witness to. There seemed little doubt that Socialist Realism is itself a defensive ideology in the same league as elevating espionage to the realm of the heroic. Soviet defensiveness is hard for an American to understand because we think *we* have been defensively holding *them* off for three-quarters of a century. But it is obvious that they think *they* will not survive if they can't keep *us* out— us in the form of our decadence, nihilism, immorality and anti-social individualism as much as our money and our prattling about the freedoms. Not just our soldiers and shekels but the whole capitalist "sickness" is what they fear, from modernism to Coca-Cola. Even a subtle, sophisticated thinker like Lukacs cannot refrain from polemic when contending with the "diabolic" character—he actually uses that word—of capitalism. Lukacs is generous enough to acknowledge with Gide that without the devil there would be no art, but the puritanical elements in the party cannot be expected to do so. Anyway, the big point is not what they *ought* to believe or acknowledge; the point is that for all shades of Soviet opinion we *are* the devil. Our recognition of that opinion of us may well be the first important step in our understanding of them.

Yet another perhaps slightly ridiculous way of looking at our relationship with them might be mentioned—a political variant on ancient Freudian gospel. To the extent that capitalism is the father of communism the Soviets are a child with an Oedipus complex and would like to knock us off. But the West is also mamma in a sense— mamma being the art and culture of the West as well as its decadence— and with mamma therefore the Soviets would like to go to bed. So the big hate-love affair goes on, and goes on with them in the child's role despite the youthfulness of *our* culture. It is our press that insists we be the adults who know everything.

La la. So we flew off to Georgia after four days of mysterious Leningrad, and being warmly met in the middle of the cold night at the empty airport of Tbilisi we began another round of parties. Some of the food made our American stomachs queasy, food like boiled brains, kidneys, oddly pickled fish and nearly raw suckling pig; but the drinking was fine, the toasts endless and we spun along grandly except at one party where I forgot my ignorance and rose unwisely to my Solzhenitsyn routine. I made a speech when I proposed a toast to our host—everybody had been making speeches because speeches slowed down the enormous consumption of a fine Georgian white wine—and in my speech I said that what I wanted to say I wanted to say in the friendliest way. I wanted to say that it was a tragic fact about the relations between our two countries, that for us their most celebrated living writer at the moment was a man they had exiled, and that there were others like Brodsky in Michigan who were hardly improving our image of the USSR. My good host listened. When I sat down he rose to say that in the friendliest way he spoke to me, a welcome guest in his house, to say that he felt it was improper for me as a guest in his house to say what I had said!

I was silenced. The party went on, we parted friends. Two days later we left Georgia with gifts and warm handshakes but the episode lingered in the cells of my brain devoted to paranoia. I imagined that the news of my impropriety had been passed back to Moscow where upon arrival we would find ourselves on a blacklist. At my first lecture in Moscow my fear seemed initially confirmed.

The lecture was at the University of Moscow where six weeks later Senator Kennedy would display an American imperative similar to mine by trying to take a poll of his audience's opinions of Soviet military expenditures. In *The New York Times* the headline the next day reported the Soviets *baffled* by Kennedy's conduct. But the text in both the *Times* and *The Washington Post* indicated less bafflement—they are not the idiots about voting procedures that the American press makes them out to be—than annoyance at Kennedy's effort to stir up some sort of confrontation. "Provocative" was the word of an elder in the audience to describe Kennedy's ploy, and the word seemed appropriate. Anyway, six weeks earlier at that same place I managed not to be provocative, but when I first entered the classroom I thought that news of my Georgian provocativeness had preceded me. The room had about forty students in it but the room was tiny and there were at least forty more in the hall unable to enter. As I began to speak I was pressed up so close to the blackboard that I could with difficulty turn around to use it. I was sure that the room was part of a plot to restrict my diabolism.

Yet the students were eager, attentive, easily amused. My talk went well and after twenty minutes Freda Lurie rushed in upon us to say she had found a larger room down the hall. We marched there—it was three times as large—and filled it: the tale of the loaves and fishes. I got over my paranoia for the day.

But there was much to be uneasy about beyond my indiscretion in Georgia. Modernism, capitalism, rootless cosmopolitanism, decadence, iron curtain, Solzhenitsyn—the whole mixed up in American-tourist stew. And the days were gray and damp, and when we were not programmed we would walk out on the streets, the streets being gray and damp and the humanity grayly dressed and damp, and we would feel fearful and alone in the face of so many bodies moving so purposefully to unknown destinations. On a Sunday morning beside the Kremlin the crowds were so large—and mixed in with the civilians were so many platoons of the Red army, tough young farm boys careening along in brown phalanxes—that the sidewalk seemed a great river with the current always against us, and we did not want to go to the Kremlin at all and look at those churches but go back to the hotel and shut the door. We were fragile; we might not last there.

And in the restaurants they mostly despised us. We were so stupid that we did not understand that nobody could have the main course until all the others had eaten all of their soup and salad. And why could we not learn that waiters were not to be waved at and snapped fingers at but were Soviet citizens who could stand by the kitchen door for as long as they chose before coming to serve the stupid Amerikanskys.

Thirteen days, then off to Paris. On the last Russian night, at the home of our poet host Lukonin we had the final big dose of international amity and cheers for poesy. We were all fatigued, the toasts were short, there were uncomfortable silences and only one moment of truth. This was after I had remarked to Lukonin that I hoped he would come to our country again (he had been on a tour like mine, with State Department hosting) but that if he did he should be prepared for occasional hostility. When my words were transmitted to him he knew I was being provocative again—he had been present at the event in Georgia—but he nodded at me and said with heat, through Freda, "I *bet* you, I *bet* you it will pass."

The next day Freda and the translator of John Cheever took us to the airport. There was an exchange of gifts and affection. As we passed through the passport barrier I felt sentimental: it had been good, they had been good and we had not been all devil. I walked out into the bare waiting room with my sentiment, and our lives seemed bare like the room. I hoped then, though I didn't know quite what I was hoping, that friend Lukonin would win his bet.

Now we've been home ten months wondering what it was that happened to us over there and reading the American press as it pushes the imperative and tells us nothing of Russia that is not of dissent in Russia. What I think I have finally learned is that if Lukonin is ever to win his bet it will be as much because we have reduced the pressures of our imperative upon *them* as because *they* have modified their "oversimplifications" and repression. La la.

1974

# How the Old Blind Decency Was Finally Led Away and Shot in the Name of Pluralism

THE ETIQUETTE OF RACE RELATIONS
*by Bertram Doyle*
THE DECLINE OF THE WASP
*by Peter Schrag*

Among the many announced revolutions—coming, in progress, or missed—we should not forget the revolution of manners. It has occurred and we are picking up pieces. It began in what seemed like out-of-the-way corners among artists, dissident white youth, alienated blacks—but it has now reached everywhere into the nation's life, breaking up established patterns of conduct, language and dress. It has changed the way we grow up, learn, make a living, enter upon family life and in general progress through man's seven ages. It is a big thing, so big that the question of how it should have occurred without an accompanying political and economic revolution is an American mystery of the first order. No analogy can quite catch its curious limits but perhaps it is a little like spitting in the emperor's face without the emperor noticing.

I firmly believe that the emperor is finally capitalism, and I trust that the seventies will produce among radicals a devotion to disturbing the basic capitalist machinery instead of disturbing the decorum of classrooms, parlors and bedrooms; but until revolutionaries stop thinking that they can be revolutionaries while making a dollar themselves or avoiding traffic in dollars, we are stuck with a strange partial revolution that has deprived us of one set of manners without giving us directions to a new set.

Deeply imbedded in the current fads is the conviction that manners are hypocritical; that we should have honest feelings and expressions rather than forms, conventional procedures, protocol—or in other words that manners can be eliminated. But this is to misunderstand manners. Man has manners whether he wants them or not; he usually has several sets of manners—for peers, parents, teachers, bartenders and so on—so that if one set of manners such as the Emily-Post set vanishes he may fall back on another. In the social sciences what I am talking about is called role-playing, but whatever one calls it man can't avoid it, and since he can't he might as well try to be benevolently mannerly, that is, mannerly in a way tending to help rather than hinder the reformation of our mixed-up society. What we have now tends to hinder. For what we have are discrete sets of manners for warring social groups, a condition that might make sense in a society highly stratified or regionally diverse, but does not make sense amidst the constant cultural leveling that dominates our society. Between children and parents, students and teachers, whites and blacks, citizens and officials, hard hats and softheads, and even male and female—not to mention WASPs and Jews, WASPs and blacks— the divisionary process seems if anything to be speeding up, and for what possible reformist reason?—the motion seems instead to be retrograde, back toward something that the gods of history must have thought they had disposed of.

Perhaps we can find an explanation by indirection, by looking at what happened to manners after the Civil War when the blacks had been officially liberated. Bertram Doyle's *Etiquette of Race Relations*, first published in 1937 and now reissued, describes how under slavery the Negro etiquette was devised by whites and was part of the white superstructure for keeping inferiors in their place, but that after the war this structure of race relationships had to be modified to meet the new "liberated" condition, a modification that took the form of substituting distance for place. This became the separate-but-equal doctrine. The equality part was mostly a figment of the laws, but it served to create and enforce distancing between the races, with the resulting anomaly, noted not only by Doyle and other historians but by many Southern novelists, that the intimacy between the races existing during slavery was seriously *diminished* by the abolition of slavery.

Doyle's book is cautious, level-headed and turgid; it is itself an example of a kind of mannerliness we have largely lost in the last two decades. Doyle, a black, is shocked at the record of the ruler whites of the South, and his book contains much evidence against them that a less passionate scholar might dismiss or temper. But though his passions show, so does his respect for objectivity, dispassion, judiciousness, all the archaic scholarly forms. His book is a mass of footnotes; everything is annotated, buttressed; and the prose is always scholarly cool. Let me quote a passage of evidence and commentary, partly for its extreme vision of white tyranny and partly to show Doyle's *method* of damning the Southern white, which was to let somebody else do the damning for him:

> By far the most cogent statement of the southern credo, if not indeed its most extreme viewpoint, is put forth by Bailey [whose credentials are strangely slurred over by an unrooted "op. cit." in the notes. He is Thomas Pearce Bailey, listed without comment in the bibliography as the author of Racial Orthodoxy in the South 1914], when he says, in fifteen conclusions: "1. Blood will tell. 2. The white race must dominate. 3. The Teutonic people stand for race purity. 4. The Negro is inferior and will remain so. 5. This is a white man's country. 6. There must be no social equality. 7. There must be no political equality. 8. In matters of civil rights and legal adjustment, give the white man as opposed to the colored man the benefit of the doubt; and under no circumstances interfere with the prestige of the white race. 9. In the educational policy let the Negro have the crumbs that fall from the white man's table. 10. Let there be such industrial education of the Negro as will fit him to serve the white man. 11. Only Southerners understand the Negro question. 12. The status of peasantry is all the Negro may hope for, if the races live together in peace. 13. Let the South settle the Negro question. 14. Let the lowest white man count for more than the highest Negro. 15. The above statements indicate the leadings of Providence."
>
> This, then, has been, and still largely is, the situation in the present period regarded from the standpoint of law and the mores of the South.

The Bailey conclusions seem to me to add up to a polemic by a disillusioned white against whites, but Doyle is undecided whether the views are Bailey's or a summary of the views of others. In any event Doyle manages to use the extreme remarks of Bailey and stay looking like a scholar himself: his is the academic decorum we are getting less and less of. Increasingly there is a denial of common ground where opposing forces may meet. The game now is to have stern absolutists shout at one another, or to give up communication entirely (the recent tomato-pelting of Humphrey at the scientists' convention in Philadelphia is an instance; and Patrick Moynihan's subsequent refusal to speak at the same convention, on the grounds that "if anybody is harassed everybody is harassed," may be the most effective way of responding). The new insolence may be a latter-day form of capitalistic individual enterprise but it is also, I would say, a latter-day form of the distancing process Doyle observed in the earlier period. We now have manners within our chosen or destined social or racial groups, but not manners to bridge the gaps between them.

Worse, we have been developing in the media what amounts to a grand strategy for *encouraging* gaps. Journalism cares less and less for manners, commercial publishing has rejected them, only the tube is still dominated by the ancient "hypocrisies" of middle-class whites. What began on the confrontation circuit a few years back is now regarded in most places as the fundamental mode of simple exposition, of teaching. Want the truth about sex?—let David Reuben or the Masters team speak. About war, politics, woman?—Mailer of course. About the presidency?—Philip Roth. About the state of race relations, the country's pulse, pollution?—turn it over to an instant journalist with a fixed and firm point of view who won't mess around being polite, fair, even well read.

Now I grant that one can slice the manners loaf many ways, and the instances I have here may seem most limiting. There are after all the manners of social life as well as those of scholarship and journalism, and the manners of the young as well as those of the old. It is mostly the manners of the young that parents think of as they meditate on a child who has not said please for six years. Yet both the Doyle book and the second volume on my agenda, by Peter Schrag, seem to me to share a common view of American manners as a whole (they are WASP manners) and a common view of WASPs (they are the enemy) that has led to the currently prevailing view of what to do about manners (ditch them). The books also show us the development of the hostility toward WASPs and manners, for there is a vast difference in the manners of the Doyle book (1937) and those of the Schrag book (1972): in the former we still find embarrassment about hostility, and piety about neutrality, but in the latter we find hostility made into an expressive virtue.

Schrag is extraordinarily malicious and righteous; his work is slapstick sociology, a sort of long-winded smear of the WASP. Schrag, a Jew who says he tried to become a WASP while at Amherst but later learned "better ways of being an American," thinks he is representing ethnics of all kinds against WASPs of all kinds, WASPs being the chief aspirers, he says, to a uniform Americanism, a WASP Americanism that the ethnics are expected to kow-tow to. He adds that WASPs are partly real and partly mythical since some of the WASP mystique, such as the John Wayne sort of thing emanating from Hollywood, has been "dominated by Jewish producers and saturated with ethnic per- formers" (these are "upstart Jews"). But real or unreal the WASP mystique, he insists, has dominated the country until very recently.

In the old days some of the most powerful WASPs were noted for the "cussedness and irreverence" (that is, lack of manners) Schrag himself professes to admire, persons like Everett Dirksen, John L. Lewis and Sewell Avery. Now, however, the WASPs have "been crippled by their own sanity, by their passion against the un- reasonable." And by their notions of decorum. "Why make a *Jewish* boy masturbate on the 109 bus or have him spread his sexual hangups over 274 pages distributed in half a million copies? *Because there is no WASP idiom in literature in which these things can be said"* (Schrag's italics). In other words the WASP's chief legacy to the country is a set of decencies that the WASPs imposed after they had (indecently) taken control. Now, says Schrag, decency is besieged; it is taking the form of good works like ecology and John Gardner's Common Cause (which takes a tough ten-page roasting), but it isn't getting anywhere; the movement is all the other way; "the WASP is a refugee in his own country."

The liberal is also, says Schrag, mostly WASP, and now a failure. He is the one who "was often prepared to champion the downtrodden but only rarely able or willing to teach them to champion themselves on their own terms; he was frequently a defender of civil rights and civil liberties because he wanted people to have faith in the system, not because he wanted them to have faith in themselves." How stupid of the liberal, but perhaps he didn't believe that institutions were necessarily allergic to selves. Schrag does: "Even though he [the liberal] called himself a Jeffersonian he believed more in institutions than in people, was more a nationalist than a pluralist, more a preacher than a teacher. For each problem he tried to create a new agency, a new program, a new department . . ." What should he have been doing?— "the genuinely radical faith is in fulfillment and prosperity without the melting pot," or in other words faith in a fulfillment to be achieved by working "to institutionalize wherever possible the social and cultural pluralism that we are now beginning to rediscover." But how does one institutionalize pluralism without institutions?

The book is very muddy on that point, but the underlying assumption seems to be that when the WASPs are disposed of, the country will have different *kinds* of institutions because the ruthless and hypocritical power boys will have been eliminated. If this is the assumption, the book is flimsy evidence of how in the non-WASP world the ruthlessness will be eliminated. Schrag's real trouble is that his book is itself a power play in the modern capitalist vein. It matches all the arrogance and self-esteem attributed to WASPs, and operates wholly within the currently indecorous and schismatic conventions for "making it": overstate the case, be sure, confront. Schrag's tone is persistently one of contempt, a steady verbal tomato-pelting of the WASP: "the New WASP: stiff upper lip, tight neck tendons, and mushrooming ulcer." "Even WASP crimes these days are usually dull . . . We need the Mafia because WASPs are boring the country to death." "Andrew Wyeth's work almost inevitably puts the museum on canvas, which is to say that he pickles feeling safely in the formaldehyde of retrospect. This obviously appeals to museum directors and trustees, most of them still WASPs." "George Plimpton is the arch voyeur; as a Jew he might have played schlemiel in a jockstrap, but as a carrier of every form of WASP privilege . . . he can do no more than represent the man whose dreams have long turned sour." "Now the fashionable [WASPs] send their spies [Wyeth and Plimpton] over the fence because life on the inside is too empty and dull to sustain without some help from beyond." And so on, with a page of real hysteria about Agnew and his appeal to "paunchy country club Republicans with fat pinky rings."

At the end Schrag condescendingly discovers three WASPs for whom there is some hope—Mayor Lindsay who "has *begun* to understand the problem of minorities" [my italics], Ramsey Clark for testifying for the Chicago Seven and Kingman Brewster for his "willingness to *concede* that a Black Panther cannot get a fair trial in America" [my italics]—but to praise these three, even faintly, is merely to underscore the hopelessness of the rest of the breed. The whole effect is of a sort of one-man purge of the WASP. Strange pluralism.

There remains the question of whether Schrag is right about WASPs and WASPism. I find him wrong on, essentially, two counts— wrong primarily because easy polemical generalizations about big fuzzy social entities are bound to be wrong (there are times to exaggerate but not, I think, in a 250-page "examination of the central American experience"), and wrong secondly because WASPs and WASPism, even though obviously important determinants in American capitalism, have never been the whole hog, and therefore never the clear and simple villains Schrag makes them out to be. Perhaps the best way to answer Schrag on the last point would be to accept his major premise, that WASP influence has vastly declined, and then demonstrate that the chief evils attributed to WASPs, such as unequal distribution of wealth and power with its attendant oppressions, are with us in greater earnest now than ever before. I think this could be demonstrated (it would take another book), but I don't think the demonstration would be of any use so long as confrontation is the game, and reasonableness and decorum regarded as irrelevant diversions.

I see there is a new edition of Amy Vanderbilt's etiquette book coming out in March, the essence of WASP etiquette. The mere thought of an etiquette book brings a smile in our blue-jean fuck-you culture, so I doubt that it will save the day. Yet if it is the only centrist alternative to the pluralism Schrag preaches I think I'll have to campaign for it. Up with finger bowls. Hurrah for the calling card. All the old WASP hypocrisies.

1972

# Gallup Poll

## THE GALLUP POLL
### by George H. Gallup

Reading 38 years of Gallup Poll results (in three large volumes totaling 2400 pages) is a happier siege than you'd think. There is, to be sure, no great exhilaration in discovering that 81 percent of Minnesota approved Harold Stassen for governor in September of 1938, or that 20 percent of all Americans believed, in 1939, that cancer was contagious; but a general historical illumination does settle in on a not too pious reader if he thumbs through these pages casually, without studying percentage details but keeping an eye out for long-term opinion shifts. Students of American thought will doubtless be better off historically with a hundred years of such data rather than 38—and by then somebody should have figured out a way to make the data intelligently selective rather than a great chronological lump with index—but what is at hand now is impressive nonetheless.

Or at least a certain small percentage of it is impressive, and that, interestingly, is the nonpresidential part of the Gallup industry. The results of polling for presidential preferences become very dead items after the elections themselves, while the results on questions that don't get settled by elections tend to stay lively. Looking through the answers to Gallup questions of the late thirties for example one can hardly fail to be struck by how often the voice of the people, on both major and minor social issues, was not heeded by gods and governments. In 1936: 68 percent of Americans wanted governors on cars to prevent speeds greater than 50 mph; 82 percent thought the manufacture and sale of war munitions for private profit should be prohibited. In 1937: 68 percent thought everybody should be fingerprinted. In 1938: 73 percent thought big trucks should be kept off the highway at certain hours and on weekends; and 91 percent thought all nations should agree not to bomb civilians in wartime! In 1939: 63 percent thought it indecent for women to wear shorts for streetwear, and 78 percent disapproved of a married woman working if her husband was capable of supporting her. So there.

Sometimes one can be pleased that the popular voice did go unheard. In 1937: 66 percent said they would not vote for a woman for president even if she qualified in every other respect (in 1971 that vote was reversed, with 66 percent saying they *would* vote for her—but which vote is real? And will we ever know?). In 1938: 66 percent were on Ford's side against the union during a big strike, and 76 percent opposed giving the Filipinos independence. And on any number of polls all through the thirties the people consistently insisted that a large army, navy and air force were the ticket to keep us out of war (through 1939 more than 50 percent thought we *would* stay out of a European or world war). The people were also persistently capable of displaying great ignorance, as when after four years of war a goodly number thought the emperor of Japan was named Hara-Kari or Fujiyama.

Sometimes the questions themselves were not so smart either. Should the schools teach the facts about communism, fascism or socialism? Do you believe the acts and policies of the Roosevelt administration may lead to a dictatorship? Do you think Tom Mooney was guilty? Do you favor restoring the whipping post for punishing certain criminals? So much for leading questions. Then there were the questions that were clever but perhaps merely clever, as when in the weeks before and after Pearl Harbor the pollsters kept asking whether people had colds or not (before Pearl Harbor, 10 percent; after, 34 percent). There were also the dumb questions: (on Pearl Harbor Day) Is there any one vitamin you have heard about in recent months?

But, as I said at the beginning, the most unrewarding questions seem now to have been the presidential questions, and since a good three-fourths of the energies of the Gallup enterprise were devoted over the years to these, it seems appropriate for a reviewer to ask a few questions of his own about the general direction and purpose of the Gallup venture. Why has it been so journalistically oriented? Why has it not been more spacious and imaginative in investigating the nooks and crannies of American thought? Answer: the money for the venture comes from the presidential side of it (153 newspapers subscribe to the poll, and are the poll's main source of income).

Now it is naive to suggest that the money part of the business be diminished. But let me be naive; I think there are two quite different but equally good reasons why this valuable, and now also demonstrably accurate, enterprise should reroute itself by diminishing its election coverage. First the polls do, I will bet my right arm, influence, though in ways we cannot now measure, how people vote; and second, the election emphasis gives an ephemeral, pulse-of-the-moment throb to the whole enterprise and therefore discourages its managers from asking questions of a more durable nature.

Of reason one, much has been written and spoken on the possible influence of the polls. Just before the last election both Gallup and Harris testified before a congressional committee on the subject; one denied influence, and the other thought that the influence, if there were any, would be a favoring of the underdog McGovern. I don't know how to begin to argue with these close-focus pragmatic opinions except by proposing a hypothetical situation, a situation I would dearly hope we might some day achieve: suppose no polling were *allowed* for the three months preceding a presidential election, so that there would be no late figures in the voter's mind as he entered the election booth. I submit that, given this situation, the voter *would* be freer in his determinings than he is now; and for analogy I can only refer to the long-term experience of our advertisers who seem to have discovered that bragging about Chevrolet sales helps Chevrolet sales (substitute any other popular brand, and think of the devotion of advertisers to the popularity of popularity). What I am saying is that the polls are, in their effect, advertisements even though their methods and practices may have the properly dignified bearing of objective inquiry. Now in most cases we do not allow the conventional advertising of candidates within a specified number of feet of the polls, presumably because we aspire to the notion of free elections and believe, though fuzzily, that advertising does but should not affect that freedom *at the place and moment* of voting. To the degree that the polls are also advertising it seems to me that they too should be kept at a distance from the moment of choice—and I suggest that the distance in time should be considerable to be truly effective. This is a big topic, not to be wound up here, but let me go on to related point two.

This pulse-of-the-moment science could be so much more useful and significant a source of knowledge about our people than it is now if we were *not* oriented so exclusively to the moment, to the front page. How much more it could be may be imagined by suggesting what the current mode of questioning consistently has neglected in just one, but one particularly important field, education. The poll forgot education entirely for years, and when it finally moved in on the subject it never graduated from the most elementary of queries: Should kids have more or less homework? Should they spend more or less hours in school? Have you put aside money for your child's college education? Are you satisfied with the education your child is getting?—plus of course all the journalistic questions about busing, integration, etc. *Nowhere* in the 38 years of the Gallup enterprise was there any evidence that I could find of anybody trying to find out what the Peepul think the goals of education should be.

I grant that if one were able to get a valid answer to such a question it might be something like: a good job in the glue factory. But I don't *know* that this would be the Peepul's answer and I'd like to know. Furthermore knowing would be of some assistance in the whole discouraging enterprise of educational reform—but the Gallup people don't imagine such a function for themselves. The same is true of their handling of other big issues. On taxes for example they have been consistently myopic, with the result that 38 years of their work have left us with a pile of outdated statistics (such as, in 1937 the people thought that an income of $100,000 should be taxed $10,000) but no data of any real legibility about what the average American thinks of his obligations to, relations with, his state. In other words the questions have been consistently patronizing of that average American, asking him what will bug his brain least. The results are with us, and they are not impressive.

Am I blaming Gallup for the parochial condition of the American mind? It may seem so, but no, I mean merely to suggest that the poll's proceedings have played along too readily with that condition, and thereby encouraged it rather than attempting to explore its hidden resources (let us pray the resources are there; the Constitution says they are). I would hope that a maturing of the poll's general vision of its function could now, after these 38 years, occur; and toward that and a shift in emphasis *away* from the Presidents would seem to be a primary first step.

1972

# Carl Becker

"WHAT IS THE GOOD OF HISTORY?"
SELECTED LETTERS OF CARL L. BECKER
*edited by Michael Kammen*

Carl Lotus Becker was born on a farm in Iowa, went to Cornell College (Iowa) and the University of Wisconsin, then on into the world of college teaching. Upon retirement he observed in a letter to Max Lerner that "as rackets go, teaching is a good one, but after 42 years of it one is content." Nearly 25 of those years were at Cornell University where, characteristically, he observed of himself that he had not done the great things for his students that some of them thought he had: "I (so it seems to me) have done nothing but sit around and look wise and tell them they have more capacity than they think—more sometimes than I think myself." As for his qualifications as a historical scholar, he once described somebody else's book as "giving evidence on every page of having been written by one who knows his subject down to the ground—something my books never show . . . " Of his writing talent he could be equally disparaging, complaining to disciple Leo Gershoy,

> *If I can average a page a day of completed ms, working three or four hours in the morning, with nothing to distract me, I do well. I usually write and throw away ten pages to get one that will pass. And I am fifty-one years old and have been practising the damnable art for thirty years. At your age I couldn't write anything that would bear the light of day.*

The quotations exaggerate his modesty but they do suggest his brand of skepticism. Seldom, he felt, did men come within shouting distance of their hopes for themselves.

And yet he was confident that the ones most likely to come within shouting distance were those in the teaching and writing and other artistic "rackets," not those in politics or business. He came back from a concert and wrote a friend,

> *. . . as I listened to these men what came over me with overwhelming force was the honesty and genuineness of what they were doing. The same is true of all genuine art,*

*scholarship, craftsmanship, and of all human activity which has for its primary object the creation of something beautiful or useful, or the discovery of some truth, or the doing of something helpful to others. But most of politics, and much of business, has none of these for their primary object; their primary object is the gaining of some advantage over others; and hence there is a subtle taint of unreality and accordingly of dishonesty about these enterprises that warps and falsifies the minds of their followers.*

His search for the genuine led him into history, where he kept his nose to the grindstone, except for bouts of illness and consequent depression, with extraordinary pertinacity. The letters published here, in this excellent collection covering nearly half a century, reveal to us a dedicated artist-scholar who was committed to 99 percent work and one percent play, and might have been a very dull artist-scholar indeed if it had not been for his wit and talent. As he observed for himself, when he was sprung from his normal Ithacan surroundings for a summer in the wicked city of Chicago, he was simply incapable of sowing wild oats: "with the best will in the world I can't break away from the virtuous dull habits of a lifetime. The most I've been able to achieve is to seek out, on hot nights, a gilded palace of sin where they sell ice cream sodas."

He wasn't even well traveled, and on his one trip to Europe his letters home were full of conventional tourist observations, plus a solid pedagogical display of exposition, to his son, about Holland's dikes and canals, and what "sans culottes" means. Yet he became one of our great historians. It seems necessary and right that he should have become primarily and preeminently a historian of the mind and *its* travels.

An English teacher may be presumptuous to take on a highly professional historian in a review; but as Becker was skeptical of the merit of reviews and reviewers anyway, and as his reputation is almost as high among English teachers as among his own kind, I'll take the chance. I do so because he, as a historian of the mind, turned the trick for me at a crucial time in my education; that is, in just a few pages he brought me, while I was in college, a way of looking at history that is still the way I look at it though I am now old and infinitely wise. The few pages were right at the beginning of his justly celebrated volume, *The Heavenly City of the 18th Century Philosophers*, where he notes that if a medieval man and a modern man were to sit down together and talk about "natural law" they could talk all night without making sense to one another. I hadn't *thought* about that sort of trouble before I read *The Heavenly City*, but ever since then I've thought about it too much and I blame Becker. He it was who made me aware that the grand words and concepts that wandered through my head tended to get their meanings *from* my head, or my neighbors' heads, not from some immutable, objective storehouse. Which was not to say that objectivity was not a historian's ideal—it just didn't quite exist.

Becker's whole theory of history is suggested by those few pages at the beginning of *The Heavenly City*. Throughout his career as a historian he was committed to a search for man's "unconscious preconceptions" and how these produced in any given age and culture a "climate of opinion" that governed man's ways of understanding— opinion, that is, that was antecedent to the "facts" and first premises believed in by even the best intelligences of the age and culture. (He traced the phrase "climate of opinion" back to the 17th century, and credited Alfred North Whitehead with bringing it into modern usage; but for me it has always been Becker's phrase.) Sometimes he ridiculed that climate; he would go out of his way, as he once did in a discouraged letter to William Dodd following World War I, to assert that the persistent dominance of the climate was a manifestation of how confused men's minds were, how incapable they were of thinking except with their emotions; but always he was concerned with exploring and assessing that climate. History was for him a long narrative about the changes in that climate.

After Becker brought me this news I had what I needed to be suspicious ever after of the hard-facts school of history; and as if that were not enough he also brought me an intimately related bit of news to the effect that history was a literary venture, a creating and ordering on the page. Becker was himself an obsessed creator and orderer, so much so that he frequently complained of his own obsession; for example he said he feared his second book *(The Beginnings of the American People*, 1915) was "fundamentally superficial." He added, "in places it verges closely on fine writing. I wish to write well; but I have a horror of being thought rhetorical." He also complained constantly of rhetorical excesses in others. Yet he was a brilliant rhetorician and it was particularly this brillance that set him apart from most of his academic colleagues—in English, I might add, as well as history.

But students are not, I have discovered, apt to be impressed by his powers with language. I can remember struggling for several years to interest freshmen in the verbal precision and high gloss of some of the paragraphs in *Modern Democracy*, a late book of his that became a familiar college workhorse after World War II. The freshmen remained unmoved by my praise, so I could only take solace in being myself moved; I was impressed by how sharply a broad generalization could, in the hands of a master, be honed, and how much of the whole blasted quest for truth and understanding was contingent upon such honing.

*His* hero was Frederick Jackson Turner, under whose spell he came at Wisconsin; and among the many compliments he paid that master was that he had implanted in the young Becker "the holy fear of the dishonest and the second best, of words without sense, of easy generalizations unballasted with knowledge." Naturally we would expect then that on Becker's list of *non*heroes would be found those who did not take care for precision—for journalists who make a profession out of "warping facts to make a good story"; for the writers of doctoral theses who wear muddy boots; for educators ready with new programs but unable to find minds even capable of defining the programs sensibly. His stance as a skeptic received daily aid and comfort from idealists of various shades whose chief imprecision, he kept insisting, was in confusing aspirations with possibility. A comic letter in 1926 to the editor of the *Cornell Daily Sun* takes up the sad case of "five bewildered freshmen" who have just written the paper to say that "they have been engaged in the intellectual life for more than two months and don't know what it's all about," and thereupon to call, with the apparent aid and backing of some faculty do-gooders, for a new orientation course for freshmen. The opportunity for reply was obviously a delightful one. Becker accepted it and, after worrying about the problem of how long it takes to get oriented ("life itself is scarcely long enough to find out what it's all about"), he went on to wonder who would do the orienting, and ran through a number of names before settling on H.G. Wells!

> [He] *might give such a course, and it would be a good course. I doubt if it would orient anyone or settle anything, but it would stir the students up and make them think. That is the chief merit of any course—that it unsettles students [disorients them?], makes them ask questions.*

Of course the expenditure of great energies on such skeptical disputation may leave less energy for other enterprises. Becker may well go down in history circles more for his precision than his ideological fire. He served democracy and education well, for example, as a worker in their vineyards, but not as a passionate advocate. Although he managed to get himself labeled as a Communist in the thirties, the charge was absurd (he himself documented the absurdity in a fine letter to one of the Hearst papers that made the charge), and in fact he did not fit comfortably under any political label, even that of liberal, here distinguishing himself from his friendly competitors Charles and Mary Beard. His precisions led him mostly to the unfiery conclusion that in politics men muddled through.

Also, since the pursuit of precision led him inevitably into qualifications and irony, he may not be remembered for many of the sweepingly presumptive truths (put forth, he liked to say, without fear and without research) that he loved to quote ironically when he heard them from others. To these deficiencies, if they are that, must be added the ironic "climate" difficulty that some of his works now find themselves in: they were written as formal lectures. Everybody *now* knows that formal lectures are devoid of spontaneity, energy and primal truth.

Both *The Heavenly City* and *Modern Democracy* were written as lectures, and so were many of his other mature writings, for the lecture form became, as it were, his genre. Looking at his lecture manner today I have to agree with my students that there is sometimes a forbidding formality about it. If he had been a poet—and to the best of my knowledge he was not, though he sprinkled doggerel through his letters with great glee—he would have been of the old school of iambics and quatrains, and have therefore been accused of insincerity and conventionality. But having said that I have said about all I can say against the man's words, and that isn't much. The climate for finished formal statement may have been disrupted in recent years by a hot romantic weather front out of the anti-academic hills, but we can still reasonably hope the disruption is temporary.

This is a well-edited volume that emphasizes the professional-man Becker, the writer Becker and the ideological Becker—but shows us the private life too. The private life looks not to have been a happy one, and I suspect—though a letter selection may be deceiving in this respect—that in his younger days his professional dedication made him a preoccupied and rather unsympathetic husband and father. Fortunately the early letters are more full of business than the late; the impression I receive is that he slowly lapsed from diligence into humanity. Certainly the late letters, even to his colleagues on dull departmental issues, display a generous warmth. The warmest of these are to Leo Gershoy and his wife and to the Lerners; but many

other persons were also lucky enough to have extensive correspondence with this extraordinary man.

Editor Michael Kammen is a professor at Cornell, and his volume
is obviously a labor of affection and admiration. It is trussed up with a
goodly number of footnotes we might have been spared (what and
where Martha's Vineyard is, who wrote *The Sun Also Rises*), but it has an
excellent brief introduction. I can only say, as an outsider to the
present state of affairs of history departments—or perhaps not an
outsider but a character across the hall—that looking at this rewarding
yet thoroughly conservative piece of scholarship persuades me that
the Young Turks Haven't Taken Over History Completely Yet.

Yet the academic conservatism of Becker's editor did provoke in
me as I read the volume a few depressing final thoughts about Becker's
own stance, not on footnotes—which he didn't like much—but
politics. For my hero's politics were of the in-between variety common
to intellectuals who pride themselves on their pragmatism, and his
*Modern Democracy* for all its virtues does not as a result stand up well as a
guide to action in our time—but rather as a guide to depressed
resignation.

"While a little betrayal is a normal thing," he said in *Modern
Democracy* in 1940, "the liberal-democratic revolution has been so far
betrayed, the ideal so imperfectly portrayed, in the course of events,
that its characteristic features cannot be easily recognized in any
democratic society today." He went on to add the obvious, that it was
in the economic realm that "the discord between democracy as an ideal
and democracy as a going concern is most flagrant, most disillusioning
and most dangerous." The distribution of wealth, he asserted, had
gone so far askew that the arguments of revolutionaries against the
private property system had achieved more than usually depressing
cogency. Yes, but at this point the non-revolutionary Becker backed
off. It was 1940, and naturally he liked not the look of either fascism or
communism. He could agree with socialists of various shades that a
more equitable distribution of wealth was essential, and could
acknowledge that no such distribution could be achieved without the
capitalist class surrendering in some measure the powers that the
institution of private property conferred upon it, but such thoughts
did not give him a revolutionary buzz. He felt good about the ruling
class; he denied the radical premise that the ruling class would
*necessarily* hang on to its powers "except under the compulsion of naked
force." As a result he looked not to Berlin or Moscow or anywhere else
for solutions, but to Washington and to the slow enactment by

democratic means of what FDR's administration was all about, increased governmental regulation of economic enterprise. He even naively imagined the "formal socialization of certain basic industries" by ordinary democratic legislation. His chief concern was not that democracy and capitalism couldn't accommodate themselves to the social need but that the accommodation would take time, time he feared the encroaching war would not provide.

There ended his argument in *Modern Democracy*. With the characteristic caution of an essentially conservative mind he went no further in his meditation upon what should be done.

Would he, if he were alive today, still display such caution? Time we have had in abundance. We have had another 30 years' worth of time, and we have disposed of approximately three wars without losing our freedoms and therefore the *capacity*—which is what he worried about—to transform our condition "by the pragmatic democratic method." Yet all we have to show for those years is further betrayal of the democratic ideals, greater and greater economic inequity. Hero, some of your fine words I think it would be best for you now to eat.

1973

# The Writer As Runaway*

## I.

A 14 year-old middle-class white boy of the District of Columbia ran away in the direction of Haight Ashbury during the *magnus annus* of Haight Ashbury (1968). His father picked him up in a juvenile detention home in Reno five days later and soon afterwards wrote up the story for the *Washington Post*. The boy had many beefs, but they were mostly about school. Education, he said, was a blind old lady. The complaint of his that I want to tack festively to the end of this first paragraph was that "he had wanted to take an advanced English course—one in which he could do creative writing—but his transfer was denied without explanation."

That paragraph can be looked at in a number of ways. It is a characteristic lead-in for a kind of sociological journalism familiar to all Americans, even English teachers—so familiar that we can all readily supply a typical next paragraph, thus:

> *Yearly thousands of teenagers leave home as Johnny did.* [I *could not quite bring myself to supply the 'Johnny' right in the first paragraph*]. *The runaway is America's latest problem child. Why he leaves, where he goes, and what he is searching for—these are the questions troubling parents, teachers and psychologists all over the land.*

Cruel, deadly prose. The poor singular Johnny has been exploited. From his special, private molehill has come a sociological mountain; the exceptional has been casually twisted into a norm; a minor instance

* This paper was originally written for a writers-teachers conference sponsored by the Modern Language Association and the National Endowment for the Arts in New York City, 1968. The meeting was a disaster, but not entirely because of this paper. The paper was received coldly by the professional writers and English teachers present, and I gather it was regarded as naive. One rebuttal was read complaining of the paper's total misrepresentation of the negro problem.

I am grateful to the Carnegie Corporation of New York for a grant in 1966 giving me time to work on some of the notions expressed in this paper, and I should say that though the proposals for English Department reform have been in cold storage in my mind for some years I still think they make sense.

has been hoked up into symbol in the name of science or maybe human interest. No miscellaneous runaway should be allowed to stand up front in a serious statement with his pirate flag flying. And to have him suddenly in our own English-Department midst, a boy who wanted to take Creative Writing, is infuriating. We know perfectly well that the absence or presence of Creative Writing never made that much difference to anybody. Creative Writing is a peripheral course, a minor skirmish in the education war. We were better off a couple of decades ago when we didn't have it at all.

Or at least that is one way of looking at the paragraph about Johnny—with indignation. Call it the Leavisite way. I too normally dislike such paragraphs, but I have by now met a number of Johnnies, usually 18- or 20-year-old Johnnies, and have decided they are no molehill. In other words I side with the sociological journalists here and find Johnny, for better or worse, a prime cause of the presence of my hero, the Writer, on campus as the coach of creation; and he is such a cause still, though the campus scene is much changed since the days of Haight Ashbury.

The Writer is not on campus just to talk about images or rhythms or characters or form or even, in the large, language, art, poesy and culture. Like coaches in other fields he also has a political role and a psychiatric role, because of Johnny. For Johnny, though not perhaps a representative teen-ager, is a common figure in Creative Writing; and he comes with his troubles.

What are his troubles? Johnny is a victim (now I wax sociological) of what I will call grandly, false expectations, expectations the Writer on Campus is hired to cope with.

It is commonplace to assert that our affluent society has bred not false but new expectations (the word most commonly used is 'aspirations') in the minds of the formerly dispossessed. The Black is now our celebrated instance, he who insatiably wants more the more he is told to want more—and who therefore disgraces us more in the Northern cities than in Dallas and Jackson. When a black boy in Creative Writing class writes a poem he writes about all black boys; he says "we" constantly and ominously; his expectations remain the chief social issue of our time. I think, however, that they are false as well as new expectations, because his wonderful egalitarian "we" will never emerge as he says it will except in the poems and propaganda. His is a utopian, media vision roughly foisted on him by blacks and whites of good will, whose obligation now is both to fulfill some of his expectations and disabuse him of others. For the expectations, though false, are expectations of tremendous social power, not to be dismissed or fooled around with.

Similarly the white Johnny has false expectations. These also have been foisted upon him by the culture, and they are not less false nor less powerful than the black boy's. Here is another sociological journalistic story, a story of a slightly older Johnny.

Not long ago I was the writer on a certain campus not noted for its runaways, and I had in creative writing class a bearded white student who was writing a novel. The novel, he said, was to be essentially a fantasy, but the fantasy was to spin off from the mind of the novel's hero, a man on drugs who was to retreat into a small room in the first chapter and pull the shade down for the duration of the novel. The fantasy he was to dream behind the shade was also to be concerned with withdrawal, and as the hero dreamed it he was not to eat or drink, but simply and quietly to waste away.

Now the student hadn't actually written much of his novel when I talked with him. I asked him if he planned to work on it in the coming summer. He said yes, he had a girl whose family would be away from their suburban house for the summer. The girl would be staying in the house at night but working in town during the day. She had offered him a room. He thought he would just move in, pull down the blind and write. That is the end of the story, except for the moral.

The moral is that our Johnnies are looking for self-salvation of a particular kind, salvation *from* the society in most of its forms, salvation through art, art of the self—and they are really hipped with the notion that they will *get* it. They not only aspire, they expect to get it. In an age hardly distinguished for its offerings in wild blue yonder they are out there in the wild blue yonder with their Eastern models and with a number of Western romantic anarchist poets, some of whom are Writers on campus. These poets and their new disciples mix their Zen aspirations casually with expectations that the Western world will receive them as capitalist creative heroes.

Note that while the black boy's is a "we" art, the art of Johnny is an "I" art. The difference is dramatic and important, and should be of concern to all writing teachers as well as to sociologists concerned with the Black Revolution; yet the difference should not be allowed to conceal the extraordinary likeness between the two arts with respect to the kind or quality of the expectations expressed. In both arts the expectations are ultimate, transcendental, without visible limits. That is what I mean when I describe them as false expectations.

My subject is not student expectations, black or white, but the Writer, black or white, on campus. But who the Writer is to be on campus, and what he is expected to do, cannot be settled without looking at the demands the campus will place on him. Student demands are of course not the only demands. We must consider also the demands or expectations of the faculty and the administration. And with deference to age, wisdom and authority I would have begun with them if I had not felt that their demands upon the Writer are largely determined by the students. The faculty and administration know feelingly what the students' expectations are, and they know from insistently repetitive recent experience that the expectations need to be satisfied in some measure. One of the cheapest devices is an insignificant course specially slanted the students' way that meets once a week in a basement. Such a course is Creative Writing (it hasn't the political edge of Black Studies, but is easier to stage). They therefore hire The Writer to teach it, and perhaps to act as a lay analyst for Johnny. Hence the Writer's function on campus is as much social (counter-revolutionary) as pedagogical. He may still perform the pleasant ornamental function he used to perform (of just being there, smiling and famous, having published perhaps one poem in the *Fourteenth Street Gazette*), but now he is also a mediator, a caterer to the kooky tastes of youth, potentially even a company spy, therefore much more than ornamental. It is he whom the students of false expectations are supposed to look to for satisfaction, while the *ancien regime* steams along in its *ancien* way. As a result he comes on campus a marked man. He is marked as anti-establishment, as a free spirit (for to be anti-establishment is to be free), and as an authority in general on the life of unlimited expectations. He is marked as this, and therefore frequently hired as this, no matter what relationship his own writings may have to unlimited expectations. He is marked as a romantic anarchist until he proves himself otherwise—that is, proves himself to be square or new critical or (of course) old.

Now you may say that I am building a box, a Skinner box, for the Writer on Campus that only the bad writer on campus will enter. You may be right. Perhaps rather than talking about a slavish writer I should talk about a good writer, a writer able to resist such demands upon him, a writer able to be his own man. I am sure there are a few of these, and I am sure I do them an injustice. But the point is I am not talking about those rarities; I am talking as if I were the personnel manager of a tremendous corporation, and saying that in finding Writers for ten thousand or so Campuses we must look at the Job

Specifications for these writers collectively. The Specs, I am saying, are god-awful. The Specs are determined by the current expectations of Writers on Campuses, expectations that will inevitably produce Bad Writers on Campuses, Writers who may in turn help create in their students even bigger and more unreasonable expectations.

II.

Now a momentary diversion. Johnny thinks education is a blind old lady, and I agree with him. Johnny's black brother also thinks education is a blind old lady, a lady wielding white power; and I agree with him too. I do not think highly of our schools, nor of the political and economic functions they perform. Bernard Shaw amused himself by blasting away at those functions back in 1914, in a treatise on parents and children—and his remarks still make good reading. Here are some excerpts:

> Here we have come to the central fact of the question, a fact nobody avows, which is yet the true explanation of the monstrous system of child imprisonment and torture which we disguise under such hypocrisies as education, training, formation of character and the rest of it. This fact is simply that a child is a nuisance to a grown-up person.
>
> It is a ghastly business, quite beyond words, this schooling.
>
> I did not learn my school lessons, having much more important ones in hand, with the result that I have not wasted my life trifling with literary fools in taverns as [Samuel] Johnson did when he should have been shaking England with the thunder of his spirit.
>
> If my schoolmasters had really engaged in educating me instead of painfully earning their bread by keeping me from annoying my elders they would have turned me out of the school, telling me I was thoroughly disloyal to it. . . . But in order to get expelled it was necessary to commit a crime of such atrocity that the parents of other boys would have threatened to remove their sons sooner than allow them to be school fellows with the delinquent.
>
> Of what use is it to us that there are always somewhere two or three teachers of children whose specific genius for their occupation triumphs over our tyrannous system and even finds in it its opportunity?
>
> What is the matter with our universities is that all the students are schoolboys, whereas it is of the very essence of university education that they should be men . . . If our

*universities would exclude everybody who had not earned a
living by his or her exertions for at least a couple of years, their
effect would be vastly improved.*

Shaw was an odd duck, sometimes sounding like John Stuart Mill
or Andrew Carnegie, sometimes like the socialist he professed to be.
Yet, were he alive I would gladly give him complete charge of our
Office of Education, partly because I believe we couldn't lose, and
partly because I believe with him that our schools are too riddled with
devices for preserving the *status quo* for the schools' elders (status quo
in the family, the nation, the economy and the literature) to be of much
use to Johnny. Something earth-shaking has to happen to the schools
before they will work (*if* they will work), and no Writer on Campus, be
he company spy or potential earthshaker, has the power to do much to
change them. Still, to the extent that the Writer might help Johnny
and his millions of teenage pals to some less slavish relationship to the
system, rather than to perpetuate the system by providing innocent
accommodation when trouble arises, I would be all in favor of the
Writer's political role on campus. Or Shaw's in the Office of Education.
The schools have changed since 1914, but not nearly enough.

### III.

I say I *would* be in favor of the Writer's political role—a conditional
favoring. I would be in favor of that role if only it could be endowed
with clear political objectives. Shaw in his 19th century socialist way
had clear political objectives for the schools; they were to be
functioning parts of the whole social system, not institutions designed
to keep a large part of the population out of play for 12 or 16 or 20
years. Shaw was a puritan socialist. He had a work program in mind
for everybody. He thought happiness was a condition in which you
didn't have time to sit around worrying about whether you were
happy. He said, "we must finally reckon work, not as the curse our
schools and prisons and capitalist profit factories make it seem today,
but as a prime necessity for a tolerable existence." And so he thought
of the schools as part and parcel of vast social work programs. He said:

*The child of the future, then, if there is to be any future but one
of decay, will work more or less for its living from an early
age; and in doing so it will not shock anyone, provided there
be no longer any reason to associate the conception of children
working for their living with infants toiling in a factory for
ten hours a day or boys drudging from nine to six under gas
lamps in underground city offices.*

That statement seems to me to be so central as to be positively exhilarating, maybe because I am a Puritan too. And yet when I think of the Writer's role on Campus, and its relationship to *getting* students to work, the exhilaration turns instantly to pain. For that Writer's role as now conceived—and I grant that it may be as Marx might put it, a temporary historical role, a prelude to something else—the Writer's role is largely to spring the student from work: school work, slave work, work that keeps him, as we now say, from his identity, work that keeps him from the Shaw kind of work. We may grant the necessity of this role in a bad system without, I think, falling for the notion that it is a complete role, a life's role.

Let me put the issue in different terms by going back to Johnny and his trip to Haight Ashbury. That trip was programmed for him, though of course he didn't know it, for several decades before he set forth on it, programmed by our literature and our culture's view of literature, as well as by all the slave forces in the schools that Shaw talked about. Creativity, which is what our Writer on Campus has a concession for, is probably the biggest political word in education, but it is strictly an anti-establishment, anti-social, anti-work word as now used. The way to be creative is the runaway way, the way of withdrawal and disengagement, even the lonely way of the student behind the blind.

Now there is merit in the lonely way. Doesn't everyone need his own Tintern Abbey? Not even the most earnest apostles of discipline and engagement would deny the virtues of withdrawal and disengagement, at least part-time. Out in the woods the mind's mercenaries are released from the disciplines of the week; they can sit down or stand on their heads. All the experience of creative humanity tells us the happiness of such release; hence schools worried about student morale and motivation obviously must find ways to provide it. Yet when that release is not accompanied by some provision for a trip back, we have the perfect situation for perpetuating and enforcing all the false expectations of students that I began by complaining about. There is, as the trip is now construed, no limit to the trip, no end.

IV.

And so I am back to the problem of limits. The trouble with limits is that they keep ending up in the hands of elders who, as Shaw would say, use them to maintain their tyranny over youth. In the literary world the most celebrated modern proponent of limits—and he doesn't seem very modern at all any more—was Irving Babbitt. Babbitt waxed very polemical on the subject of poets without limits, blue-sky poets. His various descriptions of romantic melancholy, for example, could be applied readily to Johnny or the behind-the-blind novelist—or even to the black boy if for the private self be substituted a racial self. Babbitt blamed all the romantic fudge on Rousseau, and said:

> . . . a movement which began by asserting the goodness of man and the loveliness of nature ended by producing the greatest literature of despair the world has ever seen. No movement has perhaps been so prolific of melancholy as emotional romanticism. To follow it from Rousseau down to the present day[1919] is to run through the whole gamut of gloom:
>> Infections of inutterable sadness,
>> Infections of incalculable madness,
>> Infections of incurable despair.
>
> One may devour life in revery and then the melancholy arises from the disproportion between the dream and the fact. For though the romanticist wishes to abandon himself to the rapture of love, he does not wish to transcend his own ego. . . . There is in fact no object in the romantic universe, only subject. This subjective love amounts in practice to a use of the imagination to enhance emotional intoxication, or if one prefers, to the pursuit of illusion for its own sake.
> The man . . . who withdraws into his temperamental or private self must almost necessarily have the sense of isolation, of remoteness from other men. We return here to the psychology of the original genius to whom it was a tame and uninteresting thing to be simply human and who, disdaining to seem to others a being of the same clay as themselves, wished to be in their eyes either an angel or a demon—above all, a demon.

Though these remarks seem appropriate as descriptions of Johnny, they were not followed up, as Shaw's remarks were, with an antidote, that is, with an educational mechanism for giving shape to Johnny's expectations. We do not find in Babbit a *program* to make Johnny's goals definite and finite, a part of contemporary life, a part of being human—though certainly Babbitt, had he known Johnny, would have been in there pitching to give him such goals. Babbitt unfortunately loved the past too much; he had schemes for another world than the one we live in.

We who come later than Babbitt and have watched his vital past grow moribund still have, I think, an obligation to the past, and to the use of it in finding reasonable limits to self expectations among our Johnnies. And though Babbitt was stuck in the past, and therefore unwilling to accommodate himself readily to social and aesthetic change, his principles remain sound. He said he was looking for what was normal and central in human experience, in past or present.

And in looking for the normal and central he was, he added, looking for "the general sense (*le sens commun* as opposed to the private sense or the sense of the individual, *le sens propre*)." He did not think he could find the general sense in the reveries of the melancholic or in weekly Gallup polls. The general sense emerged, he felt, from a solid respect for fact but for fact disengaged from "the jumble of particulars" immediately before each individual's eyes. Such disengagement took the form not of pulling down a blind but of learning history, reading the best of a culture's literature, and so on, and finding there a reliable account of humanity's capacities and limits; that is, it took the form our desperately failing courses in the Humanities still take.

I see no reason even now for despairing of the function of the Humanities, if by the Humanities we mean the search for normal and central in human experience by judicious, unself-centered "disengagement." But since Babbitt has gone down the drain, and since the Humanities have a sick look about them (are there any Humanities people running this country?), obviously there has been a terrible catch somewhere in the application of his sound principle. May I suggest that the catch is rather like the one Bernard Shaw discovered in the application of his perfectly sound theory that everyone should work. The catch for Shaw was that the nasty capitalist exploiters of work abused the theory, turned it to their own use. Similarly the Humanities have been abused by exploiters, those who would use the past not so much as an illumination of the present but as a preserver of their own troglodytic stake in the present. Which brings me back to the Writer on Campus—not a troglodyte but, against his best wishes, a servant of troglodytes.

## V.

We all know something of what he is and what he does, conventionally—so I won't spend much time on the nature of his daily chores. He runs the Creative Writing course or Workshop, sometimes with great attention to literary forms, disciplines and conventions, and sometimes with no attention to them at all. He talks with his students about images and plots and characters and what-all in their own work, and he tries to get them to read and criticize each other's work. He also has regular conferences with them individually, during which he may continue to talk to them about their creations but is more apt to serve as friend and confidant, listening to their gripes, their projected escapes from the System, and their vague enthusiasms about the life of a writer: this is his lay-analyst role. Finally, he serves as a hopeful model for his students by doing some writing himself, talking about it, reading it, maybe even publishing it.

In addition to these basic duties he is apt to teach, with varying enthusiasm and diligence, certain other regular courses in the English Department. He will have a Modern course of some kind. He may have a section of the Survey. He may have a Freshman Comp section. His teaching load will probably be lighter than other members of the Department (so he can do his creating), and he will probably be considered something of a lightweight outside Creative Writing—no PhD; but he will do these Establishment chores pretty much as the Establishment wants him to, only occasionally asserting his anti-Establishment soul by getting drunk with students or running off with the dean's daughter.

Now all of this, I submit, makes him a servant of the troglodytes. Even the Creative Writing course does this, and even the running off with the dean's daughter. His minor escapades strengthen rather than weaken the Establishment; they demonstrate that the Establishment is broad-minded until it fires him, at which time he is out of service anyway. His big educational challenge, however, is not to serve in this manner, but to devise ways of changing the Establishment sensibly, knocking off its crusty scales, making it really help the student find the normal and central in human experience. In other words, if anyone wears a reformer's hat on campus, it is the Writer.

Unfortunately his chief weapon of reform, Creative Writing, is a weak weapon indeed. Its most touted virtues—that it helps the student find himself, that it removes him at least momentarily from establishment pressures and evaluations, and that it takes the big step of turning his education over to him—the virtues are not to be denied. But as now taught it mingles its virtues so thoroughly with the vices I have described that it simply does not do what its proponents hope for it. Creative Writing is the runaway's meat, the melancholic's meat, the meat, to complicate the image, of the blue-sky world of souls behind blinds. Creative Writing merely works to satisfy the suicidal urge in our culture to put Creativity out of play.

The Writer on Campus doesn't like to think he is out of play. Nor does any writer. The Writer is hep; the Writer makes the scene; the Writer lives many lives and, indeed, *is* a writer partly by virtue of the range and depth of his experience—or so the myths about him say. A few years ago W.B. Scott of Northwestern University wrote an amusing account of the experiences apparently essential to a modern novelist's career (he was describing the James Jones era):

> *The Novelist must have* been, *by the time of his first big success as a Novelist, at least* eleven *of the following, in any order: (1) an all-night counterman; (2) a bodyguard (politician's or gangster's); (3) a carnival wrestler; (4) a deckhand; (5) a dishwasher; (6) a foundryman; (7) a gandy-dancer; (8) a harvest hand; (9) an hostler (horse or locomotive); (10) a lumberjack; (11) an oiler; (12) a pitchman; (13) a police reporter; (14) a pretty fair prelim boy; (15) a private eye; (16) a riveter; (17) a sheepherder; (18) a wiper.*

Scott then went on to describe the things the Novelist should have *done*, such as crossing the Andes on a bicycle, and the exotic jobs he should be able to perform, such as pressing his own wine from his own grapes. At the end Scott modestly posed the question of how the Novelist had any time for writing.

Obviously Scott's Writer is one small historical age away from the boy who drew down the blind, but they have a good deal in common nonetheless. Looking at the experiences of Scott's Writer I note that they are all part-time experiences, one-night stands, experiences to be gotten over to get on to the next. Also they are unpolitical and in a sense unhistorical experiences, experiences far from the places of power and responsibility in the society. The role of such a Writer—and I think Scott chose his instances carefully—is in this sense as much the role of bystander or runaway as that of the boy behind the blind. The Scott novelist is in motion, yes, and he is certainly seeing the world; but his connections with that world remain the connections of a runaway.

Perhaps sometime as a companion paper to this one I will do a casual survey of the range of subjects, forms and commitments Creative Writing courses encourage and concentrate on, but I know already how the survey will come out. It will demonstrate that the range of experiences students in Creative Writing choose to write about is extremely narrow and specialist, fully as specialist as the relevant experiences for a particular kind of economist, biologist or archaeologist in *his* shop. For one of the important consequences of the modern impulse in literature to stand outside the big social and political establishments has been that the range of literature has become increasingly limited even while literature has encouraged unlimited expectations.

No one denies that literature is a social affair; even those who are first to discount engagement theories of art insist upon the social or experiential base for art. For example, Warren and Wellek, though they would isolate the creative act, finally, from all other arts (and isolate also the subsequent critical act of evaluating the creative act), write very learnedly and eloquently about the relationship of literature and society in their *Theory of Literature*. They begin their account by quoting with approval Adolph Tomars:

> *Aesthetic institutions are not based upon social institutions; they are not even part of social institutions; they are social institutions of one type and intimately interconnected with those others.*

But having said this they laboriously deny it. They establish shop rules for literature that would be applicable in a dark room on the planet Mars, and end emphatically, "[Literature] has its own justification and aim."

The complex arguments like those in *Theory of Literature* that make literature simultaneously social and non-social are themselves shop arguments. Take one step out of the shop and it becomes clear that no matter what *theory* of literature may be promulgated to confuse simple minds about artistic engagement, contemporary practice emphatically puts most of the significant forms of engagement out of bounds, gives them over to politicians, sociologists and journalists, hence requiring of the Writer, if he is to play the shop game fair and square, that he be a Scott novelist writing about his days as an hostler, or a self-centered poet writing about his Being.

The conventions for making literature a runaway are not of course established only by critics. The writers themselves have the lion's share of the responsibility. Unfortunately their responsibility may be dismissed by observing the obvious, that a writer does what he can. If everything in his artist life—the conventions and traditions of his art, and the expectations of the audience for his art—tells him that his art must be a runaway, then it will be. And certainly in America the patrons of art and the amorphous audiences for art are as firmly persuaded that art should be out of play as Warren or Wellek or any runaway writer is. Art in our country, as I keep saying hopelessly in Washington, is something that occurs after working hours. Art is kulch. Art by the common consent of aesthete and philistine should not be, to use the continuously crucial word here, political.

No one can find a patron for art—a government patron or a private patron—unless that art is perfunctorily acknowledged to be non-political. No defenders of the freedom of art can speak up without first asserting that it is non-political. Politicians, patrons, lawyers, critics and artists seem to agree that it is, it must be non-political—and so do all the business interests who support opera, ballet, and sculptures in front of banks. And so do all our schools. Which brings me back to the Writer again. The Writer teaching Creative Writing is in the impossible position of having to perform an important political function on campus—the function, described above, of coping with the expectations of rebellious and alienated students—but of having to perform this function in a place where politics, engagement, social work and system work of all kinds are in effect *verboten*.

## VI.

What is a writer anyway, aside from an ex-hostler? Wellek and Warren agree that in our time "there has arisen in literature an 'intelligentsia,' a comparatively independent in-between class of professionals," but they are talking about the *class* of these professionals, not their character—what they think and do. Wellek and Warren thus miss the big point: modern writers, as well as practitioners in all the other arts, are indeed professionals, as narrowly conceived and fitted out as those new kinds of doctors one has to go to. In each art we find dozens of little cliques establishing their own "professional" standards, and mocking up private images of what an intellectual of each clique should look like.

Perhaps the only quality the different cliques in the arts share is a kind of nightmare vision brought on by having to expect so much from so little. I speak feelingly from a lifetime with (and without) artists when I say that collectively they seem to me to be in Purgatory. They are terribly arrogant yet terribly anguished. The three-chinned dog is yapping at them, yet they go on about their business fully convinced that it is a good business, the only business that matters. Here is a statement from an issue of the Sunday *Times*—a quoted remark by a young movie actor, yet characteristic of the obsessions of poets, painters, what-all. He is describing a movie he played in:

> *It is more basic and more* real *than any movie I've ever seen. In it I play a hippie who takes drugs, sells them, and gets chased around Manhattan with Edie Sedgwick by the Mafia.* The movie says everything there is to say about New York. [*My emphasis*].

I submit that any artist with *that* vision of the dimensions of his art (or more importantly the dimensions of New York) needs to get out of his art for a while, if only to try a different hole in hell. Some artists do, of course, but too many don't. In fact I don't think one can characterize the professional qualities of any modern American group of artists without mentioning their grandeur obsessions, and the consequent contempt they have for the poor unenlightened, insensitive, prudish world around them. Nor can one contemplate the role and effect of Writers on campus without taking these obsessions into account. The Writers are older Johnnies mostly; they are frequently as desperate as Johnny, as disillusioned and as expectant. Johnny unquestionably gets some of his qualities from them even if he never takes Creative Writing.

We teachers have pitifully little effect on Johnny's education. We therefore presumably need Creative Writing as a way in to him. Yet Creative Writing in high school or college is, as now constituted, a manifestation of the American Writer's professional obsessions; it is therefore a junior purgatory.

Purgatory is old and well-established, and somebody always has to be in it, ranting, complaining, suffering—for Purgatory is made by the world. So we have Purgatory, need Purgatory and must continue to sponsor Purgatory—there can be no talk of *eliminating* the Writer on Campus and his hole. Let us not be censors, but considerate skeptics remembering little pieces out of *The Odyssey* and *The Aeneid* where the way out of the hole is said to come about by the elimination of self. Purgatory in the old classics is a self-hole; the self enters it according to the nature and necessity of selves, and then slowly and painfully nibbles away at its enormous Being until that Being is a modest little subaltern in a field of ethereal clover. Let us be skeptical in these days of the earth, of the prospects of ethereal clover, but equally skeptical of the strange modern alternative that makes Purgatory not a way station but, ironically, a goal.

As I see it, a Creative Writing course must be designed to help purgatorial selves nibble. It is not performing its salvation function if the student writer only does his thing, his isolated self-thing, like one of those flat characters in plays that we English teachers talk about. Under such conditions it not only does not save him but it does not even help him in the minor professional ways useful to his purgatorial art. Under such conditions it does not sharpen and deepen his verbal sensitivity, as we would like it to do, or increase his knowledge of language and its properties, as we would like it to do. In other words it does not make any clear contribution to improving his writing, if we take as a measure of such improvement an increasing capacity to write clearly and sensibly about the world around him, about what is normal and central in human experience.

I am saying that when we praise Creative Writing for helping the alienated and lost to find their identities, we should at the same time worry about what identities they find. We should also worry about the course becoming merely an identity-finding operation, not a course in writing at all. Yet the course's strategic political role on campus so encourages the identity search as opposed to language study and practice, that the hired Writer on Campus conducting the course, no matter how good a teacher of language he may be, sometimes feels more like a boy scout counsellor than a majestic pedagogue. Our pedagogy may be bad, but surely then our mission as pedagogues is to improve it, not eliminate it. Hence we need to help the Writer on campus *to* pedagogy, not away from it.

As things stand now, the Writer on Campus, if he is the narrow specialist his art conventionally expects him to be, and if he conducts the Creative Writing course in the manner we have become accustomed to, may only deepen the infinite poverty of purgatorial runaway rooms. Yet if he is not the conventional specialist he may not be considered qualified, by students or faculty, for the job; so won't be given a chance to despecialize it.

How to solve this dilemma? I assume we cannot change the course of modern literature by curricular fiat, nor make any individual writer less specialized by waving an administrative wand. But I do not assume that curricular change need be wholly ineffectual; and since anyway it is the only kind of change that we as teachers have any measure of control over, I think a sensible program for us is simply to sit down and alter the character of that curricular thing we call Creative Writing. If we change the course we will change the job of the teacher of it, hence change the Job Specs. All of this will be very hard but should be done. And it should be done with the large political objective in mind of making the old lady education younger, and of bringing Johnny to education and the systems rather than giving him tickets out.

I have two rather different proposals to make, and will be self-indulgent in proposing them. The first is a fairly conservative and conventional English Department venture, and is in some schools already a fact. I have no great brief for it; it's a proposal for those who would move softly with a toothpick. The second is a more radical interdisciplinary notion I have come to in my dotage.

### VII.

*Proposal One.* Change the name from Creative Writing to, say, Advanced Writing. Make the course a normal part of the English major's, as opposed to the alienated writer's, training. Make it a study of forms, genres, themes and above all expressive motivation—what makes a writer tick, what the connections are between the thinking man and the writing man. And devise writing assignments in which imitation is the common mode.

If I were running this course I would want to tie the imitating in with reading, and with some historical and critical study of the forms being imitated, perhaps by alliance with a regular English course. I would also, however, want to sally forth experimentally into the non-literary. Therefore I would perhaps incorporate some of the exercises of my second proposal (see below) in journalism and other forms of shop talk. As for meeting the expectations of the trewe writers, those Johnnies and even those geniuses at whom the course, as now conceived, is aimed, well, I would not exclude them from the course but I would make clear to them before they took it that the course would not satisfy their runaway urge. I think it is a political mistake to formalize the discontent of runaways by making a course for them, so I would simply play lay analyst with them individually if and when I was asked to do so. I would also read their non-course creations, and would do what I could with Establishment powers to give them Independent-Study time when I thought they had talent. I would have my own time as lay analyst programmed and paid for, but I would not otherwise give their withdrawals establishment blessing. Instead I would work hard in the imitation course, and elsewhere in the Department where I could possibly encourage the runaways' presence, to show them that education was not a blind old lady. After all, we in English as a whole are not notoriously successful as searchers for the normal and central in human experience; collectively we tend to be runaways too. The imitation course, though not a radical departure from what we now have, would be part of a larger Department effort to make the Department's offerings normal and central.

But if you ask me how to go about the "larger effort" I can only reply by moving on to proposal two. In that, my senile convictions about the direction English Departments as a whole should go may be clearer, though the proposal itself, which will take me a time to get to, may not be to your tastes.

## VIII.

*Proposal Two.* Some preliminaries.

1. Learning a language is an organic process. Its words and conventions *grow* with us individually and collectively. Yet it is taught mechanically and categorically. The mechanics are not just those of grammar and syntax, but also of different language shops from journalism to creative writing. Each shop is a special language world, yet only in certain shops are the human dimensions of language acknowledged. The masters of what is known as Communication, for example, eliminate the human element entirely from the act of communication. They deal with transmitters and receivers, with messages and signals. For them a complete and profitable communication can take place in the desert between two electrical gadgets. English teachers mostly have the virtue of disliking Communicators, and of preaching the word that there are people behind communications; but they have their own shop too, to which they diligently attend (their monopoly on Creative Writing is a small instance of their restrictive shop activity), and also they have remarkably little control over the language-learning process.

The extent to which the Communicator's view of language has come to pervade the language world may be seen in the response of almost any students beyond the earliest grades to a piece of mundane, "objective" prose. They will see it as a language of facts, and distinguish it absolutely from the fuzzy other, the language of self. The language of facts will be for them almost anything in a newspaper or textbook, but unless they are very sophisticated they will have nothing to say about it except that it *is* facts. They may or may not imagine a person behind the facts, but they will have absolutely nothing to say about that person's relationship to the facts.

One of the major roles of English Departments must be to get their teachers out of their own shop, and to have them make effective demonstrations, *where the "facts" men are,* that the language of facts and the language of feelings, of science and literature, of the self and the other, or even of prose and poetry are not finally separable. Every language machine is manned by people, and the presence of their feelings, their motivations, their opinions can be seen, measured, and taken into account in assessing what the machine says. Procedures for studying these machines and displaying their human and shop characteristics need to be made a part of all shop studies. The studies should be largely of the "underground" of shop statements, that is, of the forces determining the forms, vocabularies and procedures of shop statements.

2. Getting into the alien shops for such a purpose means first combatting the forces which would preserve at all costs the integrity of English shops and *their* language, *their* literature. Unfortunately, teachers in English—and teachers in the Arts and Humanities in general—think of the "facts" men out over the hill as philistines, and are convinced that the philistine shops should not be allowed to contaminate the non-philistine shops. Much of the traditionalism upon which English and the Humanities are based is preserved by having the philistines to preserve the tradition *from.* Hence joining the philistines, or meeting them on their own grounds, will seem positively immoral to some English teachers. They have not heard, presumably, that the philistines have won—or if they *have* heard, as at my own university where the budget people are projecting transfers of teacher "lines" from the English Department to the Social Sciences—they are so furious that they can't think sensible thoughts about what they have heard.

Getting into the alien shops means also learning something about those shops. It will not do simply to sally forth and lecture about the virtues of the English shop. Yet English teachers have been inordinately righteous and sure of themselves about the sufficiency of their own shop in solving the problems of others. Not only have they failed, as C.P. Snow said, to learn the laws of thermodynamics, but they have displayed little interest in being generally familiar with our specialist culture. Critical yes, knowledgeable no, has been their rule. That condition has to be changed, and means teacher teaching in earnest.

3. The mythical figure of the Writer, which has been my subject here, is of a man of great breadth of interests and experience matched by a wealth of talent, especially verbal talent. I have already indicated my doubts about the breadth of his interests and experience, and I certainly do not imagine that we can uncover writer talent in large enough quantities to staff 10,000 campuses with Frosts and Hemingways. Yet if I compare the composite mythical Writer I have in my mind with the composite mythical English teacher, I am persuaded that he rather than the English teacher should perhaps be the lead-off man in my shop project. In the first place he has certain negative capabilities the English teacher lacks: he is already something of an outsider in English Departments; his curricular commitments are fuzzier and more fluid than the English teacher; and he has not been as effectively brainwashed by specialist graduate school programs as the English teacher. In the second place he would carry with him into alien shops the positive virtues of his myth; for in the alien shops they have not heard my exposé of his limitations, but they have heard, and know feelingly if inaccurately, the limitations of English teachers. Hence the Writer might be more readily received into an alien shop than an English teacher. And finally the Writer might genuinely profit by the experience in his own writing, and such profit would be duly passed on to the college as he became, thus, a more illustrious ornament and a more effective teacher and politician.

I mean seriously that he might profit. My own experience as a writer has been very consistent in demonstrating the value of non-literary surroundings for the production of literary things—and yet I am regarded by my severest critics as excessively literary. How frequently one can afford to leave the shop, and how far one may stray from it—these are matters to be decided by each individual writer (I have no aspirations to be an hostler); and yet getting out, one way or another, remains at the heart of the Writer's insatiable demand and need for experience. On the other side, staying in with Johnny and his little self-poems can be most debilitating. I am talking here about intellectual experiences, that is, academic experiences outside English in the various other shops on the campus; but I assume that all kinds of experience are grist for the writer's mill, the danger not being in the diversity but in the dabbling that W.B. Scott's novelist indulged. At the perfect university there would of course be several writers rather than just one, and they would not dabble; they would each choose an alien shop to attach themselves to, and they would attach themselves to it in earnest. Frost would be in Ornithology, Hemingway in Physical Education, and Robert Lowell perhaps in Colonial History. You can make your own slots for the writers of your acquaintance.

For these reasons, then, I think the Writer would be a good man to lead off my proposal two, so long as it be understood that he would be a beginning only, and that eventually a large part of the teaching of all kinds of writing by English teachers, at least in college, might be conducted outside the Department's boundaries.

I am done, nearly, with preliminaries now, and will get right on to proposal two after a few nice words for the philistines. I hope you understand from the irony in my remarks about them that I don't really believe all the people in the alien shops are philistines, nor that our own shop is devoid of them. Philistines are largely made, not born. The philistine Matthew Arnold deplored, and the philistine literary people have despaired of reaching, is a historyless, bodiless fiction. There is no such philistine, though there are many stupid, un-imaginative people and a whole world of society-created materialists. The myth that philistines are just natively materialistic, anti-cultural and intractable is a myth created and perpetuated by the society that professes to find them a problem. The society holds the philistine as scapegoat. Creating the philistine has been largely a protectivist operation to keep things as they are. Our departmental operations in the Arts and Humanities are an instance, and we should not be pleased with them. Culture, sensibility, creativity and taste—all those fine qualities that we seem to take as our private property, as if we were in real estate—do not of themselves naturally and inevitably adhere to us; we hang on them like grim death. It is time for—what? an ecumenical movement? Call it what you will, but we need to get on.

Now to the proposal. Let me be specific and assign the Writer to a specific shop, namely Psychology. Psychology is a good bet, I think, but I would be in favor of trying the Writer in almost any Humanities or Social Science shop, in Journalism or Communications, and, in the sciences, at least in Biology—so Psychology is just the model here. Most writers have had their innings with Freud and Jung, the literary stars of the Psychology world, but few of them are familiar with the current state of the Psychology shop—how many specialties there are within it, how full of scientism it has become, and how hard to read the textbooks are. The Writer's first job would be to become familiar with the shop. He would study, he would take courses, maybe even exams. Good for him. And during this period of apprenticeship he would ally himself with a friendly colleague in Psychology; for my proposal is a team-teaching project, with the magic number two controlling the team. The Writer would learn from the Colleague but he would also be responsible for teaching the Colleague, as much about the mysteries of language and creation, as these are known in our shop, as the Colleague seemed to require. In some cases this might entail enticing the Colleague to take Freshman Comp or Creative Writing; in most cases I would say not—better to face the language agenda on the spot in Psychology.

The language agenda is basically very simple. Writer and Colleague would combine to produce a double course, in which a single group of students would be confronted with both Writer and Colleague, each an expert in his own way but each immersed in the pedagogical problems of the other. The Colleague would of course have the contents of his course to get over or through in the old-fashioned way; and the Writer would presumably have a loose quota of written assignments for each student to fulfill. But even these seemingly discrete obligations would, I think, merge in some measure: the Colleague would be following the progress of the students in Psychology partly through their writing for the Writer, and he would also hopefully be twisting Psychology to the Writer's purposes; while the Writer would be enforcing the one general writing rule necessary to the team operation, that the students write frequently about matters related to the Psychology course.

I experimented with such a project with a Carleton colleague in Psychology, John Bare, some years ago (the merging was between two elementary courses, Freshman Comp and Psychology 10), and more recently with a psychology teacher, Larry Fisher, at the University of Maryland. Our experiences, which were most profitable but incomplete, suggested that we shared three pressing concerns, sufficient in themselves to justify our merger. First, we were all trying to make the students think inductively, and were all frustrated by student eagerness to accept the testimony of authority rather then their own eyes (surely this is a major problem in all writing courses, including Creative Writing). Second, we were all concerned with problems of conditioning, I particularly with attitudes, stances, points of view and where they came from in student papers, they with Skinner rats and case histories. Third, we all were persuaded that our students were insufficiently engaged in the real problems of our courses, I because the students quite properly regarded their papers as "dry runs" (the fatal flaw in Freshman Comp) and they because the students were too busy cramming textbook facts and formulas into their heads to think.

I can't describe all our other discoveries, but let me simply include here a few fragmentary conclusions I jotted down in a notebook I kept during the first experiment.

> *1) The old art of rhetoric makes crazy assumptions about the capacity of the individual speaker to effect a "behavior change." Teachers of rhetoric had best beware of Aristotle—we are no longer in an Athenian square. But the psychologists could learn a bit from Aristotle. What is this nonsense that has psychology beginning in the 19th century? Language conditioning has been too little troubled with except by the bad guys in the media.*

> *2) Some points of view are largely unarguable. Unexamined premises are not always explodable by being examined. We expect too much of our nice arguments. We need an impotence law in Rhetoric: what it won't do.*

> *3) There is too close a relationship between a perception and the point from which it is perceived, or between a perception and the perception mechanism or organism which perceives it, to make the ways of logicians and rhetoricians reliable. We are the inhabitants of our own history, no other. Rhetoric and logic only serve their function where points of view of speaker and audience are close—like in that Athenian Square.*

> *4) Still, integrity of perception is the first order of the day. So too the inductive method proceeding from it. The great rush to concept is endemic in our students. The difficulties of distinguishing between percepts and concepts are great, but a rough literary difference may usually be observed, and is tremendously useful in Psych or Comp. The students will achieve no integrity of concept without integrity of percept. Away with show-and-tell, on with look-and-see.*

> *5) The language medium is impure, but the facts people don't know it, and too many poets don't know it. First rule: recognize its impurities and study them, try to understand what they are and where they come from. Tone, attitude, stance all modify*

*facts. When will the authors of Psychology texts learn this? It's their field too!*

*6) A writer or teacher must avoid control procedures where he can, and know he is using them when he can't. The importance of perception and analysis as a counter-control procedure can't be overestimated. How to beat 1984.*

*7) Audience. Who are you writing or acting for? What are his demands? Are you sure? Why are you writing for him? Did he tell you to write this way? How would you change what you say if you were saying it for another? What other?*

*8) Why are you writing about "x"? To get down everything you know about "x"? To prove something about "x"? To finish off "x"? To praise "x"? Define "x"? And for whom?*

At the heart of the amity between my psychology colleagues and me was a common interest in behavior, mine in verbal behavior, theirs in physiological and psychological behavior. I found the Psych courses reinforcing me constantly in my attempts to get the students to look behind statements and to what I called the "underground rhetoric" of an occasion. I started with looking, moved on to points of view, and then to the determinants of points of view. All the student papers written for me were behavioral in the sense that the students were analyzing the determinants of their own and other statements. Meanwhile the Psych course went through a series of studies of the processes behind response. I was not about to throw out meaning for process, but I found it most profitable to talk about meaning by looking at its processes—and I think the students did too. The papers were uneven—but I was experimenting and some of the assignments were flabby. Morale was reasonably high. The students worked hard. Remarkably, though these were bright students with good schools in their past, none of them seemed to have looked at statement as process before.

My colleagues and I did comparative reading of a good many papers and tests, and found no serious problems in assessing them. We did not have the chance to combine our courses and assignments as thoroughly as we would have liked to, but we came out fully prepared to do so—that is, to accommodate our separate former courses to a genuine double course. The Psych teachers saw the Comp papers as an opportunity to put the Psych students more fully on their own; I saw the Psych classes as an opportunity for giving substance and motivation to student writings.

Among the many questions you may have at this point is what such an experiment, even if it were a good one to explore further for Freshman Comp, could do for the future of Creative Writing? At Stanford some time past a big and expensive experiment was tried with a whole crew of genuine Writers teaching Freshman Comp and preaching, in effect, the gospel of Creative Writing.* An experiment in the wrong direction, I think. We don't want everybody in Creative Writing; we want some of the qualities of Creative Writing out with everybody. We do not want self discovery at the expense of the self's capacity to de-self and live with systems. As I understand the Stanford experiment it was essentially a large-scale runaway program. If I have mischaracterized it I will doubtless be told so instantly; but in any event the purpose of my proposal is to immerse the creative act in the soup of the whole mind. I have little time for the specialist question:

---

*The Stanford "Voice Project" was probably the most ambitious equipment for changing the teaching of writing in college that we have had in a number of years, and it was a project that may well disprove some of the assertions about Writers and the role of Creative Writing that I have made in this paper. My paper will offend many of the backers of the "Voice Project," since it seems to propose an accommodation to the "voiceless" language of science, bureaucracy, the Machine. In fact "machine prose" is identified by John Hawkes and Albert Guerard as the villain the Stanford project is designed to fight. I can only say that I would like to fight the villain too, but fight it at home where it lives rather than in English class. Nor am I persuaded that machines are voiceless, though their voices are metallic and cracky. We need to understand them *as* voices if we are to fight them.

The activities and results of the first year of the "Voice Project" are described at length in a large pamphlet issued in August, 1967, with the support of HEW. It is a basic text for anyone who wishes to sample the prevailing view contemporary writers have of the Writer's role on campus.

I suppose my paper might be described as a minority report by a dissenter. If so I hope the dissent will be received amicably. I note several references in the Stanford report to the need for harnessing teachers outside English to the project, notably this statement by Walter Ong:

"... *Proposals for reform of this course or courses are legion across the nation. One which appeared particularly relevant to ideas in this Seminar was the use of teachers drawn from fields other than English (economics, history, sociology, etc.) and even of teachers without ordinary degree qualifications but otherwise highly promising drawn from the edges of the academic world (faculty wives, etc.) or from sectors of the civic community. There was great concern about involving other departments in the teaching of writing (especially since the unconcern of many faculty members causes students' writing to deteriorate after it has been brought to some kind of competence by the end of the freshman year), but there was also a general feeling that no practical way could be found to involve other departments.*"

May I suggest that the proposals here be considered as potentially "practical."

Unquestionably, however, the proposals here, no matter how practical, represent a clear bias on my part against private-voice pedagogy or at least against the pedagogy directed at the private voice exclusively, as at Stanford. Whether such different views can be reconciled and made to complement each other in any given course or curriculum is a question I can't answer.

Further observation (1976): The proposals in this essay have not to my knowledge been experimented with seriously on any campus even yet.

how can one be creative? for I assume that it is just as easy or hard to be creative in Psychology as in Creative Writing. In fact Psychology has the advantage over Creative Writing (as C.W. is now conceived) that it provides a variety of subjects to write about, or at least epigraphs to start with. It provides a nice big Other for the creative self to reckon with—and such provision is in my opinion finally of much greater importance than the company of professional writers talking about professional things.

I grant, however, that work in the conventional literary genres, poetry and fiction, might better be encouraged in connection with an advanced Psych course than at the Freshman level. My experiments at Carleton and Maryland were in the handling of Freshman Comp, not Creative Writing—and the distinction between the two, while one I am numb about, could readily be maintained by making Comp the all-purpose service course and C.W. the special, advanced elective. In the advanced course I imagine that much could be done with case histories and the keeping of journals; but on the tactics of assignments I would not argue with the Writer stuck with the course. I assume the course would remain in some measure a Tintern Abbey course, only controlled by its loose tie-in with Psych.

IX.

So there it is. Have I described a way of destroying the Writer on campus? and of destroying English Departments? I don't think so, but you may think otherwise. If you like the farm-out principle, the rest is incidental. Whether the Writer does his thing in Psychology or Physical Education, and whether he does it with Freshmen or Upperclassmen, with Johnny or frat boys, will depend upon local conditions and, of course, upon the Writer himself. As soon as the main principle of the proposal is agreed on, the Campus is in theory open to the Writer, and the Writer open to the Campus in ways we have not even begun to explore. But I know you may not like the principle.

The principle is that the Writer on Campus has uses and even obligations beyond his present province. It is a principle few of the high powers in literature in this country will accept, for the obvious reason that it is their province. In other words the principle suggests a diminution or watering down of the Writer's role as a minority culture hero. Heroes tend to be against diminution.

There are nobler objections to the principle, I know. The principle also suggests a giving in to forces of collectivist anonymity, a bowing to corrupt establishments, and even, I suppose, eventually a salaaming to the Pentagon, Atomic Science and the Media. For the normal and central in modern American experience ain't so hot. But no matter how far you may conceive us to have fallen, I must insist that the Writer's role is to confront, not evade the normal and central—and confront them no matter what the confronting does to the Writer's province. Particularly, I think, he must do so on campus, for it is there he has clear obligations to others than himself.

We will not make the old lady education any younger by saddling her with romantic, 19th century, great-man theories of culture. Yet we *are* saddling her with these right now, and doing so as much by the way we define the role of the Writer on Campus as by the arrogant prescriptions for, and evaluations of, the Writer we hand down from our prideful literary centers—should I mention New York? As a result the old lady sees a literature, on and off campus, largely characterized by what in science has been called the Matthew effect—to him that hath more shall be given. This is a ridiculous sight for the old lady, since her consuming difficulty is and must continue to be with him that hath not. In summary, then:

The strategic role of the Writer on Campus, as established by his place in the curriculum, should not be abused to delude him that hath not.

It should not be designed to give him a philosophy he cannot live with.

It should not be "structured"—there's the fine word—to put him behind blinds.

Nor, finally, should it be used to reinforce a seedy establishment by putting creative souls out of play.

Is the position clear? Then you may now damn it.

1968

# The Watchers, Waiters and Writers of Wall Street

My limited researches suggest that in olden times the making or losing of money, like other important enterprises, was regarded as in the laps of the gods. Thus the words "money" and "fortune" tended to get mixed up. Shakespeare's description of Antonio in the *Merchant of Venice*, though the work of a literary chap, is an apt one: between poor Antonio and his money is a wide sea full "of shadows and flats" and "of dangerous rocks;" his ships and therefore his fortune may or may not come home safe, and whether they do or not is out of his hands. Samuel Pepys similarly, though in more business-like fashion, observes that his fortunes are in God's hands. In fact he has a tic about it; one finds scores of such entries as:

> At noon dined at home, and after dinner to my accounts and cast them up, and find that though I have spent above 90 pounds this month yet I have saved 17 pounds, for which the Lord be praised!
>
> Up, and in my night gowne, cap and neckcloth, undressed all day long, lost not a minute, but in my chamber, setting my Tangier account to rights. Which I did by night to my very heart's content, not only that it is done, but I find everything right, and beyond what, after so long neglecting them, I did hope for. The Lord of Heaven be praised for it! . . . I did find myself really worth 1900 pounds, for which the great God of Heaven and Earth be praised!

On no other matters, I think, does Pepys lavish so many exclamation points. His thanks to God for preserving him from the plague of 1665 are lukewarm and perfunctory beside his grateful acknowledgments for financial protection.

What have Pepys and Antonio to do with Wall Street? A good deal I think. The language of the Street has never been marked by as much ostentatious piety as the language of Pepys, and in our time obeisance is made to the rough beast of Yeats rather than to God. But otherwise the feelings toward some apparently controlling forces outside the individual are similar.

Let me start with a low-powered figure, one of the most popular and least figurative of the images to be found describing the Street's activities: the market's "tone." I'm not sure, and I don't think most of the writers are sure, whether the word "tone" refers basically to music or to "the state of tension or firmness proper to the tissues of the body," but at any rate it would seem usually to have lost its figurative significance for our economists and to mean merely the quality or state of the market, whatever that is.

> 1891—"in the latter part of the month there was a much better feeling, the tone had improved."
> 1891—"the tone has been quite variable this week."
> 1907—"the tone at the close remained good."
> 1929—"the market started the week with a fairly confident tone."
> 1957—"the general tone of the market has been lower or mixed."

I would have you note the obvious here, that the market is being described as something with, if not life, at least a sort of will or character (pretty seedy) of its own. Anyone on the Street must sense this, particularly when the market's "tone" is bad, but no definition of a market I have seen admits the possibility. A market is usually defined not as a force in itself but as a wholly passive thing subject to forces working around, on or in it. Clearly, though, the writers I have been reading don't in their heart of hearts accept such cold-blooded definitions.

> 1891—"the markets were kept in a state of uncertainty."
> 1907—"the market was more or less in a state of depression."
> 1907—"the European markets were as much disturbed as our own."
> 1929—"the market has been weak, lower and depressed."
> 1957—"the market didn't make much of an effort."

On rare occasions a writer will get literary and note that he is speaking figuratively. Thus, "Business after once being checked never takes on its lost activity as soon as the cause or causes of the depression are displaced, any more than robust health can be the immediate sequence of the removal of the disease." But mostly the figures are not acknowledged, and I cannot with any confidence say that the omission is merely inadvertent. Particularly in times of stress the market's "character" seems very real indeed.

> 1907—"prices again ran off in an alarming way."
> 1929—"prices bounded up in the same unrestrained fashion."
> 1930—the market "broke savagely."
> 1930—"for the first time the market showed the ability to rally wholeheartedly."
> 1957—"a sinking spell . . . drove prices down."
> 1957—"many issues hit new lows, in sympathy with the Big Board."
> 1957—"the interest centered in specialties, with most of the list backing and filling."

Lurking behind most of the images presented so far is the image of a human being or an animal. But frequently the references are to inanimate nature.

> 1907—"on that day prices simply melted away."
> 1929—"the panic, as a result of which prices have melted away . . ."
> 1929—"the truth is, however, that the market is falling of its own weight."
> 1930—"a flood of selling hit the market."
> 1957—"a heavy wave of selling . . . knocked prices down."
> 1957—"the latest erosion in stock prices . . ."

Even when no figure is conjured up or implied the market still retains, simply as an abstract or intangible force, a momentum of its own. Here is a richly bombastic example of this, from a blurb about the New York Stock Exchange written in, of all times, 1930:

> Although often hidden by the rhetorical flights of orators and patriots, the celebration of military triumphs, and even the more enduring artistic and social achievements of the superstructural city life built about it, the parent market place of the city steadily performed its less striking but more basic economic functions. The daily exchange of goods among unremembered merchants, the influx of imports, and the outflow of exports, went quietly on. While on the Acropolis Pericles was planning a greater Athenian empire, while Phidias was carving the white loveliness of the reliefs on the Parthenon, or while Plato was discoursing on immortality in the academy, the purchase and sale of goods proceeded steadily

> *in the Piraeus—in the main unremarked by the poets, and*
> *yet fundamentally vital to the glory and power of the*
> *Athenian State.*

To be noted here is the fine confusion existing throughout about who, exactly, is being heroic down in the old Piraeus. The "unremembered merchants," like Gray's desert blossoms, might of course be accused, but in the course of the paragraph they, perhaps appropriately, recede into the background and the market itself becomes the quiet but heroic performer whose deeds may be compared to those of Pericles, Phidias and Plato. Thus the market is, and is not, just a market. Now in the following two quotations the market is clearly a market but it is also a force.

> *1929—"the downward movement became irresistible and*
> *efforts to check it, even of a most determined character, seemed*
> *puny."*
> *1957—"many who had been waiting on the sidelines for a*
> *better idea of the short-term course decided to sell when the*
> *market reached an historic support level and kept right on*
> *going down."*

The last quotation is very characteristic of our time—both the "many" outside the market and the market itself seem to be operating upon prices, so that the market is not given the sole credit for its miserable performance. Nonetheless it *is* given credit; notice that the "many" on the sidelines did not act until the market, apparently all by itself, had descended below the "historic support level." And yet the market is not in any way personified here; it is simply an independent, ungovernable, unpredictable force.

It is not continuously thus. There have been times when the market's malleability or ultimate responsiveness (as per definition) to recognizable persons and forces outside it has appeared to be its chief characteristic. Going back to 1870 I find, in a book entitled *Ten Years in Wall Street* by one William Worthington Fowler, the following lurid account of Street activities. Mr. Fowler begins by talking rather fuzzily about mere forces; there are, he says, always two forces: "one is a projectile force, sending the values upward; the other a kind of financial gravitation, carrying values downward." He does not, however, tell us what, if anything, motivates these forces. They seem to be simply present, like gravity or inertia. And pretty soon he abandons them in favor of people: "the effect of these forces respectively, the bulls and the bears, seek to heighten and turn to their profit." The grammar of that sentence is obscure, and I am not clear from it whether the forces are after all merely the bulls and the bears, or are intensified, egged on by the bulls and the bears. Anyway he now turns the heat on the latter, leaving the forces go hang.

> *Nearly all those prodigious oscillations in the stock market, which have startled the public for the past seven years, have been due to the influence of those powerful combinations, which have obtained control of certain stocks, and made them dance up in long erratic jumps, or have hurled them down still more swiftly and strangely . . .*
>
> *In the present decade . . . Cornelius Vanderbilt and Daniel Drew are the central Titanic figures. These men are the Nimrods, the mighty hunters of the stock market; they are the large pike in a pond peopled by a smaller scaly tribe.*

This particular comment on market activity I find delightful—but it is, of course, a most common kind of observation, and justifiably so. We have so much evidence of the activity of Titans or Nimrods in the market in the past, and their activity makes such good copy, that all sorts of books have been published describing them to the exclusion of that Titanic or Nimrod figure, the market itself. How Morgan manipulated Steel, Harriman Railroads, and Rockefeller Oil; how Morgan and some captive bankers (whom he had locked, with himself, in a room) ended the Panic of 1907; and how all the great financiers of the twenties pushed their chosen stocks up and down apparently at will—all these matters are in the histories and they are frequently described with an eloquence even exceeding William Worthington Fowler's. Still, as has been observed by Galbraith, Frederick Lewis Allen and a number of others, one of the results of the 1929 crash seems to have been to diminish the effect or at least the apparent effect that any individual or organized group may have on the market. The following quotations are from *Barron's* over a period of less than two months. In them there is a striking progression from faith to disillusion in the efficacy of certain private efforts to stop the market's decline.

> *July 7, 1930—"The abundance of Wall Street credit offers a constant temptation to big interests to attempt a sunshine movement in the stock market to counteract the wave of pessimism."*

*July 21—"Last week was the third consecutive week of advancing prices. The courageous operations for the rise inaugurated the week before by the so-called Meehan group . . . gradually restored confidence."*
*July 28—"The campaign for higher prices is still under way. Last week saw the publication of advertisements . . . "*
*August 4—"The 'personally conducted' bull tour struck another obstacle last week."*
*August 11—"The big campaign of two important houses to enlist public participation in advance of an autumn rise was a complete fiasco."*
*August 18—"All the broken bulls became the brilliant bears."*

The market may be unmanageable; it may be subject to neither a whip nor a burnt offering; but it is, or at least it is piously hoped to be, predictable. So the prediction business remains a fat one, and it seems to stay fat no matter how bad predictions in any given season are. This does not mean though that the predictors are less impressed by the market's curious capacity to settle its own destiny than are the mere recorders of its actions. No, the predictors—particularly those who prophesy what the whole Board is up to—are a pious and humble lot. They treat the beast gently, are careful not to offend him, not to make arrogant remarks about what He will do.

Their submissiveness is evident in most of their prophetic writings, of which perhaps the most characteristic quality is the insistent unsaying of whatever has been said. Nowhere in the world is there to be found such a group of judicious balancers of figures, forces and phrases. At first this stance seems strange for them. After all they are writers of opinion, prophets of the future; and in other fields where opinions and prophecies thrive—in politics, for example, and in journalism—one of the basic rules is that any man expressing himself on any matter about which there is any room for doubt should express himself as if he had never had a doubt in his life. Be forceful, the handbooks say. Speak as if you know what you are talking about, especially when you don't. But the prophets of Wall Street don't apparently read these handbooks, and we should perhaps be grateful. I estimate (and my only basis is casual observation) that for every prophet who will say, with certain gentlemen from Babson Park, that Canadian Oil is "champing at the bit, displaying all the eagerness for a bull market of horses at the starting post"—for every such prophet there are 10 ostensibly scholarly prophets who will mutter something like this:

> *Despite a marked advance in most [Canadian Oil] stocks since the first of the year, the group continues to have merit on a selective basis.*
> —Merrill Lynch, Pierce, Fenner & Beane

There's an obvious reason for avoiding the Babson kind of statement—suppose Canadian Oil goes the other way. In that event Merrill Lynch can point to the word "selective" and even to the lukewarm phrase "continues to have merit," while the Babson people can't. But this reason is not a vital one—most of the prophets are thoroughly adjusted to the consequences of giving bum steers. More important to them than mere rightness of opinion is correctness of manner. A certain hearty jazziness is permissible at the outset of an Investment Survey, but when the door is closed and the doctor draws up his chair to make his examination and diagnosis, then the air must get heavy and the sentences must get balanced. For in a profession where the state of the patient's health can never be precisely determined the professional man is mostly professional because he looks that way. Palmists and crystal gazers know this; so do the purveyors of old-time patent medicines—and perhaps the professionals of Wall Street should be compared with them rather than with our doctors. Or compared to Willie Loman. Willie Loman, remember, was way out in the blue riding on a smile and a shoe shine. The Wall Street prophets are always way out too, but they have to wipe the smile off when they get to their pitch; and in addition to the shoe shine they have to have a ceremonious and muggy style which will, under the shadow of the Big Board, pass for wisdom.

I have just two texts to illustrate this style: a *Security and Industrial Survey* by Merrill Lynch for August, 1957, and the *Bache Review* for about the same period. I should of course have others, for these two are clearly sheets for the masses, not for the boys on the inside. But as I am not on the inside myself I have to take what I get—and anyway the manner I am referring to is probably most pronounced when the professionals are cavorting before the masses. Let me begin appropriately at the beginning of these two publications.

> *At this point, when the stock market averages are knocking at the door of their old highs, the investor might well ask himself, "Are things really this good?" The answer would probably*

*have to be a qualified yes—qualified because things are not
uniformly nor universally good.*

—Merrill Lynch

*The start of the second half and the surge of stock prices toward
record levels makes this a particularly appropriate time to
pause and attempt to read the business barometers' forecast
for the months ahead. The readings, at the moment, would
seem to indicate bright skies for some industries, storms for
others and reasonably fair weather for the economy as a
whole.*

—Bache

Here is the preliminary light touch. I see the writer at his desk, clever,
assured, confident of his capacity to sell anybody anything. He runs off
a few *bon mots* and then gets down to business.

*The accepted measures of the nation's financial health are
mostly at or close to the highest levels ever reached . . . but
there are soft spots. Some industries and some companies
have been feeling the pinch of . . .*

—Merrill Lynch

*. . . an analysis of business in the first half of 1957 reveals
strikingly mixed trends.*

—Bache

Then a few figures are brought in to demonstrate our economy's
confusion.

*Office equipment shares rose 37.5 percent; ethical drugs were
up 31.1 percent . . . at the other end of the scale cement stocks
were down 5.4 percent, copper off 8.9 percent.*

—Merrill Lynch

*Over-all, first quarter net· was at a rate of $23 billion
annually after taxes, up from the $21.6 billion level of first
quarter 1956 but a shade under the $23.1 billion rate of
fourth quarter 1956.*

—Bache

A few more run-of-the-mill contrasts are provided (the kind you can
find almost any season anywhere) and then the general discussion
comes to a close with these words:

*All things considered, we would suggest that the investor proceed with caution at this point.*

—Merrill Lynch

*While inflation will continue to be one of the prime factors in determining security prices over the longer term, the present level of the market makes discrimination in choosing stocks more important than ever.*

—Bache

Now this pattern for a general discussion of market conditions seems to be conventional, and I should in fairness point out that it is one of the least harmful of Wall Street conventions. Nobody, reading such pieces, is prepared either to move or not to move "investment-wise"; he is merely prepared to turn—cautiously and/or with discrimination—to the figures which usually begin in quantity on the next page. Still, the convention would not, I think, be what it is if these writers really thought that they had the market by the tail. No, the language as well as the matter is ritualistic, a necessary part of the ceremony of placing a bet, but unconnected with the bet itself. The bet itself as a matter of fact is played down; for when the investor turns to the next page, hoping to get to the problem of the bet itself, he finds his prophet or tipster wriggling and squirming like the dickens to avoid specificity.

There are many forms of such squirming—and they are not the subject here—but the Merrill Lynch method is sufficiently characteristic to stand for them all. First the stocks are divided into four kinds: *Investment Type; Liberal Income; Good Quality—Wider Price Movement;* and *Speculative* (sometimes the *Investment Type* is broken down into two types: *Growth* and *Stability*). Then the prospects for different stocks within these categories are complicated by the introduction of qualitative distinctions between various industries (autos, airlines, etc.), these distinctions being *Relatively Favorable, Average,* and *Relatively Unfavorable.* Finally the stocks are listed, by industry, and by how stable or liberal or speculative or growing they are. By such a procedure a tremendous number of possible favorites can be put down; in all, for example, Merrill Lynch "selects" well over 400 common stocks, as well as some bonds and Canadian securities; Bache and Company "selects" 150. And by the mere listing of so many favorites the authors are incidentally made to look mighty profound. At the same time, by this procedure a "speculative" stock in a "relatively unfavorable" industry can be recommended with as much aplomb as an "investment type" in a "relatively favorable" industry. All this takes some doing.

It takes some doing just as it takes some doing for a crystal gazer to figure out a future that will fit anybody—and in both cases the results can be pretty terrible. This season they seem to be especially bad. I have been conducting a short study of the actual recommendations of Bache and Merrill Lynch in the surveys I have quoted from, and the results are as follows.

Merrill Lynch fared just a trifle worse over the eight-week period than did the Dow-Jones stocks, and Bache's newly selected stocks came out even with them. Now as I understand it the Dow-Jones stocks are chosen because they are representative of the market as a whole (in fact they're called "65 representative stocks"). But representation of the beast, I must insist, is precisely what our two brokerage firms are not selling. No, the words with them these days are "selectivity" and "discrimination." As Bache put it, "This, once again, underscores the vital element of discrimination in security purchases." Indeed the two firms pride themselves on their staffs of experts who are in an infinitely better position than the Average Investor (or the Dow-Jones averages) to tell a pig from a poke. Yet these experts did not beat the averages. Furthermore, Bache and Company went to the trouble to add 18 and delete 26 stocks from their master list, but in the eight-week period the additions and deletions fared nearly the same. Then too—to get over to Merrill Lynch and break down their 44 "selected issues"—their 11 "Investment Type: Growth" stocks declined 20.2 percent while their 15 "Good Quality: Wider Price Movement" stocks declined only 9.1 percent, and their 7 "Speculative" stocks declined only 10.1 percent. What price Growth, I say.

I realize that I have cited just one eight-week period, a period of what Bache has called "strikingly mixed trends." Furthermore I don't profess to be a prophet myself (though I might venture a bet, even money, on Dow-Jones for the next eight weeks). But I do think that the notable current failure of the prophets points up my point, to which I now return. The point is not why they call themselves prophets, or experts, or trained staffs—obviously it is profitable to do so; and obviously a lot of figures and rating systems, even when they come to nothing, are impressive. No, the point is that I cannot believe all this is mere show for the customers. A good deal of it must be for the trained staffs themselves, for whom a simple list of good and bad stocks unaccompanied by a respectable amount of mumbo-jumbo would be unsatisfying—as unsatisfying to them as to the yokels who can't tell a Bull from a Bear. Neither they nor the yokels would have faith in that list if all the "business" around it were eliminated; and if the "business" were eliminated perhaps that Nimrod, the market itself, would be offended.

Thus I think there is a sense in which the prophets are not simply buttering up their clients but are also buttering up the acknowledged Presence in their midst, by trying to show Him that they're doing their very best to appreciate Him as the fine reasonable Invalid or Goat or Wave or simple Force that He is. And all the time they know—they must know—that they don't understand Him at all, that He is thoroughly unreasonable, and that, like Pepys and Antonio, their money is in His hands, not theirs.

1957

---

Note: Since this essay's appearance, there have been many learned articles explaining the incapacity of professional investment funds to keep up with Dow-Jones, and also articles pointing to the unrepresentative quality of the Dow-Jones stocks. But the general point—that the inanimate Dow-Jones averages just shouldn't be as learned as those learned brokers—hasn't changed.